Eurocrats at Work

Eurocrats at Work

Negotiating Transparency in Postnational Employment Policy

Renita Thedvall

Stockholm Studies in Social Anthropology, 58

2006

Eurocrats at Work
Negotiating Transparency in Postnational Employment Policy

Doctoral dissertation

© Renita Thedvall

Stockholm Studies in Social Anthropology, 58

Department of Social Anthropology
Stockholm University
S-106 91 Stockholm
Sweden

ISBN 91-7155-186-7

Printed by Intellecta Docusys, Stockholm 2006

This book is distributed by
Almqvist & Wiksell International
P.O. Box 7634
S-103 94 Stockholm
Sweden
E-mail: order@akademibokhandeln.se

For my mother, Göta

CONTENTS

ACKNOWLEDGEMENTS

At the end of a dissertation project there are many people to be thanked. First of all, my supervisor, Christina Garsten, who has been an inspiration both as a person and as a researcher asking the important questions, being supportive, guiding me through the process, and being phenomenal in securing funding. Thank you, Christina!

I would like to thank the people in the Department of Social Anthropology at Stockholm University who have helped me retain my anthropological identity when sitting in a multi-disciplinary research centre, through seminars, conferences, doctoral council meetings and of course evenings out on the town. I have yo-yoed (Wulff 2002) back and forth to the Department to get anthropological stimulation and I would especially like to thank Ulf Hannerz, who has been my assistant supervisor, and who has provided invaluable comments on different versions of my manuscript. I am truly grateful, Ulf!

I would also like to thank Anna Hasselström, Johan Lindqvist and Mattias Viktorin who were all gracious enough to read the entire manuscript and asked me the tough questions, making me more aware of what I wanted to say. In addition, Eva-Maria Hardtmann has given helpful comments on the methodological part of the dissertation.

I would 00especially like to thank Daniel Genberg, who was the first to point out that there are informal ways of getting a traineeship in the Commission and who, together with his family Gaelle Garnier, Tea and later on Julia, made my stay in Brussels much easier and more enjoyable.

Regarding my everyday colleagues at Score, I would like to begin by thanking them all communally for making the workplace inspiring, interesting and fun to go to. I would especially like to thank the administrative personnel who, apart from being good colleagues and lunch companions, make everyday working life easier. Gudrun Aquilonius, who makes sure that invaluable tools such as the photo copying machines and the computers run smoothly; Ann Loftsjö, who puts up with my questions on financial issues and travel allowances; and Ingrid Nordling, who sees that information is distributed among us both on research and on a more personal note through the internal information bulletin.

The inspiration of being in a multi-disciplinary environment has been invaluable for me as a researcher on growth. It has helped me understand and value other research disciplines' perspectives, but has also made me – as everyone at Score knows – more protective of my 'own' discipline. Here I would like to thank Jan Turtinen, who was at Score at the beginning of my doctoral studies. As an honorary anthropologist (or maybe I was the honorary ethnologist), he and I had many similar experiences of being in a multi-disciplinary environment and could give each other support in retaining our identities as 'anthropologists' and 'ethnologists'.

During the writing of my dissertation I have taken part in three projects at Score that have partly or wholly financed my research. First, TREO, (Transnational regulation and the transformation of states, financed by the Swedish Research Council) where I would like to thank the people involved in the project, and especially the project leaders Bengt Jacobsson and Kerstin Sahlin-Andersson, for inspiring discussions and helpful comments during different parts of the process. Second, the Regleringsprojektet (The new regulation, financed by the Bank of Sweden Tercentenary Foundation), led by Göran Ahrne, Nils Brunsson and Christina Garsten. Here too I would like to thank the people involved for stimulating discussions and valuable comments during different parts of the process. Third, the EU project, EUROCAP (Social dialogue, employment and territories. Towards a European politics of capabilities, financed by the European Commission), led by Professor Robert Salais, Ecole Normale Supérieure de Cachan, Paris. As part of the Swedish team, together with Christina Garsten, Jessica Lindvert and Niklas Jambrén, I have enjoyed interesting research discussions with all the national teams, pleasant travel to different European cities and many laughs.

Through the years I have also had different office colleagues who have made the workdays more fun as well as providing spontaneous opportunities for discussing the research questions to hand. Thank you, Jonas Bäcklund, Göran Sundström, Anders Ivarsson-Westerberg, Jessica Lindvert, Åsa Vifell, Anna-Maria Lagrelius and Erik Malmstig.

Åsa and I have also, together with Kerstin Jacobsson, shared a research interest in the European Employment Strategy (EES), which has been the source of many productive discussions.

Others I want to thank are Göran Ahrne and Kristina Tamm-Hallström, who have made useful comments on different versions of the chapter on meetings. I would also like to thank the people who commented on various chapters at a Ph.D. Candidates seminar at Score: Laila Abdallah, Susanna Alexius, Daniel Castillo, Erik Malmstig, Ebba Sjögren, and Åsa Vifell. In addition, I want to thank the authors of chapters in the book *Kloka regler*, which includes one of my dissertation chapters (in revised form and in Swedish). Discussing different versions of the chapters in this book for the 'allmänt intresserade allmänheten' I have benefited from comments from the other authors: Magnus Boström, Staffan Furusten, Kerstin Jacobsson, Anna-Maria Lagrelius, Ebba Sjögren, Linda Sonneryd, Karin Swedberg-Nilsson, and especially the two editors Karin Fernler and Claes-Fredrik Helgesson.

I would also like to thank the people, who towards the end gave me insightful comments that improved my argument, Jessica Lindvert who, with her general knowledge on labour market policy, read the whole manuscript, Kerstin Jacobsson who, with her specific knowledge of the EU and the EES, commented on Chapter 1 and the concluding chapter, and Bengt-Erik Borgström who, with his broad knowledge of the EU in relation to the regional and the national, commented on Chapter 1 and the concluding chapter.

Finally, I want to thank my informants, Abigail, Anders, Annika, Bernard, Catherine, Gudrun, Hedda, Karin, Lars, Malin, Manfred, Maria, Marie, Mark, Michelle, Miguel, Peter, Robert, Susanne, Tage, Tanja, Thom, and Wilhelm. I think maybe you know who you are in the text. Without your generous sharing of your time and daily working life this dissertation could not have been written.

To my family and to my friends who have been interested and supportive of my studies, while at the same time reminding me that there are other things that are important in life.

To Jonas, my partner in life. Without you, this journey would have been so much more difficult.

ONE

INTRODUCTION

EU BUREAUCRACY: IDEAS, PRACTICES AND PEOPLE IN EU
POLICY-MAKING

Abigail walked into our office in the Directorate General of Employment and Social Affairs in the European Commission in Brussels. It
was morning and I had arrived just a few minutes before her. As I
looked up to greet her I saw a pin on the sleeve of her (winter) coat. It
read: 'Ask me. I am a civil servant.' It was an ordinary pin that could
have portrayed a pop idol or a protest against racism. As she was
hanging up her coat, the thought went through my mind. What did she
mean? Was she serious? By wearing the pin she was flaunting the fact
that she was a civil servant, a bureaucrat in the service of the European
Union (EU). Was this a wise thing to do in the city of Brussels where
many of the people not working in the EU institutions feel disadvantaged in comparison? In addition, my own understanding of a bureaucrat was more in line with the popular view and what Herzfeld has
identified as the stereotype of the bureaucrat (1992:71), namely a rigid,
inflexible, boring person. Was that something to celebrate? However,
Abigail was working in the European Commission for a few years as a
national expert from one of the member states and I had come to
know her as a great storyteller, who often made the rest of us in the
unit laugh during lunch and coffee breaks. I was thinking of alternative

ways of interpreting the pin and finally decided that she must be
joking.

During my fieldwork as part trainee and part researcher in the Directorate General of Employment and Social Affairs (henceforth
identified as the Directorate General) in the European Commission
(hereafter referred to as the Commission), my thoughts returned to the
pin from time to time. As I was drawn into the world of bureaucracy
and bureaucrats, I came to understand the rules and the roles. I was
intrigued by the bureaucratic games, both formal and informal, when
making policies. Bureaucracy became fascinating. Bureaucrats have the
power to influence and decide on issues that may affect us all. Now, a
few years later, I think of the pin as a protest against the well-estab-
lished idea of bureaucracies as '…slow, lumbering giants that
accomplish little and are generally unresponsive to public preferences'
(Wood and Waterman 1994:2) and bureaucrats as indifferent to people's feelings (Herzfeld 1992:4). This does not mean that they might
not be. However, they are people of flesh and blood with different
personalities and are driven by different goals. Some of them have
political ambitions and driven by the urge to make the world a better
place, and some are just trying to do their job and perhaps climb the
career ladder. Some of them live up to the stereotype of the bureaucrat
going strictly by the book. However, most of them are, of necessity,
flexible people (also see Albrow 1997:74). In fact, being flexible is part
of the job, as we shall see in the negotiations in the EU committees,
working groups and councils in the following chapters.

Whatever Abigail's pin was intended to signal, as a cultural construct Weber's (1958 [1946]) notion of the ideal bureaucrat and the
ideal bureaucracy still exists today. Bureaucracy is often seen as a
hierarchical system governed by rules, characterised by specialisation
and impersonality, and administered by officials in different roles, loyal
to the system rather than to persons (Weber 1958:196ff, also see Blau
and Meyer 1956:9; Meyer et al. 1994:181-182). If Weber saw this as an
ideal model, something to be aimed at, in later years this model has
been questioned. Bureaucrats and bureaucracies are constantly challenged for not understanding and taking into account individuals'
everyday living situations, and basing their decisions on the interests of

the bureau rather than the people (du Gay 2000:2). However, even if this is the case, as Albrow points out, '[r]igid, inflexible, cold behaviour is just as emotional as warm and loving responses' (1997:120).

Nevertheless, we love to hate bureaucracy and bureaucrats (see for example Ahrne 1989:11; Beetham 1996:1; Blau and Meyer 1956:3-4; Wood and Waterman 1994:2). However, our dislike of them has mainly focused on what Lipsky (1980) has labelled as street-level bureaucrats,[1] i.e. bureaucrats in, for example, the public employment office or the social insurance office who meet the general public. This study is not about street-level bureaucrats. It is about bureaucracy in the meeting rooms of the EU institutions and in the corridors of power in the member state's government and in the Commission. It is about the bureaucrats who work in the service of the politicians. These individuals rarely meet the general public in their capacity as bureaucrats. They are sometimes questioned for having too much power in relation to the politicians, but they are seldom the focus of the great majority's dislike.

Bureaucracy has been an integral part of the organisation of Western society for centuries. The concept of bureaucracy dates back to eighteenth century France (Albrow 1970:16) and in the beginning it simply meant 'rule by the bureau', the bureau usually being the hereditary monarch's ministerial advisers in her or his cabinet (Beetham 1996:3). Today, the concept of bureaucracy is connected with government and public administration. Bureaucracy and bureaucrats are what makes the state work. It is the bureaucrats who administrate and put forward the basis for policy-making. This may be done in different ways, and the many varieties of how it is and should be done have occupied many researchers over the years – the most obvious example being Max Weber (1958).

Much has been written about state bureaucracy in relation to nationalism and national identity (Graham 1999; Handelman 2004; Herzfeld 1992), and in relation to democracy (see for example Peters 2001; Premfors et al. 2003; Wood and Waterman 1994). All these

---

[1] For more studies on street-level bureaucracies and bureaucrats see for example Ahrne (1989); Graham (1999); Herzfeld (1992); Heyman (1995).

studies address the issue of power (also see Weber 1958). While democracy theorists are particularly interested in power relations between
bureaucrats and elected politicians, anthropologists and sociologists
have focused on the power of bureaucrats to classify and shape our
ideas and mould our lives and how these classifications are then used
(see for example Bourdieu 1994:16; Britan and Cohen 1980:10; Cohn
1968:16 Douglas 1986:100-102; Graham 1999:18-19; Handelman
1981:6, 1990:26, 1995:280, 2004:22ff; Herzfeld 1992:39; Perrow
1986[1972]:5). Through classifications, state bureaucracies determine
who and what is included and excluded, and in that way they exercise
power (Handelman 1995:280). As Herzfeld (1992:125) points out,
classifying and labelling people makes it possible to draw them into the
conceptual control of the state. This makes bureaucracies, bureaucrats
and their policy-making processes an important subject for scrutiny,
since bureaucratic power, to classify and interpret, influences how we
see ourselves and how we may live in the world.

Aim of the study

This is an ethnography of the work of bureaucrats in the European
Union institutions and the member state governments, in particular in
the European Commission and the Swedish government. The aim of
the study is to investigate the workings and dynamics of policy-making
in the area of employment, as an integral part of the fashioning of the
European Union. Policies are channels for the cultural flows of ideas
and notions and are in this way a part of forming 'society' (Shore and
Wright 1997:4,7). The process of policy-making is consequently an
important subject for scrutiny. More specifically, the study explores the
processes of making policy decisions quantifiable and transparent, and
the assumptions underlying these processes.

The focus is the so-called *Eurocrats*, who travel back and forth to
EU committees, working groups and councils. These are people who
work in the service of the politicians and assist them with their special-
ised knowledge of the elaboration of EU policies. Broadly speaking,
they are highly educated people, in this case with degrees in law, the
social sciences and economics and with experience and expertise in

labour market policy, labour law and econometrics. Focusing on the bureaucrats rather than the politicians reflects the fact that much of the EU policy-making takes place in committees and working groups with bureaucrats and experts as members (Larsson 2003:27). In fact, Christiansen and Kirchner have labelled the EU policy-making process *committee governance* (2000:8). The work of the Eurocrats is thus significant for the making of the European Union.

In EU policy-making, employment and social policies are of particular interest, since they have to do with the perception of citizens and their social rights. In relation to EU employment policy, the study takes a closer look at the negotiation process of deciding what indicators should measure 'quality in work' in the member states' labour markets. The notion of 'quality in work' represents an attempt in the EU to frame the idea of 'Social Europe'. The operationalisation of 'quality in work' by means of indicators constitutes an effort to make 'Social Europe' measurable, thereby making it possible to compare member states and devise EU targets. The perspectives on how to make employment and social policy vary a great deal among the member states, thus opening up the meeting rooms for negotiations, compromises, and conflicts. The Eurocrats have to balance their role as experts on statistics with the handling of political and national interests.

Policy-making in the EU brings to the surface the tensions and relationships between a postnational EU and an EU made up of sovereign nation states. The Eurocrats have to be able both to articulate their own 'national' perspective and to recognise the other member states' 'national' perspectives, at the same time as they have to decide on a common EU perspective. This balancing act is to a large extent a matter of how transparent the member states want to be in relation to each other. How visible do they want their employment and social welfare to be to the other member states? On the one hand, policy-making is about positioning and clarifying national priorities; on the other hand, it is about creating elbowroom for the protection of national independence as well as keeping that which is nationally intimate invisible from the other member states. This is what Herzfeld has labelled *cultural intimacy* (1997:x), i.e. keeping 'control over the external images of a national culture' (1997:ix) so as not to shame or embarrass the 'national' image. There is a clash between the postnational and the culturally intimate that is spurred by the idea of transparency and makes visible the national order of the EU. This conflict will be discussed further in the following chapters.

Background: 'Social Europe' in the making

When Bercusson et al. wrote their article 'A Manifesto for Social Europe' in 1997, it was still unclear what road 'Social Europe'[2] would take: a minimal EU employment and social policy or a more closely integrated EU employment and social policy in which the 'European social model' would become as important for the citizens of the EU as the nation states' models. They argued for the latter, with social rights and citizenship not only connected to the nation state but a natural part of EU politics (Bercusson et al. 1997:190). The debate they took part in, on how involved the EU should be in employment and social policy, has had a long history within the EU,[3] but had taken a new turn since the beginning of the 1990s, when the member states formed the internal market with free movement of people, money, services and goods.[4] There was a choice to be made as to whether the EU should be primarily an economic Europe or a 'Social Europe' as well – a 'Social Europe' that would be '…built on democratic institutions and democratic participation, a high level of social welfare, and a distinctive "European Social Model"' (Carson 2004:8).

---

[2] The idea of 'Social Europe' put forward the EU as a caring project, as suggested by the slogan on the back of the Commission's publication, *Social Europe*: 'For a different view of Europe read "Social Europe"' (CEC 1986).

[3] Employment and social policies have been on the EU agenda since the establishment of the legal acts: the Treaty of the European Economic Community (EEC) and the Treaty of European Atomic Energy Community (EURATOM), the so-called Treaty of Rome signed in 1957 and which came into effect in 1958. For an historical overview see, for example, Cram 1997:28ff; Jacobsson and Johansson 2001:11ff; Liebfried and Pierson 2000:267ff; Pochet 2005:37ff; Thedvall 1998; Westerlund 1995.

[4] In the Treaty of the European Union, also called the Treaty of Maastricht signed in 1992 and which came into effect in 1993.

One argument for a 'Social Europe' was based on the fact that, through the Treaty of the European Union, the so-called Treaty of Maastricht of 1992, people move freely between member states working wherever they want. They should therefore have the same working conditions, wages, social security and so forth wherever they work. There had been attempts to work together in the employment area. At the European Council[5] meeting in Essen in 1994 the Prime Ministers and Presidents (the EU term being Heads of State and Government) decided that the labour and finance ministers should monitor employment development and then report to the Council of the European Union[6] (from now on referred to as the Council or Council of Ministers) (Westerlund 1995:73). However, the United Kingdom had not signed the 'Protocol on Social Policy' in the Treaty of the European Union, which meant that there was no real mandate for EU employment and social policy-making.

At the same time as the Bercusson et al. article was published in 1997, a new intergovernmental conference[7] was being held in Amsterdam, at which the Treaty of the European Union was due to be amended. There were many people in the EU – politicians, bureaucrats, scientists – who favoured a more socially-oriented policy, and

---

[5] The European Council is made up of the member states' Prime Ministers and Presidents who meet at least three times a year to set the policy agenda for the EU, discuss and agree on responses to world events where the EU should respond with one voice, and approve decisions made by the Council of the European Union.

[6] The main responsibilities of the Council of the European Union are to pass European laws often in cooperation with the European Parliament. The members of the Council are the various Ministers in the member states' governments and they change depending on what policy issue is being discussed. In 2001 there were sixteen different Councils, one of them was the Employment and Social Policy Council (generally referred to by its acronym ESP Council). In 2002 the organisation was changed and the number of Councils was reduced to nine. The Employment and Social Policy Council became instead the Employment, Social Policy, Health and Consumer Affairs Council, generally referred to by its acronym ESPHCA Council. For more information on the Council of the European Union see, for example, Tallberg 2001; Wallace and Wallace 2000.

[7] An intergovernmental conference is a conference between the member states and the Commission where changes in the Treaties are discussed.

who had been worried about the neoliberal turn in the EU at the end of the 1980s and the beginning of the 1990s. Not least, the Commission, which had produced a number of policy documents[8] on 'Social Europe' during the early 1990s, favoured a common EU employment and social policy. The member states were also plagued by unemployment and low economic growth, and there were indications that they would be in favour of including an 'Employment title'[9] and putting the 'Protocol on Social Policy' in the new Treaty (Council of the European Union 1996:49-50).

In Amsterdam, the Prime Ministers and Presidents finally decided that an 'Employment title' should be included in the Treaty of the European Union, the so-called Treaty of Amsterdam (Title VIII Treaty of Amsterdam). In addition, the 'Protocol for Social Policy' should be removed from the annex and included in a new 'Social Policy Title' (Title XI Treaty of Amsterdam). My concern in this study is mainly with the 'Employment title' according to which the Council, together with the Commission and the European Parliament, should develop a co-ordinated European strategy on employment, now commonly known as the European Employment Strategy (EES).[10] It includes the 'EU employment guidelines' that are intended to guide policy within the member states (Art. 128, Treaty of Amsterdam). Every member state then has to write a National Action Plan for employment (NAP)

---

[8] In 1993 the Green Paper: *European Social Policy - Options for the Union* (CEC 1993a) and the White Paper: *On growth, competitiveness, and employment: The challenges and ways forward into the 21st century* (CEC 1993b). In 1994 the White Paper: *European Social Policy – a way forward for the Union* (CEC 1994).

[9] The Treaty is divided into different Titles that may be divided into different Chapters. The Titles and Chapters consist of different Articles. Among the Eurocrats of the EU it is common to refer to the number of an article instead of saying the content of the article. It is assumed that individuals know the articles within their area of responsibility.

[10] For more information on the European Employment Strategy see, for example, Behning & Serrano Pascual 2001; Biagi 2000; Foden & Magnusson (eds.) 1999, 2000; Goetschy 1999; Goetschy & Pochet 1997; Jacobsson 1999, 2001; Jacobsson et al. 2001; Keller 2000; Lafoucrière 2000; Salais and Villeneuve (eds.) 2004; Serrano Pascual 2000; Thedvall 1998; Vifell 2004.

to outline how it plans to incorporate the guidelines in national policies
(Art. 128, Treaty of Amsterdam). The national reports are then to be
examined every year by the Council via the Joint Employment Report
(JER), with the Council making 'recommendations' to the member
states on how to improve their policies (Art. 128 Treaty of Amsterdam). Altogether, this is an annual process.

It is important to note here that it is a matter of 'guidelines' and not
'directives'. It is not possible to take a member state to the Court of the
European Community if it does not follow the 'guidelines' or the
'recommendations', which are voluntary rather than legally binding.
Governing by way of voluntary regulation has been referred to as 'soft
law' in the EU literature (see, for example, Jacobsson 2004a, 2004b;
Kenner 1995, 1999; Landelius 2001; Mörth (ed.) 2004; Sisson and
Marginson 2001; Trubek and Trubek 2005). Instead, it is the process
itself that is treaty-based. The member states must write National
Action Plans in reference to the guidelines and they have to accept
being compared in the Joint Employment Report and being given
recommendations. This process has been referred to as 'a method'
within the EU, commonly known as the 'open method of co-ordination' or OMC.[11] The open method of co-ordination is built on social
control rather than legal acts. The member states' employment policies
are compared in the Joint Employment Report and analysed by a peer
review by the other member states.

In addition, the Commission also puts forward 'best practices' and
'good examples' from the member states' employment policies which
are worth following by the other member states. To be able to evaluate
the member states with regard to their progress (or failure) on the EU
employment guidelines, the member states and the Commission
develop indicators. In the Joint Employment Report, then, the member states' labour market and employment situations are compared in
both text and statistical diagrams and tables. These indicators in

---

[11] For more information on the open method of co-ordination see, for example, De la
Porte 2002; De la Porte and Pochet (eds.) 2002; Goetschy 2003; Salais and Villeneuve
(eds.) 2004; Zeitlin and Pochet (eds.) 2005.

reference to the guidelines should, according to the 'Conclusion'[12] in Cardiff in 1998 (European Council 1998), be developed and prepared by the member states and the Commission jointly, in a committee: the Employment Committee.

The Employment Committee (EMCO) was also established in the Treaty of Amsterdam. The Committee members are expected to advise the Ministers in the Council on what decisions to make. The task of the Committee is to: 'monitor the employment situation and employment policies in the Member states and the Community' and 'to formulate opinions at the request of either the Council or the Commission or on its own initiative, and to contribute to the preparations of the Council proceedings referred to in Article 128' (Art. 130, Treaty of Amsterdam). The member states and the Commission each appoint two members to the Employment Committee (Art. 130, Treaty of Amsterdam). These are high-level bureaucrats from the member states' governments and the Commission. The Employment Committee is also assisted by two sub-groups, the Employment Committee Ad hoc group and the Employment Committee Indicators group. The former (from now on identified as the Ad hoc group) prepares 'opinions' for the Employment Committee. The latter (hereafter called the Indicators group) helps the Employment Committee members to develop statistics and indicators in relation to the EU employment guidelines. Its members are usually experts on statistics and indicators in their own states.

However, the Treaty of Amsterdam and the Employment title had to be ratified by the member states' Parliaments and was not due to come into effect until 1999. The Prime Ministers and Presidents of the EU wanted the work to begin as soon as possible. An ad hoc committee, the Employment and Labour market Committee (ELC) was thereby formed, to do the same job, with almost the same members, as

---

[12] The member states rotate the Presidency of the Council of the European Union and the European Council among themselves every six months, from January to June and July to December. At the end of every Presidency period there are 'conclusions' written, generally referred to as Presidency or European Council conclusions and often connected to the place where they were made, in this case Cardiff. For more on the significance of the Presidency, see Chapter 3.

the Employment Committee would have in the future (European Council 1997). The first draft of the EU employment guidelines was written by the Commission in 1997 and then finalised by the Employment and Labour market Committee. The Employment and Labour market Committee members were also to work closely with another committee, the Economic Policy Committee (EPC). Economic, employment, and social policies were seen as closely connected (Vaughan-Whitehead 2003:4); economic policy creates the preconditions for job creation. Employment and social policy must therefore be discussed in relation to economic policy.

It was later stipulated that there should be a European Council meeting in the Spring on a yearly basis devoted to employment and economic policy. The first meeting was held in Lisbon in March 2000. A key goals included in the 'Conclusions' of the meeting was 'modernising the European social model by investing in people and building an active welfare state' (European Council 2000a:7). One of the ways suggested for doing this was to focus on 'more and better jobs for Europe: developing an active employment policy' (European Council 2000a:8). In the 'Conclusions' of the Lisbon meeting the 'social' was presented not only as connected with economic policy but as a 'productive factor' (cf. Andersson 2004:69ff; Le Cacheux and Laurent 2003:4). This was a break from earlier views of the 'social' as necessary but consuming society's economic means, rather than contributing to them.

The claim that the social is a productive factor was also inserted into the 'Social Policy Agenda' of the EU for the period 2000-2005. In the Agenda the triangulation between the social, employment and the economy was once more emphasised (CEC 2000:8). The guiding star of the Agenda was quality: 'quality in work' (CEC 2000:14). 'Quality in work' was to steer the implementation of the EU employment guidelines in the member states (Council of the European Union 2001).

When I came to work in the Directorate General of Employment and Social Affairs in the Commission in the autumn of 2001, the member states and the Commission had decided that they wanted to develop indicators for 'quality in work' in relation to the EU employment guidelines in order to be able to monitor the 'quality in work' situation in the member states (European Council 2000b and 2001a). The Employment Committee members were given the task of preparing a decision on 'quality in work' indicators before the European Council in December the same year. The notion of 'quality in work', and the idea of making it measurable through indicators, was a highly contested issue among the member states, making the policy process conflictual. It is this very policy-making process that is traced in the following chapters. Before we move on to examine this process, however, a brief overview of the interest the EU has attracted among anthropologists is needed.

Anthropological perspectives on the European Union

The study of Europe in anthropology has traditionally focused on regions, especially the Mediterranean region (Grillo 1980:3). However, a quarter of a century ago, Grillo supported (1980:4-5) the need for a European anthropology concerned with state formation, national integration, urbanisation, bureaucratisation, class conflict, etc. Several anthropological studies of Europe since then have responded to this plea for new perspectives. During the 1990s, a number of volumes concerned with European identity, European integration, and borders in relation to the nation state (see, for example, von Benda-Beckmann and Verkuyten 1995; García 1993; Goddard et al. 1994; Kockel 1999; Macdonald 1993; Wilson and Smith 1993) were published. From a broader social science perspective, European integration and its challenges have been described as processes of europeanisation (Borneman and Fowler 1997). Studies in this realm have mainly concerned the interlocking of national and EU policy-making (Cowles et al. 2001; Featherstone and Radaelli 2003; Jacobsson et al. 2004).

The focus in this study is specifically on the European Union (EU)[13] and the muddling of the member states' employment and social policies. This connects within anthropological research with how actors in the EU institutions, in particular the Commission, actively try

---

[13] For a general overview of the Anthropology of the European Union see Bellier and Wilson 2000.

to build a European identity and culture through policy-making. In a groundbreaking study, Shore (1993, 1996 and 2000) examined EU cultural policy and the Commission's strategy for uniting Europe through the promotion of a European 'culture', and the use of symbols such as a flag, an anthem and so forth – thereby mimicking the building of the nation state. Regardless of whether these attempts are regarded as successful or not, studying the process of how policies are made among the member states in the EU, and what these mean for the construction of a European identity and culture, is both socially and academically relevant.

However, whereas Shore focused on how the actors within the EU institutions operate to build the EU through the use of cultural policy, I am concerned here with the work of devising employment policies in collaboration among, and to some extent beyond, the nation states. This work is mainly carried out in committee, working group and council meetings between the states' representatives and the Commission. In this way, I focus on the nomads of the EU member states and the Commission, the bureaucrats and politicians of the member states and the Commission who travel back and forth to the EU meeting rooms in Brussels, rather than on what may be called the 'settlers', namely, the bureaucrats who work in the EU institutions in Brussels. It is in this everyday task of making and deciding on policies that what we recognise as the EU is articulated, negotiated and fashioned.

The focus on bureaucrats in motion makes the idea of the difference between the nation state and its national identity and the EU and the European identity more visible. Most anthropological studies on the difference between national identity and European identity have focused on 'settlers' in the EU institutions. These include Abélès' (1993) study of the conflict of being simultaneously a national and a European in the European Parliament, Bellier's (1997) study of the impact of nationality and the notion of becoming a European in the European Commission, and McDonald's (1997) study, which focuses on the practice of national identification and stereotypification as part of the Commission's system (McDonald 1997:61). When the nomads are in focus, the clash between the national and the European not only becomes visible, it also brings to the surface the importance of national identification and national positions in the EU's activities. This clearly emerges from Zabusky's (1995) study of cooperation between scientists and technicians in a European Space project, which shows how diversity in national identities becomes a significant part of making a European project's culture (see also Herzfeld 1987:77ff). My understanding of the notion of 'culture' is in line with that of Hannerz, namely '…culture as meanings and meaningful forms which we shape and acquire in social life' (1996:8).

Such a clash between the national and the European creates a particular *culture of compromise* (Abélès 2000:45). The concept refers to a way of discussing and agreeing so that multiple identities and ideas are harmonised without any claim to power being made (Abélès 2000:45). As Abélès points out, 'what is generated inside the European institutions is a universe of compromise where the conjugation of multiple identities is done essentially in a pragmatic fashion' (Abélès 2000:42). The idea of pragmatism is important here. Compromises are seen to be pragmatic in the sense that they are essential for political decisions to be made. However, I want to argue that the discussions in the EU meetings fluctuate between a culture of compromise and a *culture of conflict* (Cohen 1969, cf. Ross 1993). The concept of a culture of conflict refers to '[w]hen the conceptual styles used between individuals and groups are mutually incompatible…' (Cohen 1969:828). One setting in which the conflict between the national and the European becomes especially evident is when the bureaucrats of member states and the Commission try to work out common EU employment indicators that will measure the member states' progress (or failure) in national labour markets. The desire of the member states' representatives is to render invisible that which is culturally intimate.

National and postnational tensions

In the context of the EU the nation state is the foremost organising principle of geography, people, decision-making, politicians, and bureaucrats. It is the nation state that is at the centre of the bureaucratic culture of policy-making in the EU. At the same time, the ideology of the EU points towards the building of the EU as a postnational unit, a community of nations in which political, financial and social ideas are not only reducible to nation states. There is a pendulum between the notion of the EU as made up of separate and sovereign nation states and that of the EU beyond national borders. The concept of *methodological nationalism* (Smith 1979:191) points to the dominant practice in the social sciences of taking the national entity as a given in scientific research. The traditional methodological approach has been not to question the prevalence of the nation state, but rather to use it as a backdrop and given unit for cross-national comparison.

Given this idea, in an organisation such as the EU the notion of the nation state may be used favourably as an instrument, a method, to make sense of the EU. It is difficult to understand, for example, the discussion on 'national' identity or 'national' positions without assuming that the EU is an organisation of nation states. It is also difficult to understand the negotiations and discussions in the EU committee, working group and council meetings without taking into consideration that the members represent nation states. This *national order of things* (Malkki 1999[1997]:53ff) is so rooted and unambiguous in the way of thinking in the member states' representatives that the idea of, as they say, a 'national' interest is seen as natural. In fact, organisations such as the EU assume and even reinforce the national order of things (also see Ben-Ari and Elron 2001:275-276). The Eurocrats, who convene at the meetings, are there as representatives of their nation states and should act in the national interest. Jacobsson and Morth (1998:199) argue that the work in the EU has forced the member states to adopt a 'national' position where there has not been a need for one before. In this way the notion of the 'national' and the 'nation state' is upheld in the work of the EU. At the same time, the policy-making process and the EU decisions made on common policies constitute a postnational EU, in which policies become something more than just the sum of national interests.

A postnational EU in the making

The concept of *postnational* figures frequently in the literature on citizenship. Soysal (1994:1) argues that in the world today there are different types of citizenships that transcend nation states' borders as well as national identity. The notion takes on postnational characteristics by emphasising citizenship based on criteria other than legal rights and obligations connected with a nation state. Koopmans and Statham (1999:655-656) point out that the notions of 'guestworker', 'immigration', and 'transnational migration' have meant that the idea of citizenship, where identity and rights were previously closely connected with the nation state and nationality, has now been decoupled from them. The idea of the nation and the state being intimately connected is thus becoming more and more difficult to uphold. In recent years the state has increasingly separated itself from the cultural project of forming national identities and creating national communities (Appadurai 1996:168-169; Delanty and O'Mahony 2002:169-170). Individuals' identification with postnational and transnational organisations and movements has instead increased. Other forms of identities such as scientific epistemic identities, transnational ethnic identities, religious identities, movement identities are, for the citizens of the world, becoming more, or as, important as a national territorial identity (Appadurai 1993:419, 1996:167-169; Delanty and O'Mahony 2002:169-170, 185).

Recently, it may be said that the EU is showing signs of postnationality. Habermas (2001:89) even argues for the need of a postnational democracy in the EU. The concept of postnational has a slightly different meaning in this context. It refers to the notion that the nation state, both nation and state as constructs, is losing sovereignty to the EU, and we are thereby seeing the emergence of a postnational community where the nation and nationalism no longer constitute the prime legitimising ground for its existence (Delanty and Rumford 2005:190). In addition, the creation of a monetary union, and the continued development of EU policies on employment and social issues, suggest that the EU member states can no longer be seen as 'states' in the classical Westphalian sense, i.e. as sovereign territorial states distinguishing between domestic and foreign affairs, and acting among each other with the imperative of 'balance of power' and the model of *raison d'état* as guiding principles (cf. Cooper 2003; Delanty and O'Mahony 2002; Habermas 2001).

Cooper (2003:26ff) puts forward the argument that the typical traits of the modern state, such as keeping transparency and openness within domestic life, with secrecy vis-à-vis the rest of the world, are now being challenged, as the EU is moving into a postmodern era. He argues instead that, in the EU, the idea of *transparency* between the member states has replaced the imperative of balance of power and *raison d'état* as master ideas (Cooper 2003:28,36-37). In this way membership in the EU should make the member states' policies and political institutions more visible to each other, thereby weakening grounds for suspicion. As a result, the arena for conflict then becomes the meetings in the EU, rather than the battlefields of war (Cooper 2003:35-36).

However, the present study is not so much about the postmodern as about attempts to create a postnational order of things. In the EU the contours of the national are continuously being negotiated and the national communicates and negotiates with the postnational. Hence, we may argue that the nation state is gradually taking on another form based on multinational identities and the acceptance of state affairs being internationally transparent and 'meddled' with by other member states in the EU. In addition, the notion of the postnational brings forward other possible identities such as the people of Europe identifying themselves in categories as groups of 'unemployed' or 'working women'. Whilst multinational and transnational are concepts that signal that the national is the strongest identity marker for people, ideas and things, concepts such as international and supranational assume that the state is at its base national. These identities are very much valid in some parts of the process of policy-making within the EU, but when a policy decision is made, something new is created: postnational policy.

Nevertheless, even if member states' policies are becoming more integrated and the national identity is no longer the only identity available, the nation and the national are still of importance. Cooper (2003:28, 36-37) may argue that the replacement of the modern European system of security – through the balance of power and *raison d'état* – by transparency through interdependence is a sign of the nation state being replaced by the post(modern)national state. However, the techniques for making EU member states' policies transparent are also articulating and separating the member states, making us more aware of the nation and the national.

But what does it mean that the EU bureaucrats are creating *transparent* policy processes and policy decisions?

Transparency in process?

In the Western world today, concepts such as 'transparency', 'benchmarking', 'accountability', 'evaluation', 'audit', 'best practice', and 'indicators' are becoming more and more familiar. In general, these used to be the language and managerial techniques of private organisations, but during the last quarter of a century they have also infiltrated the language and practices of state bureaucracies (Sahlin-Andersson 2000b:1), among them the EU institutions (McDonald 2000; Harlow 2002). In the context of public organisations, these ideas and practices have been labelled New Public Management (Hood 1991; Stewart and Walsh 1992) and have spread around the Western world[14] in different forms but with roughly the same language (Sahlin-Andersson 2000a:4). New Public Management is based on the conception that goals have to be set and then evaluated by results, preferably in the form of indicators and statistics. This spectrum of ideas in New Public Management may be seen, in Appadurai's terms, as an 'ideoscape' (1996:36-37), i.e. a network of connected ideas and practices.

Such an ideoscape of ideas and practices in the EU derives its direction to a large extent from the notion of *transparency*. The concept of transparency generally refers to making things or processes visible (Garsten and Lindh de Montoya 2004:5). It has to do with openness (Florini 1998:50). Transparency has become a buzzword during the last ten to fifteen years in international and transnational organisations, state governments as well as private corporations (Sanders and West 2003:1-2, Florini 2003:33-34). Part of the concept's attraction has to do with 'its power as a mechanism for revelation, disclosure, and cleansing' (Garsten and Lindh de Montoya 2004:5). It carries promises of flushing through and revealing that which is hidden (ibid.). Florini

---

[14] In, for example, New Zealand, Australia, the United Kingdom, the USA, Sweden, Norway, Switzerland, Germany and France (Sahlin-Andersson 2000a:6).

discusses transparency as 'regulation by revelation' (2003:34). The idea is that by making information about policy-making processes, decision-making, environmental and labour practices or budgets accessible to the public, international and transnational organisations, governments and corporations are forced to be accountable and trustworthy. Transparency thus works as a regulatory mechanism.

Transparency, then, gives the impression of being all good and neutral. However, as Strathern states, there is nothing innocent about the idea of transparency (2000b:309, also see Garsten and Lindh de Montoya 2004:12). Sanders and West (2003:16) point to what it might instead hide. They ask:

> 'What, after all, is claimed when the operation of power is described as transparent? What is *seen through*, and what, then, is *seen? Transparency,* as it is used in contemporary global-speak, presumes a *surface* to power that can be seen through and an *interior* that can, as result, be seen. If the processes through which power functions constitute its interior, what, then, constitutes its surface? Its (ideological) representation? If so, can such surfaces ever be rendered transparent; can they ever be completely stripped away? Or can they only be transformed/replaced/covered over? And by whom?' (Sanders and West 2003:16).

They discuss in terms of the 'veil of transparency' and point to the fact that making something transparent may hide as much as it reveals, since what should be made transparent is a matter of choice (Sanders and West 2003:26). The member states' and the Commission's discussions and negotiations about what should be seen and what should remain hidden are thus determined by what the member states want to make transparent, rather than actually making policies transparent. This makes the policy-making process of creating transparency an important subject for scrutiny.

The 'epistemic culture' of numbers

One way the EU is currently trying to make policies more transparent is by the use of statistics and indicators. Indicators are used to audit and evaluate policies in order to make them transparent. This is part of an *audit culture* (Strathern 2000a), drawing on Power's notion of the *audit society* (1999[1997]), which implies that both individuals and organisations are becoming subject to increased scrutiny and control. The need for auditing is based on a lack of trust in the process (Power 1999[1997]:2-3) and a tendency to place trust in the seeming objectivity and political neutrality of numbers (Strathern 2000a:4). Auditing is thus believed to restore trust and make the process efficient and transparent (Power 1999:122-123).

The use of numbers and statistics in political processes has a long history in bureaucracies and governments in the [Western] world (for an overview see Johannisson 1988; Porter 1995). The idea that we can know ourselves through numbers is one of the most distinctive features of modernity (Asad 1994:79; Hacking 1990:1). The obsession with turning politics into numbers has been examined in anthropology (Asad 1994; Paley 2001; Shore 2000; Strathern 2000a; Urla 1993) as well as in other disciplines (Alonso and Starr 1987; Cohen 2005; Johannisson 1988; Miller 2001; Porter 1995, 2001; Rose 1991, 1999; Stone 1997[1988]; Zimmermann 1996). The work of classifying individuals and their social life in numbers and statistics is part of what Handelman calls the *bureaucratic logic* (2004:5). The concept refers to the ordinary, everyday practices in bureaucracies and the corridors of power of inventing and applying classification (Handelman 2004:5). These practices to a great extent shape the objects of policy-making, in that they provide definitions of what is desirable, possible and thinkable. The classification of individuals in births, deaths, diseases, literacy, crimes, occupations and the like has occupied policy-makers since the end of the nineteenth century. In Hacking's terms, it is a way of 'making up people' (Hacking 1986:222).

As a field of knowledge the science of statistics, as described by Power (2003a:14), is dominated by two perspectives, *calculative idealism* and *calculative pragmatism*, in which advocates of calculative idealism believe in numbers and mathematical models as representing reality, whereas advocates of calculative pragmatism see numbers as 'attention-directing devices' with no real claim to correspond to reality (Power 2003a:14). The first view of statistics has been duly criticised. It has been pointed out by several people that indicators are developed in a political and cultural context, which means that they are bearers of implicit meaning (see, for example, Starr 1987:31, Alonso and Starr 1987:4, Asad 1994:77-78, Porter 1995:3ff).

However, it is also important to note that even though indicators and numbers are perceived by many as 'attention-directing devices' or ways of administering society, the people in this study, and most likely people in Western societies at large, are part of an *epistemic culture* (Knorr Cetina 1999:1-2) *of numbers* in which statistics and indicators are believed to be, or at least should be, objective and politically neutral. In this epistemic culture, EU citizens and member states' representatives should be able to follow statistically how their member state is performing compared with other member states. Statistics is supposed to provide the policy-making process with democratic legitimacy (cf. Power 2003b). In addition, the results may be 'benchmarked', i.e. compared with each other to bring out 'good examples' and 'best practices.' The outcome of these comparisons may then lay the basis for new policy-making and have the potential to be the source of social reform. Urla (1993:834) points to the outcome of a census on Basque language-use as a catalyst for more emphasis being put on using the language in public and in teaching in schools. This makes the power of numbers and their ability to transform our lives evident. Regardless of whether one believes in numbers as capable of representing reality or not, numbers may thus be useful political instruments. The presentation of a cause or a political message may be perceived as more professional and politically neutral with the use of statistics (Paley 2001:136). Numbers make political decisions appear objective (Miller 2001:382, Porter 1995:8) or 'disinterested' (Rose 1999:199), rather than based on political values.

In this way, statistics and indicators are used as instruments to guide and govern. Foucault's concepts of 'governmentality' (Foucault 1991:87ff) and 'political technology' (1988:146) are useful here. The concept of governmentality points to the perception that political technologies such as statistics are internalised in individuals' minds, bringing with them certain norms and ideas that then become shared and indisputable. When norms and ideas become internalised, governing is performed by controlling the frame of mind, the mentality, rather than by fear of punishment. The use of statistics then becomes a way

of governing by numbers (Miller 2001:379). That which is political
moves from what may be seen as interests and values into expertise
and technologies such as indexes, indicators and statistics.

Numbers transcending borders

Traditionally, statistics has been developed within the framework of
the nation state – for the nation state and about the nation state (see
for example Scott 1998; de Swaan 1998). Indeed, the concept of statistics means 'facts about the state' (Starr 1987:10). However, during
recent decades more and more statistics are produced within international and transnational organisations such as the EU. In the context of
the EU, statistics may be seen by its proponents as a *lingua franca*, where
member states' representatives have different mother tongues but can
share the language of statistics. As Porter (1995:ix) and Mallard
(1998:573) point out, numbers and quantification are often assumed to
transcend local borders and transform that which is local or time-
dependent into something general and universal.

The view of numbers as a *lingua franca* that transcends borders fits
well with the idea of transparency. The local in the context of the EU,
in this case the nation state, is in a sense made culture-free by the use
of numbers. EU policies are thereby believed to become transparent,
since the numbers are assumed to be culturally and politically neutral.
In this way the numbers unite the EU member states since they become a language that everyone can understand. *Euroistics*, paraphrasing
the notion of state-istics, or, as Shore suggests, *euro-statistics* (2000:31),
i.e. statistics developed in the context of the EU, is able to pull people
together by creating a postnational Europe where other classifications
than nationality become fusing categories that go beyond the nation
state's borders. Euroistics plays an integral part in the creation of a
community beyond the nation state, i.e. the building of the EU (Shore
2000:31).

At the same time, statistics makes it possible to make comparisons
between the EU member states. This makes the process of developing
indicators particularly important to the member states (cf. Salais 2004).
It is in this process that what should be revealed and what should
remain hidden under the veil of transparency is decided. What finally is

made visible is a matter of negotiation and compromise. In this way, statistical numbers may hide as much as they reveal since what should be measured is a matter of choice. This is not particular to the development of statistics between nation states, but is valid for statistics in general. However, to develop statistics between nation states adds an important dimension. The states' concern with how they appear in relation to other nation states becomes an issue of concern to their representatives.

Keeping the culturally intimate hidden

With the decision to measure 'quality in work' by indicators, the national order of the EU became especially evident. The member states wanted to look good and 'their' interests to be represented in the EU diagrams and tables. What was to be measured and how were therefore highly important. If, for example, the definition of an indicator for measuring the number of 'unemployed' include those in 'activation programmes', this would produce a different score from that if the unemployed in activation programmes were excluded. In the interest of the nation, then, that which the nation state did not want to be displayed should not be measured.

Herzfeld's concept of *cultural intimacy* (1997:x,ff) is useful here. Herzfeld's (1997:ix-x) point is that there is often an external, government-produced, presentation of the national culture, which may be completely different from the individual citizens' presentation of their 'nation state' and 'national' characteristics. The key point is that cultural intimacy is created within the group through knowledge of what is *not* presented by the state as 'national culture'. According to Herzfeld it is often that which is a source of external embarrassment that is not displayed and that therefore creates sociality (Herzfeld 1997:3, 6, 9).

However, whereas Herzfeld (1997:5) focuses on the states' harmonious display of what they want their 'national culture' to represent versus the everyday practice, I focus here on the practice of the state in shaping the national display in the context of the EU. The member states' representatives try to act in their nation state's 'interest' by arguing for the use of one indicator rather than another or the definition of one indicator being changed to another. The member states and the Commission present conflicting arguments, which have to be moulded into a compromise. The 'EU' position thus becomes displayed as a shared way of thinking with common rules and practices that may be said to be postnational. Nevertheless, this postnational position is formed in a context in which the member states try to keep hidden what is culturally intimate to them. There is a clash between what should be displayed as transparent, on the one hand, and the culturally intimate, on the other hand, that has its roots in the tension between the postnational and the national in the EU. This will be discussed further in the following chapters.

Meeting in the postnational order

Whilst the bureaucratic logic transcends national boundaries and the EU nation states are becoming more integrated in different policy areas that until now have been national in character, the governments and bureaucratic institutions are more firmly located in their respective nation states or in the EU districts in Brussels. In regard to the structure of the EU in terms of governments and bureaucratic institutions, it is useful to think in Castells's terms of the EU as a 'network state' (1998:311). In the EU, decision-making can be said to be carried out in networks rather than in a central political structure. These networks have nodes rather than centres. Castells (1998:332) points out that there might be nodes, i.e. states, that are more powerful than others. However, there is no node in the network that can be ignored, as would be possible in a central political structure where the centre is in control of power. If nodes were ignored, the whole system would be called into question (ibid.).

However, the people in a network have to meet somewhere. Today, people in top positions such as politicians, civil servants or company managers, live under extreme meeting pressure (van Vree 2002:3). In today's complex societies members may be dispersed all over the world and the only times they meet face-to-face are often in pre-scheduled meetings. This is also the case with the EU. As in most organisations, formal decisions in the EU are made in meetings. The importance of meeting face-to-face has been widely discussed in the social sciences, not least by Goffman (1963:17, 1983:3) who argues that it is easier for people to read each other's purposes and intentions when they have a visual face-to-face encounter (Goffman 1983:3). There is also a richness in information flows that seems to be difficult to replace by any other medium and, not least, face-to-face meetings facilitate feedback (Goffman 1963:17). In addition, the meeting pressure has not decreased, despite the spread of media technology such as the internet, e-mail and virtual conferences (Garsten 1994:144). In fact, Boden (1994:81) argues that electronic communication expands rather than replaces face-to-face communication.

A 'meeting' may be defined in different ways. Goffman (1983:7) distinguishes between conversational encounters and meetings, the difference being that in meetings there is a chairperson who controls turn taking and relevance. Boden (1994:84) defines meetings as planned gatherings where the participants have a perceived role, where there is some forewarning of the event, and where the event has a purpose, a time, a place and an organisational function. Schwartzman (1989:62-64) distinguishes between scheduled and unscheduled meetings. Scheduled meetings have a set time, show a high degree of formality, and the participants are formally responsible, while unscheduled meetings have no set time, are rather low-key, and the participants are not formally accountable to other groups (Schwartzman 1989:63). While the weight given to different aspects of the meetings may vary, the combined views of these three authors provide a useful perspective for analysing EU meetings. The focus here is on formal, scheduled meetings with formal rules for making decisions. In this sense the meetings I have studied may be seen as 'instances of bureaucracy'. In the Weberian sense they are governed by explicit rules, the participants are regarded as experts, and the products of the meetings are written documents (Weber 1958:196-244).

The study of political meetings and how decisions are arrived at in meetings such as councils or committees has a tradition in anthropology. In the 1971 volume edited by Richards and Kuper decision-making and political process are discussed in a number of contexts; in an English town council (Spencer 1971), a council among the Merina of

Madagascar (Bloch 1971), or the councillor system of the Bemba of Northern Zambia (Richards 1971). Schwartzman's (1989) study of the importance of meetings in an American mental health centre is another example. A more recent example is Abram's study of rituals in Town Hall councils and committee meetings in Norway (Abram 2003:152ff). Meetings and decision-making in organisations are intimately connected. To follow a decision-making process evidently involves studying meetings as processes of negotiation and the articulation of perspectives. The meeting format – the scheduled time, the rituals in the meetings and so forth – thus also affects the decision-making process. The empirical material in the present study is mainly based on following the decision-making process of agreeing and deciding on 'quality in work' indicators in the different EU committees, working groups and council meetings that were involved in the process.

Fieldwork: following a decision-making process in EU meetings

This study is a policy process study, i.e. I have followed a decision-making process, the classifying of 'quality in work' into different areas, and the elaboration of 'quality in work' indicators based on these areas, through different localities during a period of two and a half years, in particular for one and a half years from the autumn of 2001 until the end of 2002.

I began by conducting semi-structured interviews with bureaucrats in the Commission[15] and taking part in conferences[16] on EU employment policy as part of familiarising myself with the field. Later on I carried out participant observation through a trainee position at the Directorate General of Employment and Social Affairs at the Commission during three months in the autumn of 2001, where I

---

[15] I did 24 interviews with bureaucrats at the Directorate General for Employment and Social Affairs on three different occasions in 1999, 2000 and 2001. In 2004, I did two additional interviews with one bureaucrat in the Directorate General and one in the Swedish Ministry.

[16] I took part in the Social Policy Agenda conference in Brussels in September 2000 and the Work Life 2000 – Quality in work conference in Malmö, Sweden in January 2001. More on these events in chapter two.

began to follow the decision-making process of developing 'quality in work' indicators. I continued to follow the process during 2002 by taking part in the preparatory meetings on the 'quality in work' indicators in the Swedish Ministry and then following the Swedish delegation to the Employment Committee meetings in Brussels, where the indicators were negotiated. I have followed the process in nine Employment Committee meetings lasting one to two days – including the Indicators group (six in number) –, one Social Questions Working group meeting, one Permanent Representative Committee (Coreper) meeting (more on these committees and groups in Chapter 3), and three preparatory meetings. My first meeting was the Employment Committee's Indicators group meeting on 24-25 September 2001 and my last was the Employment Committee meeting on 21-22 November 2002. The process of elaborating 'quality in work' indicators conveniently 'ended' at my last meeting.

When I began my study I had a general interest in how EU employment policy was formulated, negotiated and decided on in relation to the Swedish government and the EU institutions. This led me to work with the European Employment Strategy, which is one of the main strategies for EU employment policy. My interest in classifications soon steered my focus to the process of elaborating 'quality in work' indicators. This was especially interesting since the task of finding indicators to measure 'quality in work' brought differences in opinion between the member states to the surface. The work with developing indicators was also something that had increased in the EU during the last ten to fifteen years (as mentioned above), so it appeared to be an important subject for scrutiny.

Reinhold (in Shore and Wright 1997:14) uses the concept of 'studying through' to describe the method of following a policy process. She argues that by studying through, the 'webs and relations between actors, institutions and discourses across time and space' will be revealed (Reinhold in Shore and Wright 1997:14). She suggests that the study of policy should be carried out in the network in which the policy moves in order to capture the interaction between different places and levels in the policy process. To follow a policy process in this way is to use research techniques that pay attention to movement and tracing, such as following a people, a thing, a metaphor, a story or the like (Marcus 1995:106ff). Participant observation by following a policy process will thus have a different character from conventional, localised fieldwork. A policy process goes everywhere, and to follow a policy process therefore means to follow it through different localities. Marcus points out that: '[e]mpirically following the thread of cultural process itself impels the move toward multi-sited ethnography' (1995:97).[17]

My multi-local fieldwork moved between the Directorate General of Employment and Social Affairs in the Commission, the EU meeting rooms and the Swedish Ministry of Industry, Employment and Communication, (hereafter called the Swedish Ministry of Industry, as it is generally referred to). At the outset of my fieldwork, when I had a trainee position in the Commission, I was moving between the Directorate General and the meeting rooms, while living in Brussels during that time. During the second part of my fieldwork, when I was doing participant observation in the Swedish Industry Ministry and in the Employment Committee, the fieldwork had the character of what Wulff has labelled yo-yo fieldwork (2002:117), the yo-yo symbolising the going back and forth, and in and out of the field. It is important to point out, however, that the concept of multi-local may give the impression of having separate fields, whereas it is rather 'several fields in one' (Hannerz 2003:21), since a policy process may move across sites, but be connected into parts of a single field.

Working as part trainee, part researcher

As discussed by Nader (1972:302), one of the difficulties in 'studying-up' may be the problem of access. However, the problem with access and making rapport is difficult in more 'traditional' fields as well (ibid.). In my case the problem of access was for the most part solved as soon as I obtained a trainee position (*stagiaire*[18]) in the Directorate General.

---

[17] Multi-sited, multi-local or translocal fieldwork has been discussed by several anthropologists (see for example Garsten 1994; Hannerz 2003; Ortner 1997).
[18] In Brussels the trainee positions are referred to by the French term *stagiaire* regardless of language. There is a whole culture around being a *stagiaire*, or doing a *stage* as the

The EU institutions are accustomed to having researchers working in their corridors, which was made clear by the label *stagiaire universitaire*[19] that I received. The trainee position made it possible for me to walk freely in the corridors, search on the intranet, and attend meetings that would otherwise have been difficult to attend. In return for the opportunity to be a trainee I had to do something for them. At the end of my stay I left two papers at the Commission: 'Active Labour Market Policy or Workfare' and 'What Can Research Say on the Impact of the European Employment Strategy within Member States?'

However, it was not in the corridors but in the meetings that the organisation became most visible for observation, since people in the Directorate General and in my unit often worked on 'their' topic, by themselves, in their offices. The (almost) weekly unit meetings informed me of what people in the unit were doing and who to ask about particular policy areas. Other meetings that were important were the meetings I attended as the assistant of the Commission. However, the meetings that stood out as most interesting were the decision-making meetings between the Commission and the member states, in particular the Employment Committee meetings. It was there that the work of the Commission (together with the member states) was debated by the member states and the Commission.

My 'strategically situated ethnography' (Marcus 1986:177) is thus mainly based in the Employment Committee meetings. However, the field of the Employment Committee was made up of different localities. The central nodes in the network were the Employment Committee meetings, but for the meetings to function as intended, i.e. as decision-making arenas, other nodes in the network had to play their part. The member states' representatives had, for example, to adopt a 'national positions' in order to be able to negotiate their case in the Employment Committee. In this way the negotiations and decisions

---

English say. There are *stagiaire* organisations divided into different national groups and Directorate Generals and they organise lunches, parties and other social events. Every weekend there is most likely at least one *stagiaire* party somewhere in Brussels.

[19] A trainee who is in the European Commission as a researcher.

made in the Employment Committee were affected by discussions, negotiations and decision-making processes somewhere else.

The view from the Employment Committee made it possible to see the different negotiations, discussions and decisions made by all the member states. In this sense it became a multi-local fieldwork, but in one place. It enabled me to see how member states were able to form decisions on the 'quality in work' indicators. To work in the Commission was important, since it is there that all the documents, papers and opinions are prepared before they are discussed in the Employment Committee. However, to better understand why members said what they did in the Employment Committee meetings, I also had to study how member states prepare for the meetings. To do participant observation in all the member states, I would have had to be in several different places at the same or nearly the same time, in order to be able to grasp all the participants' perspectives on the same issue. For logistical reasons, this proved impossible. To get at different perspectives I chose instead to follow the Swedish members in the Employment Committee by taking part in their preparatory meetings in the Swedish Ministry of Industry. In this sense, my choice of field may be described as a 'strategically situated multi-local ethnography'.

Yo-yo-ing between Stockholm and Brussels

My fieldwork position, as part of the Swedish delegation in the Employment Committee, gave me insights into how representatives of one member state discuss things before the meeting. Earlier, when I was taking part in the meetings as a representative of sorts of the Commission, I had become familiar with some of the discussion in the Commission before the meeting and I had seen some of the Commission's 'opinion papers' in advance. What I wondered when I sat in the meetings was why member state so and so said what it did. Being part of the Swedish delegation gave me insights into that process. I also believed that it was important to understand what happened in a member state before the meetings.

In the preparatory meetings in the Swedish Ministry of Industry I also realised that I had missed out on the dealings and negotiations that take place outside and between the meetings with the Commission and other member states. As I was part of the Swedish delegation, this knowledge gap became more and more evident. A trainee position[20] in the Swedish Ministry of Industry would have given me access to these log-rollings on a more day-to-day basis. I now had a broad idea, more elaborated than if I had only done interviews, but not as elaborate as would have been the case, had I had a trainee position.

Being an observer in the Swedish delegation made fieldwork somewhat different from when I worked in the Commission. My fieldwork moved more significantly between different geographical spaces and made me aware of the significance as well as the insignificance of geographical as well as cultural borders. I went back and forth between Brussels and Stockholm on a number of occasions. I also moved back and forth into the field. During my internship in the Commission I had lived in the field for almost four months. Now, I went back and forth into the field from my university life, to the Ministry of Industry, to the Employment Committee meetings and back to my university life.

This yo-yo fieldwork meant that the excitements, as well as anxieties, of entering a field were repeated at every entry. Anxiety, because before every meeting I always imagined that they had changed their minds and that I would not be allowed to attend. Excitement, because my fieldwork was progressing and I would be learning more about the field. It also meant that I was not present in the field all the time. However, as pointed out by Wulff (2002:122), the movement back and forth into the field did not mean that I left the field completely in between. I was still in touch with the people in the field through e-mails and lunches, to make sure that I had not been forgotten and to get their perspective on questions I had when going through my notes and the documents from the Commission and the Swedish Ministry of Industry. I also followed what new policy areas were coming up on the agenda on the Directorate General's website and read policy

---

[20] I applied for a trainee position in the Swedish Ministry of Industry but was turned down. Instead, it was agreed that I could take part in the preparatory meetings for the Employment Committee and then follow the Swedish delegation to the Employment Committee meetings in Brussels.

documents to keep myself informed about the policy area in general
and the 'quality in work' indicators in particular. In addition, everyone
else came to the Employment Committee meetings from a life elsewhere. The Swedish members had, for example, to varying degrees,
other areas they worked on as well as the work connected with the
Employment Committee. In that sense my informants and I were in a
similar position.

Observing in meetings

In the meetings my role was primarily that of an observer. I never took
part as an active member. I sometimes helped the Secretariat of the
Employment Committee with handing out papers or running the
overhead projector when I was working in the Directorate General,
and I sometimes commented on issues in the preparatory meetings in
the Swedish Ministry of Industry when I was travelling with the Swedish delegation, but I was never a participant in the way the people I
observed were.

However, I do not believe this was a problem. The role of an observer made it possible for me to give my full attention to all the
members in the meetings instead of preparing my input or thinking of
it in relation to the other members, as the regular members were doing.
Nevertheless, if I had, for example, been working in the Secretariat of
the Employment Committee, I would have been more involved with
what was happening both inside and outside the meetings. In fact, the
outside of the meeting room was the most difficult place in which to
do fieldwork. It was impossible for me to follow all the delegates
around. There were about a hundred individuals directly involved in
the work of the Employment Committee at the Ministries of Labour or
Industry in the member states and in the Commission. In addition,
there were experts from other units in the Commission or in the
Ministries in the member states involved.

When I took part in the Employment Committee meetings I sat in
the back row, observed and took notes of what was said. The meetings
usually lasted two days and they were very hectic – not least for me,
since I tried to write down everything that was said. Of course that was
not possible, but at least I got a pretty good sense of what was said.

There were some difficulties, however. Sometimes I did not fully understand the discussion since they might be using concepts with which I was not familiar. At other times I was unable to follow the discussion because I was too busy writing what had been said before, so that I missed some of the beginning of the next speaker.

Nevertheless, even though I hardly have any direct quotations from the meetings – when I do they are in quotation marks – in the chapters which follow I have chosen to write, for example, 'the Swedish representative said' and then continue as if it was a direct quote. There are two problems with this. The first and obvious one is that I give the impression in the text of statements being direct quotations. Second, many of the quotations are meta-quotations since they are also translated by a translator and then written down by me. My purpose in doing so is that I may not have captured everything word for word, but the words in the text are still close to what was actually said. I believe that there is a point in writing 'the Swedish representative said'[21] since it makes it easier to understand the dialogue in the committee. If I had chosen to make an interpretation of what they said, the ethnography would lose out in richness. I am confident that I have written and understood what they meant in the so-called citations. The fact that I decided to follow one question, the elaborating of 'quality in work' indicators, was important here. During the different meetings I had come to gain a fuller understanding of the discussions and their implications, and by the end of my fieldwork in the Employment Committee meetings, I recognised arguments and sometimes knew how

---

[21] The choice of writing 'the Swedish representative' instead of using her or his personal name has to do with the formality of the meetings. In the meetings the members are referred to as 'Sweden' or 'Italy'. This signals a difference between the roles of individuals inside and outside the meeting. When outside the meeting, they are mentioned by personal name. When referred to by both first and last name they are not anonymised. When called only by first name they are. I have distinguished between public individuals such as Ministers who are then mentioned with first and last name and individuals working as bureaucrats behind the scenes, who are mentioned only by first name. However, sometimes bureaucrats appear in public such as in conferences and then they are given their real name, which is distinguished again by using both their first and last name.

different member states were going to react before they even took the floor.

Another problem with the constant writing of what they said was that I did not have much time to see their facial expressions or bodily movements as they talked. However, their tone of voice often revealed their state of mind. But does this mean that I could just have listened to recorded tapes of the meetings in the way Weiss and Wodak (2000:80) did? One answer is, of course, that if I had not been at the meetings I would not have been able to access the discussions going on there. There are no recorded tapes of the meeting. A second answer is that I also got a feel for the atmosphere in the group and in the room that I would not have had otherwise. In addition, even if I did not see and analyse all the facial expressions and bodily movements in regard to what the members expressed in the meetings I was still in the midst of the action.

An additional problem was the language. When member states spoke anything but English (or Swedish, of course) I had to listen to the interpreters. As Aull Davis points out, translations are far from theoretically neutral (1999:113). The interpreters did a remarkable job, but as I got to know the topic being discussed better I sometimes had to interpret their interpretation. They might, for example, have used another term than the one agreed upon in the Employment Committee.

However, what may be more challenging in a field this close to home is the overlapping of the emic and the analytical. The informants have a similar, at least on the surface, type of language, an academic language, and a way of reasoning similar to mine. Policy development in the Commission is performed in dialogue with the social sciences. Concepts and ideas studied by the social sciences such as 'governance' are soaked up by the Commission and made its own through the process of writing Communications, White Papers or Green Papers,[22]

---

[22] The Commission produces different policy documents. The Commission Communications, often referred to as COM-documents, include proposed legislation or other communications with the Council, the member states governments, and other institutions. Green Papers are discussion papers published by the Commission with the

as well as the other way round. As Bourdieu points out, '[s]tate bureaucracies and their representatives are great producers of "social problems" that social science does little more than ratify whenever it takes them over as "sociological" problems' (1994:2). This makes it difficult to see the way the meaning is made, which in turn makes it more difficult to analyse. The fact that we often have a language similar to our informants may give the impression that we share perspectives (Aull Davis 1999:108). In fact, as Garsten (1994:41) points out, field-work in an environment where the academic language is shared be-tween the informants and the researcher requires an even more critical stance. To reach this critical perspective required a period of distancing from the field.

Outline of the study

At the core of my research is the tracing of a decision-making process in the EU. I follow the policy process of framing the political vision of 'Social Europe' in the EU, by the idea of 'quality in work'. Particular focus is placed on turning this idea into 'quality in work' indicators. The notion of turning politics into numbers by using indicators is part of a wider problem related to the nation state losing political power in the postnational era, and the practices of transparency creating new classifications and categorisations in the context of EU policy-making. In this bureaucratic culture of policy making the Eurocrats move between different EU meetings to negotiate, discuss and decide on common 'EU' positions, in this way creating a postnational Europe. The different bureaucratic tools and political ideas that are put forward in these processes of communicating diverse perspectives and negotia-tions and how they are affected by the 'national order of the EU' and practices of transparency are the focus of the chapters that follow.

In Chapter 2, the focal point is on how 'quality in work' got on to the policy agenda in the EU. The notion of 'Social Europe' is pertinent

---

intention of creating discussion that may then lead to legislation. White Papers are papers published by the Commission that include proposals for action in a specific policy area. Green Papers are thus papers to create debate and White Papers to put forward an official proposal.

here, since it guides employment and social policy in the EU. Particular focus is placed on the work with the Commission's Communication on 'quality in work' and how the member states tried to shape the classifications in the Communication. The Prime Ministers and Presidents had asked the Commission to classify 'quality in work' and propose possible indicators. However, at the same time the member states had an interest in trying to influence the classifications in the Communication in order to direct 'Social Europe' in the interest of 'their' particular state. The member states, as seen in the chapter, attempted to influence the Commission's classifications by suggesting, in official events such as conferences, Councils, and European Councils, possible ways of measuring. These different 'classification-sets', i.e. sets of definitions of 'quality in work', drawn up by different actors had diverse meanings and shaped the idea of 'quality in work' in disparate ways. However, in the end the Commission's Communication was published and the classification became formal. Here, the bureaucratic logic of making classifications formed the policy-making process in the EU by steering it into defining concepts. These classificatory exercises are thus part of the bureaucratic culture of policy-making in the EU.

In Chapter 3, the emphasis on the bureaucratic culture of policy-making is put forward from another perspective. Here, the focus is on the time scheduling and temporal organisation of the decision-making process. When the Commission's Communication on 'quality in work' was published at the end of June 2001 it suggested possible indicators to measure the classification-set defining 'quality in work'. The Prime Ministers and Presidents had agreed in the European Council that indicators needed to be worked out before the end of the Belgian Presidency in December 2001. This set in motion a rhythm of meetings in which the members had to discuss, negotiate and argue on the indicators in order to come to a decision. The meeting schedule was thus determined by this hierarchical order of decision-making, in which the members in one Committee, Group or Council had to give 'their' opinion before the participants of the next Committee, Group or Council could give 'theirs'. The order of decision-making is part of making formal decisions legitimate. In this way the policy-making process is pushed towards a decision by the scheduling of the rhythm of the meetings and the actual meeting days. In addition, the changing of Presidencies every six months also moves the decision-making process forward, since the member state holding the Presidency wants to leave its mark on the EU by having decisions made during 'its' Presidency. Given that decisions are generally referred to by the particular meeting in which they were made and/or where they were made – 'decided on in the European Council in Nice' – makes the Presidency state part of the EU chronology. The changing of Presidencies and the rhythm of the meetings and their meaning for moving policy-making towards a decision are the focus in Chapter 3.

In Chapter 4, the emphasis is on the meeting format as such, as a significant feature of the bureaucratic culture of policy-making in the EU. Particular focus is placed on meetings as ritual processes of negotiation, communication and decision-making. In addition to timing, the ritual processes in the meetings are an important subject for scrutiny since they move the policy processes towards decisions. Here, I focus on the Employment Committee, which is the first Committee in the series of meetings to discuss, negotiate and decide on the 'quality in work' indicators. It is in the Employment Committee that most of the actual negotiations take place and it is here that the decisions are often taken in practice. The meeting format in the EU is based on the member states adopting 'national' positions, which are then negotiated and discussed in the meetings until the members can agree on a compromise. The relation between the meeting as frontstage and the preparations for the meeting as backstage reinforces the tension between the national and the postnational, which in turn shapes the policy-making process. Here, the focus is on how the ritual process of the meeting handles the conflict, thereby creating room to make compromise decisions.

In Chapter 5, the focus is on the idea and practice of forming indicators to evaluate policy. The practices of transparency are based on the foundation that numbers make decisions politically neutral and objective. The notion of giving political decisions legitimacy through scientific knowledge in the form of statistics is part of the bureaucratic logic in the Western world today. Here, specific attention is devoted to the development of indicators in one of the classified areas of 'quality in work', 'diversity and non-discrimination', and how this policy issue moves towards a decision through the rhythms of the meetings. The negotiations in the Employment Committee are a particular focus since, as described in Chapter 4, this is where most of the negotiations take place and often where decisions are, in practice, made. The chapter explores the interplay between statistics as 'objective' and the different political views on what should be measured in the member states. These differences are emphasised by the forming of 'national' positions. However, the perceived neutrality of the indicators also handles these political differences. There is a distinction made between the 'political' and the 'technical', where the technologisation of political ideas into statistics is believed to make them objective and context-free. This handles the conflict between the different national positions, since knowledge is used to make the decision politically neutral. The knowledge of these tools, the 'political' and the 'technical', is pertinent for the members to know how to argue their case in relation to the other members. The use of the notion of the 'political' and the 'technical' is thus part of the bureaucratic culture of policy-making, which makes decision-making in the EU achievable.

In Chapter 6, the development of 'quality in work' indicators is explored through the policy process of negotiating different perspectives in the Employment Committee and thereby finding a compromise decision. The member states are encouraged to have different national positions that often are conflicting in the meeting. Here, particular emphasis is put on how the member states, in this case Sweden, try to push for 'their' position in the Committee and how their success is determined by their ability to argue their case, with the use of bureaucratic tools such as the 'technical' and the 'political' or the use of 'key' and 'context' indicators. In addition, the need to have support from other member states is crucial. This does not mean that there has to be a majority in favour, but the other members have to see the relevance of discussing the issue as well as taking an interest in reaching a conclusion. The member states are partly made aware of 'their' concern for a policy proposal in the process of forming a national position. This forms the bureaucratic culture of policy-making in the EU, in which the national is the precondition for creating postnational transparency across the EU labour markets.

In the concluding chapter, Chapter 7, I discuss the making of transparent member states further. The idea of making member states' employment policies transparent is part of fashioning the bureaucratic culture of policy-making in the EU. Based on this, I explore the possibilities of the EU moving towards a postnational European community. The euro-statistics and indicators developed make the EU mappable, forming a particular kind of postnational community based on the calculable. This community is, however, heavily negotiated with reference to what the member states want to make visible and what they want to keep culturally intimate. In this way it may be said that calculability is an important starting point for forming a postnational European community.

Finally, in the Epilogue, I return to the field as it appears in 2005 and explore what has happened since I did my fieldwork in 2001 and 2002. Ten new member states have joined the EU and the scope and organisation of the European Employment Strategy have changed twice. How do these changes influence and shape the EU employment policy-making process? What has happened to the idea of 'Social Europe' and the 'quality in work' indicators? How has the accession of the ten new members affected the national and postnational tensions? These questions will be discussed and reflected upon in the Epilogue.

TWO

BUILDING 'SOCIAL EUROPE'

Introduction: 'more and better jobs for Europe'

'More and better jobs for Europe' the Presidents and Prime Ministers of the EU member states advocated in the European Council meeting in Lisbon in March 2000 (European Council 2000a). Social and employment policy was at the top of the EU agenda and the idea of 'Social Europe' and of employment and social security among individuals was seen as the prerequisite for economic prosperity in the EU. Already in 1984, the Council had agreed that the Community would not be able to strengthen economic cohesion if it did not at the same time strengthen social cohesion (Council Conclusion in Cram 1997:38). However it was not until now, at the beginning of the 2000s, that the idea of 'Social Europe' was pursued actively. There was a new employment and social title in the Treaty, and a willingness among the member states to collaborate further on social and employment policy within the EU.

The EU has been formed by different political processes, from the establishment of the European Coal and Steel Community (ECSC) at the beginning of the 1950s to working together to form joint EU employment and social policies at the end of the 1990s (Treaty of Amsterdam 1997). These different decisions, in the form of treaties, have connected the EU member states more and more closely by making it possible for them to be engaged in each other's external as well as internal policies. Through the texts of the treaties, ideas such as 'Social Europe' set the framework for what the EU is all about.

'Social Europe' may thus be seen as a *key symbol* for the EU, in the sense that it is a key element of the culture of the EU (Ortner 1973:1338). Or, to narrow the focus, 'Social Europe' may be seen as a *root metaphor*. Following Ortner, key symbols with great elaborating power may be identified as *root metaphors* (Ortner 1973:1340). A root metaphor is '…a symbol which operates to sort out experience, to place it in cultural categories, and to help us think about how it all hangs together' (Ortner 1973:1341). 'Social Europe' may thus be seen as a category for the ordering of conceptual experiences. By making sense of and establishing a certain view of the world, root metaphors help suggest '…valid and effective ways of acting upon it' (Ortner 1973:1342).

However, it is the everyday activities of making policies and policy decisions that create and re-confirm what we identify as 'Social Europe' (cf. Mörth 1996). In this chapter the focus is on the policy-making *processes* and how policies are 'muddled through' and moved towards decisions. The everyday policy-making processes are important areas for scrutiny, since these mundane performances of 'muddling through' (Lindblom 1959) and making decisions sustain the notion of the EU. The content of root metaphors is continuously created and re-created by individuals, in this case by politicians and bureaucrats (and sometimes by researchers). It may change with political trends in the EU, or depending on whether there is a majority of left- or right-wing governments in the member states. Even if the member states were in agreement that a 'Social Europe' was needed for the establishment of a prosperous 'Economic Europe', and in that way might help guide political ideas towards the social, what the concept would actually mean in practice would be quite another matter. 'Social Europe' is in Gallie's (1956:169) terms an 'essentially contested concept', i.e. a concept '…which inevitably involves endless disputes about [its] proper uses on the part of [its] users' (Gallie 1956:169).

The EU member states as well as the Commission have different ideas about what 'Social Europe' might mean (cf. Gallie 1956:170-171). What 'Social Europe' should mean in the EU has therefore to be discussed, negotiated and compromised on in order to achieve a common definition. Words are invented that signal particular political aspirations and ideals. At the beginning of the new millennium 'quality in work' was at the top of the EU agenda for 'Social Europe'. The Commission was asked by the European Council to produce a Communication, i.e. an official EU policy document, with classifications and possible indicators on 'quality in work' (European Council 2000b). At the same time, the member states' governments were interested in influencing the Commission's classification according to 'their' own visions and political ideals. They had to try to influence the classifications before they were published in the Commission's Communication. The everyday policy-making game played by the different actors trying to influence the words used to frame 'Social Europe' and to classify 'quality in work' is the focus of this chapter.

'Social Europe': a postnational 'society' in the making?

The notion of 'Social Europe' having a common employment and social politics within the EU creates a space for the 'social' to be connected to other spheres than the nation states. It may be seen as a basis for creating a postnational 'society' in the EU. Employment and social policies are in this way *society-creating* (Hoskyns 1996:47, also see Carson 2004:71) and may serve as the glue creating a sense of belonging among individual citizens in the EU.

For the politicians and bureaucrats working with EU policy, 'Social Europe' also has another unifying power, which is based on the 'other', in this context the perceived 'non-social' United States (also see Andersson 2004:69). The representatives of the EU member states are thus interpreting Europe as the continent that is 'doing good'. When the Prime Ministers and Presidents advocated 'more and better jobs for Europe', the words carried with them these ideas. The EU member states wanted to put forward that their policies are about 'more and better jobs' not just 'more jobs', as in the US. Defining Europe in relation to the 'other' is a way of forming 'us', a feeling of the EU being united. The 'social' then becomes something distinctively European.

The idea of a 'Social Europe' and the creation of a 'European social model' have been part of the EU since the Treaty of Rome, and different ideas, guidelines and directives have slowly been added during the decades of the EU's existence.

Building a 'European social model'

In the beginning the EU, or the European Coal and Steel Community (ECSC) (1952), as it was called at the time, was a peace project. The thought was that if the member states[23] were involved in each other's economies and armaments industries, there would be fewer opportunities for starting a war. However, for the founding fathers, Churchill, Spinelli, Rossi, and especially Monnet, Schuman and Spaak,[24] this was only a first step towards a united Europe (Carson 2004:95). The vision was to build a United States of Europe. There were forces both against and in favour of this vision, but in Rome in 1957 the member state Prime Ministers and Presidents were able to take steps towards such a vision. There, they agreed on the Treaty of the European Atomic Energy Community (EURATOM) and the Treaty on the European Economic Community (EEC), the so-called Treaties of Rome. The two new treaties, together with the European Coal and Steel Community, became (in 1958) the European Community (EC).

Through the European Economic Community the member states established a common market with common trade barriers and common trade policies with free movement of goods, persons, services and capital. In the European Economic Community Treaty, the conception of a 'European social model' also first saw the light. The Treaty gave the member states a legal basis for cooperation on employment, labour legislation and working conditions, industrial safety, social security, industrial hygiene, vocational training and the rights to establish associations and to negotiate (see Jacobsson and Johansson 2001:11-12).

However, social policy issues were of minor concern for the members of the European Community during the decades to come (Cram

---

[23] The member states at the time were Belgium, France, Italy, Luxembourg, the Netherlands and West Germany.

[24] For an overview of the creation of the EU and the people involved see Carson 2004:85ff. In the EU quarters in Brussels the visitor is constantly reminded of the founding fathers with the Rond Point Schuman and the Spinelli and Spaak buildings in the European Parliament.

1997:31). Some small steps were taken during the 1970s and 1980s. In 1974, for example, the first Social Action Programme was agreed on. This advocated 'equal treatment for men and women in the workplace, pay, and access to employment' as well as a 'common labour law on working conditions and health and safety at work'. Nevertheless, the programme only mentioned that co-operation should be encouraged. Instead in 1987, through the Single European Act, a social dimension was added to the Treaty. It was agreed that only qualified majority voting was needed in the Council for measures securing workers' freedom of movement. This was an important step towards a more 'Social Europe' since it gave more room for actual policies to be created. In addition, it was agreed in the Treaty that the member states should work to harmonise their policies on 'health and safety at work' as well as promoting a 'social dialogue' between the social partners at the European level. The terms of 'should work to' or 'promoting' were quite vague, but the fact that the idea was included at all has been attributed to the Commission's President at the time, Jacques Delors (Cram 1997:41). Delors was a strong advocate of a 'European social model' (Vaughan-Whitehead 2003:4).

A few years later (1989), in the Community Charter of the Fundamental Social Rights of Workers, or the Social Charter, it was laid down that, through the expected formation of the European Union, with a more closely connected common market, the 'social' also had to be an issue for the EU. Employees should, for example, be guaranteed social protection in the event of unemployment regardless of whether they were working in their native country or not (Westerlund 1995:79). This can be said to be the first step towards a more pronounced policy concerning social issues within the EU.

However, it was not until the 1990s and the Treaty of the European Union (1992), with its annexed Protocol on Social Policy that social and employment policy became a more substantial part of the Treaty. Through the Protocol on Social Policy it was agreed that it was possible to make decisions in the Council with qualified majority voting in a number of new areas: 'health and safety at work', 'working conditions', 'information and consultation with employees', 'equality between men and women with regard to labour market opportunities and treatment at work', and 'the integration of persons excluded from the labour market' (Art. 2, Protocol on Social Policy). The Protocol also made it possible to make unanimous voting decisions in the areas of 'social security and social protection of workers', 'protection of workers where their employment contracts is terminated', and 'representation and collective defence of the interests of workers and employers' (Art. 2, Protocol on Social Policy). In addition, a European 'Social dialogue', which before had only been 'promoted' was now established between the Social Partners and the Commission (Art 3 and 4, Protocol on Social Policy).

Even though the Protocol was only annexed to the Treaty – because the United Kingdom was opposed to it – the fact that it was decided that in many areas only qualified majority voting was needed was an important step for the member states advocating more social policy within the EU. A few years later, when the Treaty was being rewritten in 1997, the United Kingdom had changed to a more left-wing government and the Protocol on Social Policy and an Employment Title were able to be included in the Treaty of the European Union. Since then the member states have also been working more closely together on employment and social policies through, for example, the European Employment Strategy. Thus it is possible to see the EU project as moving from being concerned with peace and economy to also including the 'social', in this way creating a postnational 'society'.

Keeping the social 'national'

Whilst employment and social policies have emerged as significant policy areas within the EU, they have traditionally been connected with the nation state. In Sweden, for example, there is a long tradition of valuing the importance of work for the development of social identity and of placing great value on employment and labour market politics for the imagining of the 'national'. 'The Swedish model' as an employment policy instrument has had great symbolic value in the creation of a Swedish national identity. This Swedish national identity is, if not challenged, then at least affected by the notion of 'Social Europe'.

Nevertheless, most EU Directives in these areas are less stringent than the national laws (Bean et al. 1998:9). Many of the employment and social policies are based on procedures rather than laws, such as the open method of co-ordination used in the European Employment Strategy. In fact, the Commission, after spending a decade fighting with the Council, toned down its approach during the 1970s and 1980s by not pressing for substantial legislation in the social area (Cram 1997:36-37). Instead it became involved in producing research and promoting small-scale social programmes. It also devoted extensive energy to policy analysis, not only of its own policies but also of the member states' national policies, in order to exert influence by the producing 'knowledge'. The approach has been called a 'softening up process' (Majone in Cram 1997:38), and has been the Commission's approach when trying to promote employment and social policy ever since. This softening up process is usually referred to as 'soft law', as mentioned in Chapter 1.

In addition, the member states have different visions of what the state, or in this case the EU, should be involved in, in these areas. Even if the EU has included the Employment title and the Protocol on Social Policy in the Treaty of Amsterdam in 1997, and the member states have agreed that social cohesion is a prerequisite for economic prosperity, there is still room for interpretation of what 'Social Europe' should be about. For example, the United Kingdom Prime Minister together with the Spanish, Italian and German Prime Ministers drew up a number of different documents during the end of the 1990s and the beginning of the 2000s arguing for greater flexibility and less labour market regulation, in the same spirit as the neo-liberal United States, and less co-operation in this field in the EU (Vaughan-Whitehead 2003:26-27). At the same time, the Commission, together with, for example, France, Belgium and Sweden, favoured more co-operation on employment and social issues in the EU, albeit with different views on what and how much.

This clash between different perspectives on what employment and social policy should be concerned with culminated at the European Council in Lisbon in March 2000. Again, it was emphasised that 'Social Europe' should be connected to better articulation between the economy, employment, and social cohesion (European Council 2000a). The connection of the social with the economic solved the problem about different views on employment and social policy, since there was room for understanding this connection in different ways in the member states. However, and as we shall see below, there were at the same time attempts to frame 'Social Europe' in a more specific way, connecting it to certain concepts and ideas.

Framing 'Social Europe': working symbolic analysts

To guide what 'Social Europe' should be about, the politicians and bureaucrats make efforts to frame the direction by inventing concepts that are intended to describe what 'Social Europe' means. These concepts may be termed 'keywords' in Williams' sense, i.e. '...they are significant, binding words in certain activities and their interpretation; they are significant, indicative words in certain forms of thought' (1976:13). In the process of forming classifications, the meaning of 'Social Europe' is, in this way, interpreted through keywords, i.e. words that are particular to, and which have particular meaning in, the EU context, such as 'quality in work'. These words are imbued with ideas that narrow the focus of what 'Social Europe' might mean.

The classifying of ideas into concepts is part of forming society. The work of inventing new concepts to identify, explain, and solve problems, is an activity that Reich has labelled 'symbolic analytic' work (1992:177). He identifies diverse professionals such as researchers, engineers, public relations executives, lawyers, consultants of all types, art directors, architects, film editors and producers, journalists, musicians, who might all be viewed as *symbolic analysts* (Reich 1992:177-178). According to Reich, symbolic analysts 'solve, identify, and broker problems by manipulating symbols. They simplify reality into abstract images that can be rearranged, juggled, experimented with, communicated to other specialists, and then eventually, transformed back into reality' (Reich 1992:178). Categorising notions – as well as people and things – into different boxes, such as 'flexibility' or 'quality in work', is a way of framing political decisions. As symbolic analysts, politicians and bureaucrats simplify reality by classifying the abstract idea of

'Social Europe' into a particular classification-set, namely, a number of related words that together make up the classification, in which the 'boxes' are supposed to be orderly and coherent. Words are used, rearranged, and juggled to find the 'perfect' classification.

Keywords, then, may be said to exist at different levels where one concept provides the definition of another. One keyword may also in one context constitute a definition of another keyword, and in another context the second keyword may provide a definition of the first. However, what signifies them is that, despite changes in meaning and level in the classification system, the words are often the same or similar over time. Defining root metaphors, such as 'Social Europe', or keywords framing root metaphors, such as 'quality in work', is a constant process. However, while root metaphors are wider in their interpretation, keywords are in this context more precise and tend to rotate, having, for example, 'flexibility' at the top at one time, while at the next having 'flexibility' as a definition of 'quality in work'. The meaning and the classification system change depending on the politicians' and bureaucrats' opinions at the moment. Nevertheless, regardless of their inconsistency in hierarchical structure, keywords work as guidelines for the perceived pathway for policy-making. If 'Social Europe' is a root metaphor, the keywords narrow the focus on what 'Social Europe' could mean. The language becomes, in Gustafsson's (1994:206) terms, 'ritualised', which means that concepts are given a more formalised definition.

In addition, when keywords are used in new contexts, old meanings may gain new importance, or the existing meaning may take on new and unforeseen developments, a process that has been described as a 'discursive transformation' (Garsten and Jacobsson 2004:274). As Garsten and Jacobsson point out: 'Discursive transformations may not involve a complete turnover of basic assumptions, but more often entail a gradual shift in understanding and framing' (2004:274). The keyword may, then, be the same but the understanding of it may be different in different times and contexts. This has consequences for what meaning 'Social Europe' will have, in turn influencing what route employment and social policy will take in the EU.

From 'flexisecurity' to 'quality in work'

The notion of 'flexibility', was introduced in the EU employment
policy agenda through the White Paper: *Growth, Competitiveness,
Employment. The Challenges and Ways Forward into the 21ˢᵗ Century* (CEC
1993b:64). One of the cures during the 1990s downturn was seen to be
a more 'flexible' labour market (CEC 1993b:64). Nevertheless, the EU
member states wanted to distinguish the EU from the US, where
employment politics was understood to be all about 'flexibility'. The
EU member states wanted to emphasise that the 'European social
model' was based on other values than the neo-liberal ideals of the US.
They therefore put forward the importance of 'social security'. The
'European social model' should instead be based on 'flexibility <u>and</u>
security', or 'flexisecurity' as it is sometimes called. In the EU guidelines for employment at the end of the 1990s it also read that the
member states should 'promote a modern work organisation with a
flexible but secure workforce' (Council of the European Union
1999:7).

'Flexibility and security' was seen in the context of the EU employment guidelines as an aspect of 'adaptability' (ibid.). To find out
how adaptable workers and work organisations are in the EU, the
Commission decided that indicators needed to be worked out to
measure this. However, 'adaptability' first needed to be classified.
Miguel, a principal administrator in the Commission, developed a
definition of adaptability into ten classifications: 'labour supply availability'; 'health situation of the labour force'; 'level of education and
training of the labour force'; 'capacity to utilise new technology';
'degree of flexibility in working time'; 'industrial relations'; 'labour costs
flexibility'; 'labour taxation'; 'contract flexibility'; and 'labour mobility'.
The classification-set was intended to reflect the idea of flexibility and
security in combination. However, the main focus was on the employees' ability to be flexible, versatile in task performance and to accept
flexible working hours and flexible contracts, rather than on their
security.

At the beginning of the new millennium, EU employment politics
changed its agenda from 'flexisecurity' and 'adaptability' to 'more and

better jobs'. The idea of 'better jobs' was related to the 'other', in this case the US, as well as the perceived notion that in the future there would be a labour shortage within the EU, because of the declining birth rate. People needed to be encouraged and to have the strength to stay in employment longer. To make that possible, work had to be 'qualitative' and 'attractive' (European Council 2000:a). The slogan 'more and better jobs for Europe' was, after the European Council in Lisbon, heard and seen everywhere in policy documents in the context of EU.

The notion of 'more and better jobs' was soon translated into 'full employment' and 'quality in work' in the Commission's proposal for the European Social Agenda, which was published in the summer of 2000 (CEC 2000:14). The idea of 'quality in work' was not new. In the 1960s and 1970s there had been a big movement generally referred to as 'quality in working life'. According to Miller and Rose, '[t]his ideal was articulated in the name of the mental health and personal fulfil-ment of the worker, the ability and morality of the manager, the quality of the product, the efficiency and competitiveness of the enterprise, and the political legitimacy of the corporation' (1995:439-440). The idea was that the best interest of the workers also lay in the best inter-est of the companies. Efficiency, competitiveness, and the quality of the product would be better if the workers had stimulating, motivating jobs in which they could use their creativity. This also contributed to a new view of the individual as '...an active and motivated individual, seeking autonomy, control, variety, and a sense of worth' (Miller and Rose 1995:441). Experiments were conducted at workplaces in, for example, Norway during the 1960s, but the ideas were never really incorporated into working life in Norway or any other country during the 1960s and 1970s (Miller and Rose 1995:440). The exceptions would be Volvo and Saab Scania in Sweden, where team working and dock assembly replaced the assembly line in many factories during the 1970s and 1980s (Miller and Rose 1995:446, also see Huzzard 2003).

In the US the idea of 'quality in working life' was very much alive in the 1970s. Several national organisations concerned with the 'quality of working life' were formed (Miller and Rose 1995:451). However, few factories actually implemented the ideas and in the 1980s a new political ideal emerged in the US as well as in the United Kingdom in the period of Reagan and Thatcher. This new ideal has generally been referred to as neo-liberalism, and it fostered a new view of individuals as seeking 'to conduct their lives as a kind of enterprise of the self, striving to improve the "quality of life" for themselves and their families through the choices that they took within the marketplace of life' (Miller and Rose 1995:455).

Now, what does 'quality in work' mean in the 2000s in the context of the EU? What discursive transformations has the concept undergone? The member states were not in agreement in the European Council in Lisbon. In the Lisbon Conclusions the Prime Ministers and Presidents were able to agree that 'more and better jobs' would mean 'improving employability and reducing skills gaps', 'giving higher priority to lifelong learning as a basic component of the European Social Model', 'increasing employment in services, for example, the telecommunication and internet industry', and 'furthering all aspects of equal opportunities' (European Council 2000a). The idea was that there would be 'quality in work' if individuals were more employable and if more jobs were created in the telecommunications industry. In this context, it is safe to assume that the Prime Ministers and Presidents thought that 'to be employable' meant that, through training, individuals would have the skills needed for the jobs available. It also meant training individuals in work so that they would have the ability to follow changes in, for example, technical shifts in the factory or to enhance computer literacy in the office. And finally, in order to make jobs more qualitative and attractive, everyone would have to have an equal chance to get and keep a job and to advance in it. These classifications, however, were not seen as sufficient since the member states agreed in the European Council in Nice the same year that indicators needed to be developed to determine the 'quality in work' in the member states (European Council 2000b). To make this possible, the notion of 'quality in work' needed to be <u>formally</u> classified.

Towards a classification of 'quality in work'

The focus in this section is on the political process of classifying the policy goal of 'quality in work'. The making of 'quality in work' is manifested in different events in which the future of 'Social Europe' is being shaped in a 'battle' between different actors to find the 'right' keywords and classify them in the 'right' way – the 'right' way being in line with the political visions of the member state governments, as well as presenting them in an attractive way when it is time to turn them into indicators. This conflict between perspectives is visible in the different events and policy documents.

In this chapter, I am interested in what politicians and bureaucrats communicate in events such as policy conferences or different EU meetings. The focus is on what is said rather than the structure of the event and what the event itself represents. Events are important loci for the expression and communication of politics, where politics is given more definite contours. In addition, formal policy documents are often the outcome, the protocols and conclusions, of events such as meetings or conferences.

As mentioned above, the assignment to find classifications and possible indicators for 'quality in work' was given by the Prime Minis-ters and Presidents in the European Council to the Commission (European Council 2000b). However, the member states all tried to influence the outcome of the classifications through different policy documents and speeches at political events and scheduled conferences. The member states and the Commission were thus attempting to agree on what needed to be done to achieve 'quality in work'. Regardless of whether these were deliberate attempts to influence the classifications by proposing preliminary definitions, it is safe to assume that these attempts did, in the end, influence the 'final' classifications by the Commission.

The bureaucratic logic of classification, to make society readable, has usually been connected with the political interests of the nation state (see, for example, Scott 1998, de Swaan 1998). But in the EU it is not only political preferences that are in play but also national interests.

The idea of 'Social Europe', with the capacity to hide different competing interpretations, was one of its strengths, since the member states
could interpret the concept in accordance with their own national
context. Hannerz's term 'creolisation' (1992:265) is useful here for
understanding the dynamic between the use of a common language
within the EU and at the same time the making of one's own particular
national or local interpretation. To narrow the possibility for national
interpretations, however, the member states, pushed by the Commission, tried to agree on common classifications.

This narrowing of focus meant that there was more at stake for the
member states. Since they knew that the classifications would be the
basis for developing indicators, it was important for them to influence
the classifications so that 'their' member state would 'look good', i.e.
show high 'quality in work', in the comparisons. In addition, the classifications needed to be aligned with the political preferences in 'their'
member state. The fact that classifications may stir up policy-making in
the member states, since what is measured sets in motion political
processes, was important here. Previously, when the Prime Ministers
and Presidents agreed that 'Social Europe' should be partly defined by
the notion of 'quality in work', they steered possible future directions
that policy could take in this area. Now, when 'quality in work' was
going to be defined, it was even more important to influence the
outcome, since it would narrow the possibility for member states' own
interpretations.

The Commission campaigning for 'its' classification of 'quality in work'

At the end of September 2000 in Brussels, at the conference on the
Social Policy Agenda[25] in the European Parliament, the Commission
introduced its suggestion for the European Social Agenda for the next
five years, 2000-2005. The Commission's draft European Social
Agenda (CEC 2000) had been published in June and the Commission
and the Parliament now organised a conference on the policy issues

---

[25] For more information about the conference visit:
http://www.europarl.eu.int/hearings/2000_en.htm Last visited 2005-12-09. Print-out
in author's possession.

presented in the Agenda, to which researchers and policy-makers had been invited to discuss the topics.

The conference took place on the third floor of the Paul-Henri Spaak building of the European Parliament. At the conference were researchers from different universities and research institutes, including myself. Some of them were there as presenters and others as listeners. However, the majority of the audience were policy-makers: bureaucrats from ministries and state agencies and the EU institutions, social partners from both the European level and the national level, and other agencies such as consumer interest organisations.

In the Commission's European Social Agenda document, the question of 'quality in work' was in the spotlight. The idea of 'more and better jobs' from the European Council in Lisbon a few months earlier was translated here into 'full employment' and 'quality of work'. It read:

'Full employment means promoting more jobs; Quality of work includes better jobs and more balanced ways of combining working life
with personal life' (CEC 2000:14).

To be able to accomplish 'full employment' and 'quality in work' six possibilities were introduced in the European Social Agenda that would help create what was sought. These were: 'improving people's employability and reducing skill gaps', 'promoting entrepreneurship and job creation', 'enabl[ing] job creation in services', 'giving more priority to equal opportunities', 'pursuing economic reform of product services and capital markets [...] strengthening the employment con-tent of growth', and 'lifelong education for all' (CEC 2000:16). Several of these ideas were recognisable from the Conclusions of the Euro-pean Council in Lisbon.

The opening session on the first day took place in a big meeting room where the seats were ranged in a semi-circle rising in steps with room for hundreds of people. The presenters sat on a platform facing the audience. A representative from the Parliament, Anne Van Lancker, and a representative from the Commission, the Commis-sioner for Employment and Social Affairs, Anna Diamantopoulou, introduced the proceedings. They both showed the 'triangle' from the

Commission's draft on the European Social Agenda on the overhead projector:

Social policy
Social quality/Social cohesion

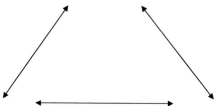

Competitiveness/Dynamism   Full employment/Quality in work
Economic policy   *Employment policy*
                                                      (CEC 2000:8)

The 'triangle' would later show up in different policy documents and be presented in different political events. At the time, it constituted the focus of 'Social Europe', where the thought was that social policy, employment policy and economic policy all influence each other. Certain keywords were also attached. Within the area of economic policy, the EU member states should focus on making the EU 'competitive' and 'dynamic'. In the area of social policy the focus should be on 'social quality' and 'social cohesion', and in the area of employment policy the focus was set on 'full employment' and 'quality in work'.

On the second day, in a workshop called 'Full Employment and Quality of Work – The Microeconomic Side', one of the speakers is Karl-Johann Lönnroth, Director at the Directorate General of Employment and Social Affairs. His opening remarks focus on the shift in discourse from 'more and better jobs' to 'quality in work'. He says:

> Before we used to speak about more and better jobs, but it is not until now that quality of work has come into the limelight.

He asks rhetorically what 'quality in work' is and then goes on to suggest ten criteria: (i) 'Sustainable wages'; (ii) 'Health and safety at work'; (iii) 'Full labour rights'; (iv) 'Freedom to choose to occupy a job'; (v) 'Producing environmentally sustainable products'; (vi) 'Providing equal opportunities for men and women'; (vii) 'Social rights'; (viii) 'Individuals having the opportunity to develop skills and capacities'; (ix) 'Jobs that are not only for one, for example ethnic, group'; and (x) 'Inviting also older people to stay on longer'.

In other words, Lönnroth, with this classification-set, was arguing that, for the Commission, 'quality in work' meant having a reasonable wage for the job one is doing, having a healthy and safe working environment, enjoying full labour rights, the freedom to choose a particular job as well as to refuse one, working in an organisation that produces environmentally safe products, working in an organisation where men and women as well as immigrants have the same opportunities, enjoying full social rights such as social security, working in an organisation where one can develop one's skills and capacities, and working in an organisation where the experience of older employees is valued.

If 'quality in work' had previously been talked about in terms of ideas on what needed to be done to aim at 'full employment' and 'quality in work', now stricter classifications were being set up instead. This entailed a categorisation of what 'quality in work' could mean, in which it was divided into different sub-areas to facilitate the measurement of each. The classifications constituted a hierarchical system (according to the bureaucratic logic of classification), where 'quality in work' was at the top with different subgroups underneath. In such a hierarchical system, every idea is to be put into a neat box and each idea has its given place. However, as we shall see in Chapter 5, these boxes are not always so neat and clear.

This attempt to classify 'quality in work' was followed by others. The classification process is thus a political process, in which politicians and bureaucrats argue, negotiate and present their ideas of what 'quality in work' might mean. It is important to bear in mind that the 'first' definitions made public may, and often do, guide future definitions. Accordingly, it is important not only to negotiate and argue with one's peers, but also to make one's views public and known among the member states in the EU in order to find allies and influence the Commission's Communication.

Attempting an EU classification of 'quality in work'

A few months later, during the French Presidency, the Prime Ministers
and Presidents met in the European Council in Nice in December
2000. They then decided, in line with the Commission's suggestion in
the European Social Agenda, that they needed to get at the 'quality in
work' in the member states by developing indicators, in order to be
able to measure 'quality in work' and compare the member states. The
Commission was given the assignment to write a Communication on
'quality in work' suggesting classifications of the concept and possible
indicators before the summer of 2001, in order to reach a decision on
'quality in work' indicators before the Belgian Presidency's last European Council meeting in Laeken in December 2001 (European Council
2000b Annex). So as to make an impact on the classifications of the
indicators, the Prime Ministers and Presidents attempted, for the
second time (the first was in Lisbon), to agree on a common classification of 'quality in work'. In the European Council Conclusions they
agreed that 'quality in work' was concerned with: 'working conditions',
'health and safety', 'remuneration', 'gender equality', 'balance between
flexibility and job security', and 'social relations' (European Council
2000b Annex).

It is possible to deduce from this definition that the Prime Ministers and Presidents believed that an employee feels that there is 'quality
in work' when an organisation has good working conditions, a healthy
and safe work environment, when one receives compensation for the
work done, when there are equal opportunities for both men and
women, when there is a balance between flexibility and security, and
when social relations between employees and employers are good.

In comparison with the Commission's classification, the definition
of the European Council was more focused on the employees' social
rights in the workplace, while Lönnroth had a broader definition,
which included the workplace's products as well as the quality of life in
general. These discursive transformations of the concept would thus
give 'quality in work' a slightly different meaning.

Sweden promoting 'its' definition

During its Presidency, in the first half of 2001, Sweden arranged a conference on 'quality of work' in Malmö. The organiser, the Swedish Ministry of Industry, had, together with the National Institute of Working Life,[26] the Swedish Work Environment Authority,[27] the National Labour Market Board,[28] and Prevent Sweden,[29] been preparing for the conference for four years. The conference had been preceded by sixty workshops during this period. Swedish researchers had headed the workshops, but they had invited researchers doing research on employment and labour market issues in 'their' own states. The aim of the workshops had been to identify the policy challenges and possible strategies to cope with working life in the future.

The conference aimed to summarise what had been said in the different workshops. At the time the first workshop took place in 1997, and in any of the other workshops for that matter, it is safe to assume

---

[26] The National Institute for Working Life is a national centre for issues concerning working life. It carries out research and development covering the field of working life, and on commission from the Ministry of Industry, Employment and Communications. See its website for more information: http://www.arbetslivsinstitutet.se/about/default.asp Last visited 2005-12-09. Print-out in author's possession.

[27] The Authority's objective is to reduce the risks of ill-health and accidents in the workplace and to improve the work environment in a holistic way, i.e. from the physical, mental, social and organisational viewpoints. For more information see its website: http://www.av.se/english/default.shtm Last visited 2005-12-09. Print-out in author's possession.

[28] The Swedish Labour Market Board (AMS), which is the central authority in the Swedish Labour Market Administration (AMV), has the task of putting Swedish employment and labour market policy into practice. For more information visit its website: http://www.ams.se/englishfs.asp?C1=223 Last visited 2005-12-09. Print-out in author's possession.

[29] Prevent – 'Management and labour improving work environment' works on behalf of the Swedish Confederation of Enterprises, the Swedish Trade Union (LO) and the Federation of Salaried Employees in Industry and Services (PTK) to improve the working environment and prevent accidents. For more information visit its website: www.prevent.se Last visited 2005-12-09. Print-out in author's possession.

that the researchers did not have in mind selling 'quality in work' as a new EU policy agenda. One may also presume that the policy-makers in 1997 did not regard 'quality in work' as the most important EU employment policy issue either. But at the time of the conference it was very much the focus, and the name of the conference also spelled this out: 'Work Life 2000 – Quality in Work'. The conference was thus framed according to the prevailing EU political programme.

The opening session took place in a room decorated with the blue and yellow colours of the Swedish Presidency, and with the Swedish Presidency logo behind the podium of the presenters. The participants were a mix of researchers and policy-makers, with most of the re-searchers as presenters and most of the policy-makers as listeners. The conference was aimed at policy-makers in the EU, but there were also people from countries outside the EU such as Bulgaria, Egypt, Estonia, Georgia, and Norway. Mona Sahlin, Minister at the Swedish Ministry for Industry, gave a supporting speech about her expectations of the conference and the importance of promoting 'quality in work' in the labour market. The conference proceeded with different Round Table discussions and workshops to present the results from the preparatory workshops.[30] At the end of the conference Mona Sahlin returned to sum up the proceedings. She said:

> 'As I mentioned in my opening address, I have had huge expectations on this conference. I also hoped that this conference would contribute to the discussion on what quality in work is and how we can achieve it'.[31]

---

[30] After the opening session there were parallel workshops mixed with Round Table discussions on the four themes of the conference: 'Diversity in Working Life', where the focus was on both workforce and workplace diversity; 'Labour Market', where the focus was on new employment, labour law and social rights, social changes and employment and IT, and the new media industry; 'Work Organisation', where the focus was on health, human resources, future workplaces and work life, and the information society; and finally 'Work Environment', where the focus was on physical and chemical risk factors, health effects, risk assessment and control, occupational health and safety management and medical surveillance.

[31] Visit http://www.eu2001.se/eu2001/calendar/meetinginfo.asp?iCalendarID=1842 to find the written speech. Last visited 2005-12-09. Print-out in author's possession.

She emphasised the importance of having good working conditions, not only for the sake of the individual worker, but also in the interests of having competitive enterprises. She also thought it important in regard to working life issues to take into account diversity, the working environment, skills development and all other questions that have been discussed as components of enhanced 'quality in work'. She argued that there will be no economic growth if there is no 'quality in work'. One way to achieve 'quality in work', in her view, is to make sure that individuals can adapt to new changes in the labour market. She concluded by saying that an important task is to define 'quality in work' more clearly and to develop a method so that the policy approach can be implemented in European and in national policy. She said that a first step would be to develop 'quality in work' indicators and that she had been co-operating with the Belgian Minister, Onkelinx, on how this could be done. The work on finding definitions for the indicators had thus already started and the present Presidency, Sweden, was co-operating with the next Presidency, Belgium, to make it possible to have indicators in this area.

Minister Mona Sahlin, in her summation, thus identified the conference as part of the 'quality in work' EU policy agenda. She wanted to emphasise the Swedish view of what Sweden thinks 'quality in work' is and how it should be classified. Like the Prime Ministers and Presidents in the European Council, her classification-set was also focused on the employees' rights, working conditions and the environment. However, she also mentioned the importance of having competitive enterprises, thus broadening the concept beyond the individual to the industry's conditions in line with the Commission.

Advancing the EU classification

Later that Spring the Swedish Presidency was host to the informal Employment and Social Policy Council,[32] which took place in the northern town of Luleå on 15-16 February 2001. In her opening

---

[32] 'Informal' refers to the fact that no formal decisions are made. Instead it is a time for discussion. The informal Council meetings take place once or twice in every Presidency within all the different Councils of Ministers.

speech,[33] Mona Sahlin stated that it is difficult to define 'quality in work' and that what quality is, is subjective to the individual, but that she still thought it important to try to identify those features that are essential. She suggested seven criteria: 'lifelong learning', 'gender equality', 'diversity', 'adequate working conditions which are also conducive to good health', 'sound, flexible work organisation', and 'employee participation'. To her, and to the Swedish government, 'quality in work' would mean a workplace where lifelong learning is encouraged, where gender equality and ethnic diversity are valued, where there are good working conditions and a healthy environment, where there is a flexible work organisation with secure personnel, and where employees participate in decisions.

The classification-set the Swedes put forward this time had shifted slightly towards being only about the individuals' working situation. Depending on which classification-set is chosen, the idea of 'quality in work' would have different meanings and produce different possible ways of interpreting them. As mentioned above, while the classifications of Karl-Johann Lönnroth (the Commission's representative) were a mix of the employees' social rights in the workplace and in life in general as well as of the quality of the companies' products, the classification made in the European Council and by the Swedish Minister at the informal Council meeting in Luleå focused only on the employees' social rights in the workplace. In a comparison between the European Council's classification and the Swedish classification, it is possible to see some similarities. However, wages were not in the Swedish list, but instead 'lifelong learning' and 'diversity' were, two policy areas that had been at the core of the Swedish working life policy agenda in the late 1990s and the beginning of the 2000s, were included.

On a general level, the definitions put forward by the Commission's representative and the Swedish representative were also similar to the classifications all the member states had agreed on in the European Council first in Lisbon and later in Nice. The focus on what

---

[33] For a copy of the speech and more information on the meeting in Luleå see website: http://www.eu2001.se/eu2001/calendar/meetinginfo.asp?iCalendarID=151   Last visited 2005-12-09. Print-out in author's possession.

'quality in work' could mean in the EU context was already narrowed. Here, the notion of 'Social Europe' guided the member states and the Commission in a way that limited the possible classifications that might be made. The member states and the Commission had on former occasions agreed on common definitions of 'Social Europe'. These also coloured the classifications now. Issues such as 'health and safety at work' and 'gender equality', which were the only ones in all three classification-sets, had been on the EU agenda since the Treaty of Rome and were therefore agreed common ground, while 'remuneration' and 'diversity' were potentially much more difficult to agree on.

However, the use of different concepts for nearly the same meaning suggests that the actors were trying to develop their own classification-sets independently of the others in an attempt to make 'their' mark on the process. The differences between the concept 'health and safety at work' in the European Council and the Commission's suggestion and 'Good health' in the Swedish proposal suggest that every event has its own agenda, making the process of classifying 'quality in work' into 'parallel processes' (Jacobsson 1987:85) rather than one process. Different ideas and possible classifications were prepared for every occasion. As long as there was no formal EU definition made public the field was open. The member states' and the Commission's representatives were defining what 'their' member states or the Commission believed that 'quality in work' should be about, which they ventilated at different events, making their views public. If 'their' perspective was then to become that of the entire EU, it would be considered a victory. The classifications would subsequently be understood as in line with 'their' member states' political preferences, which would make the development of indicators and the prospect of comparisons between member states in these areas less threatening.

The (final) discursive transformation: making the classification of 'quality in work' formal

All the different attempts to classify 'quality in work', in the Work-Life conference, in the informal Council in Luleå and in the European

Councils, were for the most part made in order to influence the formal classification in the Commission's future Communication on the subject. It is reasonable to presuppose that there were other attempts by the member states to influence the outcome. The Belgians, who would take over the Presidency after Sweden, did, for example, employ a research team to write a report on possible indicators for 'quality in work'.[34] The politicians and bureaucrats knew that when the classification-set was formally decided in the Commission's Communication, this would be the classification that would function as the point of departure for any further attempt to change it. Before this was done, the Commission and the member states were free to make their own attempts. Afterwards, everyone had to work from the same classifications.

The job of drafting the Commission's Communication was given by the Commissioner to the research unit on employment policy at the Directorate General. Miguel, a principal administrator in the Directorate General, and his team were given the main responsibility and at about the same time as the 'Work Life 2000 – Quality in Work' conference took place, they began work on the Communication. In an interview, Miguel said that he had been inspired by the conference when they were attempting to classify 'quality in work'. With the help of the rest of the people working on these issues at the Directorate General, he had to find classifications that reflected what 'quality in work' should be about, for them and for the EU.

In addition, even if there is probably an infinite number of ways of interpreting 'quality in work', there is a much smaller number of possible interpretations in the context of the EU, as mentioned above. There are sets of possible classifications that would be most likely to appear in the context of EU employment policy-making. Issues that have been important before, such as 'flexibility and security', turning up again, as well as 'health and safety at work' and 'gender equality'. The number of classifications, a round number such as ten, is also a good departure point. It would not be the first time the Commission

---

[34] This report entitled 'Belgian Presidency/Mapping Indicators' was written by research centre, TNO Work and Employment, which published a draft report in April 2001.

had classified by ten. Karl-Johann Lönnroth did so at the Social Policy Agenda conference. Miguel had done it before, when he was defining 'adaptability', and now he was considering it for the 'quality in work' classification.

In June 2001 the Commission presented its Communication: *Employment and Social Policies: A Framework for Investing in Quality* (CEC 2001), in which it had classified 'quality in work' and suggested possible indicators to measure it. The Commission proposed ten classifications in which indicators were meant to be developed. It distinguished between two different levels of classification: 'the characteristics of the job itself' and 'the work and wider labour market context'. The classifications were:

Characteristics of the Job Itself:

1. Intrinsic job quality

2. Skills, life-long learning and career development

The Work and Wider Labour Market Context:

3. Gender equality

4. Health and Safety at work

5. Flexibility and security

6. Inclusion and access to the labour market

7. Work organisation and work-life balance

8. Social dialogue and worker involvement

9. Diversity and non-discrimination

10. Overall economic performance and productivity (CEC 2001).

The concepts were recognisable from the classification-sets above, even if some were new and they appeared in different constellations. In each of the ten classifications there were indicators, three in each area, suggested for measuring what, for example, a 'flexible and secure' working life means in the member states. The classification system was getting bigger when another level in the hierarchical system was added, namely, that of the indicators.

To summarise, the different classification-sets were given different meanings that would frame the problems and possible solutions in different ways. Even if the classification-sets underwent only small changes as the process evolved, such apparently minor discursive transformations shifted the way 'Social Europe' was understood and changed the course social and employment policy would take in the EU. A focus on employees' working conditions as well as general conditions of life implies another meaning and policy direction than if the classifications take only working conditions into consideration. This may in the long run have real impacts on individuals' lives. The classifications in the Commission's Communication suggested focusing mainly on the employees' working situation, but there were also attempts to bring in the employers' perspectives by measuring the 'overall economic performance and productivity' of the workers. Nevertheless, the classification of 'quality in work' was hereby relatively fixed, at least for the moment. However, the suggested indicators were another matter. These still remained to be discussed and decided upon. The negotiations and discussions on these will be considered in the following chapters, in particular in Chapter 5 and 6.

Conclusion: 'Social Europe' between visionary ideals and working definitions

The idea of 'Social Europe' has guided EU employment and social policy for decades. The concept and the ideas connected with it, as argued in this chapter, may be seen as a root metaphor for the EU, where one of its features is the need for the 'Social', i.e. a 'European social model' and social policy, in the form of social protection and social cohesion for the EU's citizens, if there is to be a prosperous EU.

Policy-making, in general, and in the EU in particular, is partly made up of inventing concepts to describe in which direction the politicians want their politics to move. Part of the work of inventing concepts is also to classify them so that interpretations of ideas are as compact and as well defined as possible. This is especially evident in the EU where not only party politics encourages different interpretations but also the fact that there are different national ideas present that differentiate between the member states. The different classification-sets of 'quality in work' above may illustrate the attempts to classify as well as the struggles to be the 'first' to define, or to be the member state that has the most influence on the 'final' definition.

In addition, the politicians and bureaucrats anticipated what the future measurements of the phenomena might mean and often tried to act so that comparisons between member states would show the right kind of 'transparency', namely, keeping the culturally intimate hidden from view. In other words, not revealing aspects of cultural identity that might be considered a source of external embarrassment, but making visible those in which a member state takes some pride (cf. Herzfeld 1997). The concept of 'Social Europe' has on a general level a unifying power, in that it may contribute to creating a postnational 'society' in the EU. But, at the same time, trying to agree on what 'Social Europe' means is a process fuelled with potentially divisive ability to make national differences in social protection systems and social policy more visible.

Nevertheless, the member states and the Commission ultimately have to agree on a (final) classification of 'quality in work'. This is because they have decided to develop indicators in the area and for that to be possible a common classification has eventually to be agreed upon. What this classification will be is important for the direction 'Social Europe' will take. Even if there are only minor discursive transformations, it will have consequences for policy-making. It is a question of how social 'Social Europe' should be. In the context of the EU, it is also a question of who should have the power to decide on the social – the nation state or the EU?

In this chapter the 'informal' process of influencing formal EU documents, such as Commission Communications, by the member states has been the focus. Furthermore, different notions about what 'Social Europe' and in particular 'quality in work', might mean have been scrutinised. As we have seen, policy-making is a process, a 'parallel process in one'. These different parallel processes are thus, if not all contributing, all merged into one policy document, the Commission's Communication, where the classifications are made explicit and formal. This document is from then on the point of departure for further discussions. It is also the point of departure for the rest of the chapters in this study, where the empirical focus will be the work with developing 'quality in work' indicators. This is now no longer an informal process of influencing EU documents but a formal pre-determined process in which different meetings are scheduled for discussing the issue and where there is a specific order of, and in, the meetings that has to be followed in order to make the policy-making process legitimate.

The issue of time is significant here since the time to influence the document is determined by when the Communication needs to be finished, which in turn has been agreed on by the Prime Ministers and Presidents in the European Council in Nice, namely, before the last European Council during the Belgian Presidency in Laeken in December 2001. The scheduling of decision-making time, i.e. in meetings, becomes imperative for what decisions are made. Timing and its influence on the decision-making process are the topic of the next chapter. Everyday life is filled with reminders of how individuals' and organisations' existences are governed by time – working-time, birthdays, weekdays and weekends, national public holidays. Time is also determined by the bureaucratic logic of classifications through years, months, days, hours, minutes and so on. The limiting and managing powers of time are an important factor for policy-making, and particular focus is placed on the policy-making process and how it moves towards a decision through the organisation of Presidencies and decision-making in meetings.

THREE

EU CHRONOLOGY: THE RHYTHMS OF MEETINGS

The Council of the European Union had asked the Employment Committee to finalise the 'report' on 'quality in work' indicators before the Council of the European Union meeting at the beginning of December 2001. There had to be a conclusion in time for the European Council and the end of the Belgian Presidency. Several meetings had preceded this final Employment Committee meeting before the Council meeting, at which the member states and the European Commission had had to negotiate and discuss the indicators. Today, the decision had to be made. The European Commission had made a 'report' and the Secretariat of the Employment Committee had written a 'draft opinion' that the members had to take into account. As the members arrived in the meeting room everyone expected two long and hard working days; there were several problems with the 'report' that had not been worked out during the preceding meetings and now they really had to be re-solved. The Committee members were stressed.

Introduction: EU chronology

The above story contains all the ingredients of what this chapter is about, and which may well be heard in an interview with a Eurocrat in the corridors of the Commission when asked about the EU formal decision-making process on employment policy. As may be detected in the story, the changing of the Presidencies is one of the most significant EU institutions, and is important for setting policy-making processes in motion. The rotation of the Presidency of the Council among the member states every six months pushes processes to a decision. The member state holding the Presidency and the very shifting of the Presidencies dictate when a decision has to be made, and in that way the bureaucratic process of shaping a decision is set off. The notion of time is imperative here.

The anthropology of time is as old as the discipline itself.[35] For example, Malinowski discussed systems of time reckoning among the Trobriander (1927). The perception of time within the EU is mainly connected to 'linear time'.[36] Time in this sense is often seen as time with a purpose: '…time-for-the-sake-of-God, -state, -shop, -self, among other possibilities' (Greenhouse 1996:22). It becomes a bureaucratic instrument for controlling individual and organisational behaviour (Greenhouse 1996:22) within the EU as well as fashioning that which we identify as the EU. Thus, linear time creates a history, a present and a future. The EU policy process of making common decisions creates a sense of belonging among the member states by creating a shared history, a mutual chronology (cf. Handelman 2004:110). This history may then be the basis for creating a future.

On the other hand, the changing of Presidencies, as well as the repetitive rhythm of meetings, together constitute a sense of cyclical time. There is a certain circularity on its own in these events, that provides a ritualised temporal structure to the EU policy-making processes. Hence, linear and cyclical time work in parallel to shape the temporal structure of policy-making.

Using the notion of time to create a common history and a sense of belonging has been strongly connected to the nation or the nation state (Anderson 1983:31, Handelman 2004:110). However, in the EU, bureaucrats and politicians, though not all EU citizens, share a time calendar complementary to, and sometimes conflicting with, to their

---

[35] For an overview see, for example, Gell 1992 and Munn 1992. For a critical examinations of the anthropology of time see Greenhouse 1996.

[36] In the study of time, time is usually divided into 'linear time' and 'cyclical time.' The clock and the calendar are based on linear time where time is perceived as moving forward and where it produces a history, a present and a future. Cyclical time is connected to the seasons and the circle of life, where time is perceived as being repeated (Greenhouse 1996:23).

nation state's time (cf. Jacobsson 2004b:365). This calendar is part of a postnational EU time, through which the EU is creating its own history, present and future. There are thus different 'time rationalities' in play (cf. Noon and Blyton 1997:75-76). EU time is to a great extent shaped by the changing of the Presidencies and the EU meetings schedules, while member states' time may have other time schedules for their budget years, parliamentary calendars or meeting schedules. Also, at the same time as bureaucrats and politicians are creators of time, they are also managed by it. Their time schedules are based on the clock and calendar of 'standard time',[37] which controls the time in which decisions can be made in the EU. This may clash with member state time. However, the member state bureaucrats and politicians have to follow meeting schedules and the changing of EU Presidencies every six months to be part of the EU.

I argue that the changing of Presidencies creates the EU chronology through the rhythms of the decision-making meetings, and in this way fashions the making of the EU. By exposing the decision-making process of developing 'quality in work' indicators, I shall show how the hierarchy of meetings, at which the experts' meetings prepare for the politicians' meetings, shapes decision-making in the EU. The meetings are scheduled in sequence, with one meeting followed by another in a specific decision-making order and with some meetings for discussing, arguing and negotiating and some for deciding. This order has to be followed for policy decisions to be legitimate. The actual meeting day becomes important here; particularly critical is the final meeting before a decision has to be made in order for a policy issue to move to the next level in the meeting hierarchy. However, we turn first to the creation of an EU chronology by the rotation of Presidencies.

The changing of the guard: the EU Presidencies

The everyday work in the EU of writing policy proposals, preparing decisions, preparing papers for meetings, writing Communications, White papers, Green papers and the like is run by the Eurocrats in the

---

[37] 'Standard time' was first introduced by the railroad companies to make possible a timetable for trains running between cities and countries (Kern 1983:12).

different EU institutions: in the Directorate Generals in the Commission,[38] in the member states' governments[39] and Permanent Representations to the European Union (hereafter identified as the Permanent Representation),[40] in the Directorate Generals and the General Secretariat of the Council,[41] and in the parliamentary committees and working groups in the European Parliament.[42] However, the

---

[38] The staff of the actual organisation, the Commission, are organised into different departments known as Directorate Generals (DGs) and services (such as the legal service). Each Directorate General is responsible for a particular policy area and is headed by a Director General who is answerable to one of the Commissioners. It is in the Directorate Generals that the work of devising and drafting the Commission's proposals takes place, but these proposals become official only when 'adopted' by the Commissioners' College (also referred to as 'the Commission') at its weekly meeting. The Directorate General responsible for employment issues was in 2001 and 2002 the Directorate General for Employment and Social Affairs, usually referred to by its acronym DG EMPL.

[39] The Swedish government is made up of Government Offices. These Offices included in 2001 and 2002: the Prime Minister's Office, the Ministries (10 in number), the Permanent Representation of Sweden to the EU, and the Office of Administrative Affairs. The Swedish Ministry responsible for employment policy is the Ministry of Industry, Employment and Communication.

[40] The Permanent Representations to the European Union, generally referred to as the Perm Rep, are the member states' embassies to the EU. In Brussels, Sweden has an Embassy that works with Belgium and a Permanent Representation that works with the EU. The members of the Council's working groups usually work in the member states' Permanent Representations.

[41] In 2001 the General Secretariat of the Council of the European Union, headed by the Secretary-General Javier Solana, included 9 Directorate Generals from A to J. Employment policies were handled by Directorate General J, which employed nine people. The Secretariat is run by the member state holding the Presidency, with the help of bureaucrats in the General Secretariat.

[42] In 2001 there were 8 Directorate Generals in the Parliament. The bureaucrats working on employment policies were in Directorate General 2. However, in the Parliament the politicians also work on the EU everyday policy-making in parliamentary committees, the committee responsible for employment policy being the Committee on Employment and Social Affairs.

agenda is set and decisions are made by the EU Commissioners,[43] the member states' Prime Ministers, Presidents, Ministers and parliamentarians,[44] and the parliamentarians in the European Parliament.[45]

Nevertheless, even if what will be decided on is generally based on initiatives from the Commissioners or the Prime Ministers and Presidents in the European Council, the member state holding the Presidency has a significant power to determine what in practice will be decided on during 'its' Presidency. To hold the Presidency means to represent the EU on the international stage, to act as President in the European Council and the Councils of Ministers and their committees and working group meetings, and to be responsible for the agenda of decisions to be made in the Councils of Ministers and the European Council meetings. The fact that the member state holding the Presidency also chairs the committees and working groups and sets the

---

[43] In 2001 and 2002 the Commission consisted of the President and nineteen Commissioners with different policy areas. These constitute the College, which runs the Commission and makes its decisions. The Commissioner for Employment and Social affairs in 2001 and 2002 was Anna Diamantopoulou from Greece. The Commission has the right and the responsibility to draw up proposals for new European legislation. It is also the executive body, i.e. it is responsible for managing and implementing the EU budget and the policies and programmes adopted by the Parliament and the Council. The Commission also acts as the guardian of the treaties, i.e. it is responsible for ensuring that EU laws are properly applied in the member states. Finally, the Commission represents the EU on the international stage. For more information on the European Commission see, for example, Wallace and Wallace 2000, Tallberg 2001.

[44] The Prime Ministers and Presidents formally meet, discuss and make decisions in the European Councils. The Ministers formally meet, discuss and make decisions in the Councils of Ministers. In some member states the national Parliament has to approve a decision before the Ministers can agree to it in the Council of Ministers. However, in most member states the parliamentarians are kept informed by the governments but have no formal power to influence decisions.

[45] The European Parliament is a marginal actor in regard to the European Employment Strategy (EES), and in its extension to the 'quality in work' indicators, since work with the European Employment Strategy usually does not result in legal directives or regulations but rather in guidelines. The European Parliament is consulted, but it has no decision-making power. For more information on the European Parliament see, for example, Wallace and Wallace 2000, Tallberg 2001.

agenda for the Council as well as for the European Council, makes the
role of holding the Presidency a powerful one. One may assume that
the short terms of six months are due to this state of affairs.

In addition, the Conclusions drawn up at the end of every Presidency, in the European Council,[46] keep track of *when* something was
thought of and *when* something was decided on. In this way an EU
history is built up in which decisions and agenda settings are referred
to, by the bureaucrats and politicians working on EU policy-making, as
decided on during this or that Presidency. Decisions thus constitute
temporal landmarks for the bureaucrats and politicians. The Eurocrats
use the jargon of saying, when arguing for something or reminding
someone, 'as decided in the Stockholm conclusion', or 'it is part of the
Lisbon process', or 'it is in the Amsterdam Treaty'. Everyone is expected to know that the Lisbon European Council took place in March
2000, and that the Treaty of Amsterdam was concluded in 1997 but
ratified by all the member states and made legal in 1999.

Furthermore, this habit of naming processes and decisions by
where they were decided on geographically reveals the extent to which
this or that member state's Presidency was successful or not. In a way,
fear of not being able to organise things so that decisions can be made
often helps the EU policy processes move towards a decision.

Guarding the EU while keeping it 'national'

During its term the member state holding the Presidency is supposed
to guard the interests of the EU. At the same time, it has to show
resourcefulness in presenting the 'priorities' that it wants to push
towards decisions during the Presidency period. These priorities usually
reflect the interests the member state's government has. Here, party
politics becomes important. There is, for example, a common understanding among the people working within the EU that the Treaty of
Amsterdam would not have had an Employment title if most of the

---

[46] One of the European Council meetings is always at the end of every Presidency.
Apart from this European Council there is the so-called Spring European Council,
which takes place in March, at which the Prime Ministers and Presidents work in
particular on economic, social and employment policy.

member states' governments had not been Social Democrat at the time. However, the Social Democratic party in Sweden and New Labour in the United Kingdom work in different contexts with different institutional traditions and they have different agendas. In the context of the EU, party politics is also blurred by the interest of the member state in forming a 'national' front on what it thinks is important. The priorities are also always referred to as 'national', as, for example, the 'Swedish Presidency's priorities'.

To manifest progress it becomes important to decide on what the national priorities should be. When Sweden held the Presidency in 2001 its priorities were the three Es: Employment, Enlargement and the Environment (EEE). Two of them, employment and the environment, are policy areas in which Sweden is considered to be well advanced, sometimes even the 'best in the class', as on employment. These policy issues are also considered by Sweden and other member states in the EU, to be typically 'Swedish' concerns that all parties in the Swedish Parliament could have put forward (though with different political content and weight). Enlargement, on the other hand, had been on the EU agenda for several Presidencies and the Swedish Government, being in favour of bringing ten new members into the EU, was anxious to push through a decision that would contribute to making enlargement possible (which was also the outcome of the Conclusions from the Gothenburg European Council (European Council 2001b). In this way the Swedish Presidency's priorities were focused both on typically Swedish concerns in which Sweden could be the best in the class and take on the role of 'teacher', and on policy issues that the EU had been working on for several years. The priorities thus presented the Presidency member state in a favourable light and also related to issues that were important for the EU in general.

The fact that there are issues that need the time of several Presidencies to reach a decision leads to the formation of alliances between the member states. The prerogative for the member states' governments deciding what should be on the agenda during their Presidencies opens up the possibility of alliances between the states next in line for the Presidency. In fact, it is hardly possible to reach a decision without having discussed the issue during earlier Presidency periods, since these

are so short. Thus, the sequence of Presidencies may lead to the formation of (unexpected) allies, such as France, Sweden and Belgium (in
order of Presidency) on the issue of 'quality in work' and 'quality in
work' indicators.

There is interplay between the national and the postnational here,
where the changing of the Presidencies every six months[47] makes the
member states push for EU decisions and work together, at the same
time, as their agendas may indeed be highly national. It enables member states to put national marks on EU work by steering policy in line
with their governments' intentions. At the same time, it is important
for a member state to show that it can organise its Presidency so that
processes such as EU enlargement move towards a decision during its
Presidency. This importance given to showing progress sets EU policy
processes in motion and in this way contributes significantly to the
fashioning of the EU.

Embracing the Presidency: 'selling' your member state

When the time is drawing near for a member state to take over the
Presidency, its representatives present their priorities at press conferences and in EU meetings. Different knickknacks, such as a tie for the
men, and a scarf for the women, pens and the like, are also made all
with the Presidency logo. The phenomenon of producing gadgets for
specific projects, organisations, and nationalities is widespread and may
be seen in private organisations such as Apple Computers (Garsten
1994:17) or in public organisations such as the EU. It is a way of
representing the particular, the national, and at the same time it ex-
presses a trend towards being postnational.

The Presidency logo changes from Presidency to Presidency and
the design of the different logos is repeatedly discussed among the

---

[47] When I was doing fieldwork from September 2001 till the end of 2002, Belgium,
Spain and Denmark held the Presidency in that order. However, the Swedish
Presidency during the Spring of 2001, the French Presidency during the Autumn of
2000 and the Portuguese Presidency during the Spring of 2000 were also important for
the process of developing 'quality in work' indicators.

Eurocrats in the EU when the next logo is presented.[48] These ties, scarves, and pens are handed out to the other member states' representatives at meetings or to the people working in the Commission. Mark, a Secretary in the Employment Committee, always made a habit of wearing the tie of the member state holding the Presidency during the Employment Committee meetings. These items create EU history for the bureaucrats and politicians working with the EU, where one logo is connected with a particular period. The production of gadgets thus supports the temporal rhythm.

The Presidency member state also launches its own web site.[49] This is a means of keeping the member states' representatives and the general public informed of the work taking place in the EU, when meetings are held, etc. The work is also organised in such a way that various member states' representatives have to visit the state holding the Presidency. The informal meetings of the Councils of Ministers are usually located in the Presidency Minister's hometown. The first meeting of the Employment Committee of every Presidency is also labelled the informal Employment Committee meeting and is held in the Presidency member state as well. During these meetings, the Ministers and Eurocrats not only discuss political issues, but also visit 'good examples' in their policy area, are shown the local 'culture' on sightseeing tours and are served national food specialities.[50]

In addition, holding the Presidency is generally an occasion when the national governments put extra effort into making the EU known to the public in their own countries. Public discussions are arranged, such as that on democracy in the EU held at the Central Railway

---

[48] See different examples of Presidency logos at the left-hand top corner at the Presidency web-sites
http://ue.eu.int/cms3_fo/showPage.asp?id=695&lang=en&mode=g
Last visited 2005-12-09.
[49] See, for example, the Swedish Presidency web-site of 2001, which was still active in 2005 www.eu2001.se Last visited 2005-12-09.
[50] See, for example, reports of the informal meeting of the Ministers of Telecommunication and Employment in Luleå where they visited an IT exhibition and a Sami village. http://www.eu2001.se/static/eng/lulea/lulea_1.asp Last visited 2005-12-09. Print-out in author's possession.

Station in Stockholm during the Swedish Presidency in the Spring of 2001. Research conferences are arranged by the member states on the issues they prioritise, one example being conferences on 'quality in work' during the Swedish and Belgian Presidencies in 2001. In addition, cultural events are sponsored by the Presidency, such as the art exhibitions, design events and music events held in Brussels during the Belgian Presidency in the Autumn of 2001, all presented on the Presidency web-site.

The 'Presidency', then, is an extended series of events in which the member state's public are to be made more fully aware of the fact that they are part of the EU, and at the same time an opportunity to inform the other member states' politicians and Eurocrats about the Presidency member state. However, the picture of the Presidency member state presented to the other member states is a polished version of how it wants to be presented, and there are choices to be made to enable its 'best' side to be displayed, regardless of whether it concerns the Presidency's priorities or the places and projects shown during the informal meetings. That which is culturally intimate is kept secret and a 'national' front is displayed to the other member states.

Eurocrats adapting to the Presidencies

The changing of the Presidency and the subsequent shift of priorities shape the everyday practices of the Eurocrats engaged in writing policy documents and preparing decisions for the politicians. A particular policy issue may be on the agenda for a while, and sometimes a decision is made. However, issues are repeatedly dropped because the new Presidency may have other interests. With regard to the 'quality in work' indicators, the French, Swedish and Belgian Presidencies in succession wanted to reach a decision. When it was time to make the final decision on the indicators at the end of the Belgian Presidency, the members agreed that they had to do further work on them the following year. However, when it was time to reach a fresh decision on the indicators at the end of 2002, the Danish Presidency did not prioritise them and no decision was made. If the Presidency does not press for decisions, especially on difficult policy areas in which the EU has no real mandate, such as on employment and social policy, then it is very likely that there will be no decision and the issue might even be conveniently forgotten. This means quick rearrangements of what should be prioritised and worked on further and what should be consigned to the archives, perhaps to be brought out again later, or never again.

The Commission's bureaucrats, who prepare the papers, move from one issue to another, often not knowing if their work will lead to a decision or, a concrete policy, or not. Miguel had worked on the flexibility/adaptability indicator, but the priorities changed to 'quality in work' for which he was asked to develop indicators instead. After two years of working on the 'quality in work' indicators, the priorities changed again and the 'quality in work' documents were assigned to the archives, even if several of the indicators were put to use in other areas instead. There is a certain recycling of ideas that characterises the EU as an organisation (I shall touch on this later in the Epilogue.)

To sum up, the Presidencies, with their interest in setting the EU agenda in their member state's favour, as well as moving ongoing policy processes to a decision, set the decision-making processes in motion. The changing of Presidencies and the desire of member states to have decisions reached on their priorities during their Presidency thus push the policy-making processes to an EU decision. The 'national' is here a prerequisite for creating something postnational. In addition, the Presidencies' Conclusions are part of creating the EU chronology thereby making a shared EU history that the member states relate to and build on Presidency by Presidency.

However, if a Presidency member state is eager to have certain decisions reached during its Presidency, these decisions have to be prepared in different committee, working group and council meetings to be legitimate. This creates an EU rhythm during the year, based not only on the changing of Presidencies but also on the bureaucratic process of reaching decisions in the meetings. The Presidency period generates a pulse of meetings during its term. It is in the everyday work in these meetings that the EU is formed.

The rhythm of the meetings: the bureaucratic process

When I came to work in the Directorate General one of the first papers handed to me was the meeting schedules. There were meetings in the European Parliament, the Council's building and the Commission's buildings. There were the European Economic and Social Committee[51] meetings, the Committee of Regions[52] meetings, the Employment Committee meetings, the Social Questions Working group meetings,[53] the Permanent Representatives Committees meetings (hereafter identified according to the acronym: Coreper),[54] the Council meetings, and the European Council meetings.

To influence policy-making and decisions the representatives of the Commission and the member states have to take an active part in these meetings. Some meetings are more important than others. The Economic and Social Committee meetings, for example, are only advisory to the Commission, while the Employment Committee meetings are part of negotiating an actual decision. Most of the meetings take place in Brussels, which means that the Commission's bureaucrats or the member states' representatives in the Permanent Representations can walk to the different meeting rooms, while the representatives from the national ministries have to travel to the meetings. The EU time schedule may conflict with the time schedule at home, since some represen-

---

[51] The European Economic and Social Committee, sometimes referred to as EcoSoc, is an advisory body to the EU. It is made up of representatives from the social partners, and civil organisations in general. The Economic and Social Committee is on the EU employment guidelines in the European Employment Strategy, for example.

[52] The Committee of Regions is an advisory body to the EU. The members represent the local and regional authorities in the member states.

[53] The Social Questions Working group (SQW) is a preparatory working group of the Council located in the Council. The members are usually bureaucrats working in the member states' Permanent Representations in Brussels.

[54] The Coreper is the last preparatory committee before the Council meeting. Formally Coreper is one Committee but since the growth of its workload it has had to divide it into two groups that meet weekly. Coreper I handles employment policy issues. Coreper members are usually high-level bureaucrats from the member states' Permanent Representations, often the Ambassador.

tatives have to be away for several days and the work at home may not be in sync with the EU work.

However, the member state's representatives have to adapt to the timing of the EU in order to be able to influence its future and its history. If a decision is scheduled to be taken in the EU at the end of a particular Presidency, the member states have to try to abide by this even if the information on which the decision should be based might not be available in their member state until later. The production of national statistical data, for example, sometimes has a different timetable from what would be needed to fit in with the EU timetable. As a consequence, the desire to influence decisions might in fact steer member states' time schedules so that they become more synchronised with these of the EU. In any event, the process of preparing a decision for the Council is scheduled in a particular pre-determined order, which controls how and when a decision can be made.

Committee work: Eurocrats preparing decisions

The Ministers in the Councils and the Presidents and Prime Ministers in the European Council are supported by Eurocrats in expert committees and working groups. The experts are appointed on their merits as being experts on the policy area in question. They are also bureaucrats in the service of the national governments and the Commission, and they advise the Ministers on how to decide on policy issues. And, as mentioned above, it is in these expert committees and working groups that most of the negotiations on policies are conducted.

In the EU there are different types of committee with different responsibilities. Larsson (2003:37) makes a distinction between different EU committees depending on where in the sequence of the policy process they are situated, so to speak. There are policy-formulating committees, decision-making committees and implementing committees. The policy-formulating committees, sometimes also referred to as advisory committees (Vos 1997:211), are set up by the Commission to advise or make proposals in a certain policy area, and their members are often scientific experts representing either themselves or a member state (Larsson 2003:38-39). The members of the implementing

committees, the so-called 'comitology committees',[55] are also considered to be experts but they represent the member states. The implementing committees are set up by the Commission for the member
states to find a way of agreeing on how to implement what has been
legislated by the Council (Larsson 2003:49ff, Bergström 2003:2).

The decision-making committees, also called management committees (Vos 1997:211), are as a rule connected with the work in the
Council or the Parliament and consist of bureaucrats from the member
states and the Commission in the Council committees and representatives from Parliament in the parliamentary committees (Larsson
2003:39ff). The Council committees prepare the Council's decisions,
while the parliamentary committees prepare the Parliament's decisions.
The Employment Committee is a decision-making committee preparing for the Council and is the 'first' committee that prepares employment policy for the Council and the European Council.

What makes the Employment Committee somewhat different is
that the other decision-making committees have previously had their
Secretariats located in the Council or in the Parliament buildings (cf.
Larsson 2003:40), whereas the Secretariat of the Employment Committee is located in the Commission. This is not without importance
and was debated intensely among the member states and the Commission before it was agreed. Many of the member states wanted the
Committee Secretariat to be in the Council, so that they would have
more control over it through the Presidencies. However, it ended up in
the Commission, which meant that the Commission gained more
control over the policy-making process since the Commission members of the Employment Committee had more control over and access
to the documents prepared for the Committee.

For this reason employment issues are prepared not only by the
Employment Committee but also by the Council's working groups: the
Social Questions Working group and Coreper. This increases the

---

[55] According to Vos (1997:212) the whole system of committees in the EU may be
referred to as the 'comitology.' However, she concludes that the correct usage refers
only to the implementing committees. For more on the 'comitology' see, for example,
Bergström 2003.

opportunity of the member states to influence the process, especially for the state holding the Presidency. However, the experts in the Social Questions Working group are of lower rank than the members of the Employment Committee and the 'opinion' written by the Employment Committee members are very seldom changed in these working groups.

Nevertheless, the order of the different meetings has to be followed in order to reach a formal decision.

Asked by the European Council

In regard to the task of developing 'quality in work' indicators, it is possible to visualise the rhythm of the meetings from the meeting schedule of the Autumn of 2001. This schedule is intertwined with other meeting schedules of individuals preparing for the meetings or commenting on their outcome and opinions. There is a web of meetings that are sometimes in parallel and sometimes entangled. A policy issue such as 'gender equality' is part of a number of different decision-making processes and the bureaucrats responsible for this area have to juggle the different policy processes and try to ensure that the meeting times are set so that it is possible to follow all the processes. In addition, national and EU schedules for policy-making might conflict by focusing on the same issues but at different times. Or they might complement each other, as in the national preparatory meetings for the EU meetings.

However, if we return to the process of developing 'quality in work' indicators, the meeting schedule would look as shown in Table 3.1.

Table 3.1: Meeting schedule for the 'quality in work' indicators, 2001

Dates	Meetings
24-25 September	Employment Committee Indicators group, Brussels, Belgium
4-5 October	Employment Committee, Brussels, Belgium
8 October	Council of the European Union (ESP), Luxembourg
7-8 November	Employment Committee: Indicators group, Brussels, Belgium
15-16 November	Employment Committee: Indicators group, Brussels, Belgium
20-21 November	Employment Committee, Brussels, Belgium

26 November	Council: Social Questions Working Group, Brussels, Belgium
28 November	Council: Coreper, Brussels, Belgium
3 December	Council of the European Union (ESP), Brussels, Belgium
14-15 December	European Council, Laeken, Belgium

The prior-knowledge needed to understand the meeting schedule is that the French Presidency in the 'Nice Conclusion' (December 2000) and the Swedish Presidency in the 'Stockholm Conclusion' (March 2001) had concluded that 'quality in work' indicators should be developed, decided on and presented to the European Council in Laeken during the Belgian Presidency (14-15 December 2001).

For this to be possible, the Council of Ministers had to come to a decision before that meeting date. The schedule was set up so that this would be feasible at the Council meeting on 3 December 2001. The expert committees were then asked to make preparations so that it would be possible to arrive at a decision in the Council and a Conclusion in the European Council. The work of the Employment Committee and the Council's working groups had to begin. The Employment Committee would have to reach a decision in enough time before the Council of Ministers for the Council's working groups to have time to prepare. In this case, it meant before the meeting on 20-21 November. This in turn meant that the Indicators group had to present a final 'report' and a document expressing their 'opinion' of the 'report', generally referred to as the 'opinion' at its last meeting of the year, i.e. by 15-16 November.

In this way the meeting schedule is determined by the fact that the Prime Ministers and Presidents in the European Council want to develop 'quality in work' indicators and the Presidency member state, Belgium, wants to reach a conclusion on them in its Presidency Conclusions. I shall go into more detail on the decision-making process in regard to developing 'quality in work' indicators in the next section.

Agreeing before the Council

I enter one of the Commission's conference centres in Brussels. Ahead of me is a line of people waiting to have their bags x-rayed and themselves examined by passing through the metal detectors. I go past them flashing my Commission access card at the security guard and he nods, silently accepting my going through without having my bag x-rayed. There is a long queue for the lift, so I walk up the escalators to the third floor. The conference centre has at least four meeting rooms on each floor in the five-storey building, and just before 10 a.m. there are always a lot of people rushing to different meetings. Around me different languages are being spoken, and people have flown in or taken trains or cars from their member states to attend the different meetings in the building today.

I am on my way to the meeting of the Indicators group, whose members meet today for the first time to discuss and try to work out 'quality in work' indicators. On the third floor I find Mark, a Secretary in the Employment Committee, and, at the time, one of my colleagues in the Commission. He is talking to the President of the Indicators group. They are going through the agenda for the meeting and discussing anticipated objections and problems on the different items. I greet them and go into the meeting room to find my place. The room is furnished according to the stereotype of what a bureaucratic institution would look like, with old-fashioned furniture and grey-beige-brownish surroundings, floor-to-floor grey carpets, the tables made of fake mahogany and the chairs covered by office-chair cloth in beige. The interpreters' booths behind glass windows along the walls reveal that this is a multinational and multilingual meeting, the languages translated today being English, French and German, as indicated on a board in a corner of the room.

I find a seat behind the Secretaries of the Employment Committee, where I shall be out of the way and not risk occupying seats that are reserved for representatives of the member states or the Commission. The members are seated in a circle in front of me, with the member states in alphabetical order, according to how their country is spelt in their own language.[56] In front of each member state's row of seats is a

---

[56] In order: Belgium, Denmark, Germany, Greece, Spain, France, Ireland, Italy, Luxembourg, the Netherlands, Austria, Portugal, Finland, Sweden and the United Kingdom.

sign indicating the member state's name. The Secretaries of the Employment Committee, the President, and the Commission are seated between the United Kingdom and Belgium, i.e. at the junction of the ends of the circle. Behind the circle there are seats for observers, like myself, for alternates to the members, or for the Commission's presenters. These presenters are experts who have worked on particular policy issues and they will take their seat beside the Commission's representatives when it is time for their issues to be discussed. The presenters thus often change from question to question.

I take from my bag the papers that are going to be discussed in the meeting. Before the meeting starts, I realise I have to fetch more writing paper on which to take notes, so I sneak out to the reception area to find some. When I pass the table at the entrance I look to see if there are any additional papers that I have not received. This is a common practice that I have picked up from the members, since papers are sometimes distributed on the day of the meeting.

The national delegations and the Commission's representatives arrive and the room slowly fills up. There is a constant buzz around me of members greeting and kissing each other. The interpreters are taking their place in the translators' booths. I examine my headset and make sure that it is set to 'English'. I look around the room and observe that one-third of the members are women and that about half have brought with them an expert, the alternate member of the group who generally varies depending on the question. The members are starting to take their seats and at about 10:15 the President of the Indicators group rings the bell, everyone falls silent and the meeting begins.

The members of the Indicators group have been asked by the Employment Committee to develop 'quality in work' indicators before the Committee's last meeting in the Autumn. The job of the group's members is to help the Employment Committee members determine whether an indicator can be considered statistically 'robust'[57] and 'politically neutral'.

---

[57] The concept of 'robust' is part of the language of statistics and econometrics. In the science of statistics there is an ongoing debate about the 'robust' and 'robustness' (see, for example, Portnoy and He 2002). However, in a general sense and for the

In the letter from the President of the Indicators group,[58] which the members have received beforehand, he has explained why they have to develop the indicators on 'quality in work'. According to the letter, the Indicators group has to draw up 'a draft report on the indicators of quality in work, which will be submitted to the Employment Committee'. The group is also guided on which areas it should focus on to develop indicators. The informal Council of Ministers (Liège, 6-7 July) and the informal Employment Committee meeting (Genval, 9-10 July) that took place during the summer had scrutinised the 'quality in work' indicators suggested in the Commission's Communication and decided that the Indicators group should be mandated to try to find indicators in six out of ten areas, the ten areas being, as established in Chapter 2:

1. Intrinsic job quality

2. Skills, life-long learning and career development

3. Gender equality

4. Health and Safety at work

5. Flexibility and security

6. Inclusion and access to the labour market

7. Work organisation and work-life balance

8. Social dialogue and worker involvement

9. Diversity and non-discrimination

10. Overall economic performance and productivity (CEC 2001).

The four areas that had not been agreed on were: '1. Intrinsic job quality'; '5. Flexibility and security'; '7. Work organisation and work-life

---

bureaucrats in the EU an indicator is perceived as 'robust' when it is statistically reliable and valid.

[58] The Presidents of the Indicators group and the Ad hoc group are regular members of the Employment Committee. They also serve as Vice-Presidents of the Committee, together with the one of the members from the incumbent Presidency and one of the members from the next Presidency. The Presidents of the Employment Committee, the Indicators group, and the Ad hoc group are elected from among the members and serve for two years.

balance'; and '10. Overall economic performance and productivity'. The Ministers could not agree on whether the four areas should be measured at all or if they should be measured with other indicators. But, in the report written by Miguel, the principal administrator in the Directorate General on the 'quality in work' indicators, and his team, all ten areas were presented with suggested indicators to the Indicators group meeting.

Several of the members immediately put their member state sign on its end to signal that they want to speak. The President gives the floor to the representative of the Netherlands who says:

> We are only supposed to work on indicators in which consensus has emerged, but the indicators in the paper are not indicators where there has been consensus.
>
> (Indicators group 24 September 2001)

The President argues that they can discuss the four indicators from a 'purely technical point of view'. He is supported by the representative of the Commission,[59] who also thinks they ought to have a technical discussion on the remaining four. The representatives of Belgium and Austria are of the opinion that they can have a 'technical discussion tomorrow afternoon if time allows'. However, several of the member states (the United Kingdom, Spain, Germany) agree with the Netherlands that they should only discuss the indicators on which there has been a political decision. The President points out that there are four against and four in favour and he asks the rest of the members to express their views. There is a small majority for discussing all ten areas, and the President announces that they will discuss the remaining four if there is time at the final meeting the following day.

---

[59] The Commission has two assignments in the Employment Committee and its sub-groups. Its representatives are there as presenters of a suggested report and also as members. This means that the Commission usually has two seats in the Indicators group and three seats in the Employment Committee, two of which are often taken by the Director General and Deputy Director General, and the third by a civil servant who has worked on that particular topic and who presents the work. This 'third' member changes depending on who has worked on the issue discussed.

What was it about the four areas that made it difficult for the Ministers to agree and why were some of the group members so concerned about not discussing them, while others thought it was acceptable? It is safe to assume that the member states' representatives not wanting to discuss them in the Indicators group were the same member states that did not want to include them as areas in the Council of Ministers. From later discussions it is possible to conclude that the Netherlands, for example, with a large number of people working in a-typical jobs such as fixed-term contracts and as temporary employees, did not want indicators on '5. Flexibility and Security' and '7. Work organisation and work-life balance' that would indicate that permanent contracts are 'better' than fixed-term contracts and temporary employment, which one might conclude from the indicators suggested. The same was true for Sweden, which had a large number of part-time workers, especially among women, and which did not want indicators suggesting that part-time employment was 'not as good as' full-time employment.

The members want to protect how their member states will be viewed in relation to the others: where in the tables of comparisons between the member states they will end up and what consequences this will have for their government's politics. It is also a question of political views on what the different member states think is the right way to perform employment politics. However, in the context of the EU political views are always located in the political context of the member states, and member states' positions are viewed as 'national' rather than referring to party politics. The member state representatives want to decide what is to be revealed and what is to be kept hidden when policy processes are made 'transparent'. What is to be measured should be in the 'best interest' of all the member states.

After the meeting, Miguel and his team return to re-write the report and amend it according to the decisions taken in the Indicators group. The President, together with the Employment Committee Secretariat,[60]

---

[60] The Employment Committee is supported by a Secretariat, generally referred to as the Support team, located in the Commission, in the Directorate General. The Secretariat is made up of 3 people, Tanja and Mark (Mark later replaced by Peter) working as assistants to the Committee and especially to the Presidents, and Michelle

writes the Indicators group's opinion on the report and the documents are then sent to the members of the Employment Committee. The four areas are still included in the report from the Commission but the opinion of the Indicators group reads that the indicators were tabled at the meeting and the members only commented on the data sources.

In the Employment Committee a week later (4-5 October), the four areas are still not discussed, but in order to advise the Ministers at their Council meeting a few day later, the Committee members have to prepare an 'oral statement'[61] on the progress they have made so far. In this statement there is room to suggest indicators for the four areas in order to advise the Ministers that it is possible to work on these areas. For this reason several of the representatives of the member states insist that the oral statement must be written in the Committee instead of allowing the President of the Committee to do it himself, which would have been the case at a less sensitive stage of the proceedings. During the evening between the two meeting days the President and the Secretariat prepare the oral statement based on the discussions on the indicators during the day.

The next day, 5 October, the members go through the presentation paragraph by paragraph, word by word. In the text there are suggestions for indicators on the four areas, which will mean that if the Ministers accept the statement they will have authorised the Employment Committee members to try to find indicators for the remaining four.

There is a lengthy discussion on how these formulations on the four are to be articulated. The representatives from the Netherlands are against the formulation: 'The possibility should also be explored of

who takes care of the practical arrangements such as booking meeting rooms, making sure the members have all the papers, attending to the reimbursement of travel expenses and so forth. (None of them are now working in the Secretariat.) They are all employed full-time on the Committee's work. They are employees of the Commission, but they are the Secretariat of the Employment Committee, which includes the member states as well.

[61] The 'oral statement' would be submitted to the Council in written form but it would not be included as an official document since it was only a progress report, not a written opinion of the Employment Committee.

extending this concept to cover progression from unemployment into part-time and fixed-term work and from there into full-time and permanent work'. They argue that not all individuals want full-time permanent work and that it is a prejudicial indicator against a certain type of employee–employer relationship. Finally the text reads: 'The Committee recommends that its Indicators Group explore the possibility of indicators to measure the transition from unemployment and inactivity and the transition within employment'.

This formulation was much more open than the one above and the Ministers agreed to this as well as the texts on the other areas. This meant that the Employment Committee members were given a mandate to work on the four areas as well (8 October 2001). In this way the policy process was moving towards a decision on all ten areas. In a sense, then, this was a break-through.

However, the work of developing 'quality in work' indicators was not yet completed in any of the ten areas. The Indicators group had two more meetings on the indicators to go before it had to hand its final report to the Employment Committee members. The members of the Employment Committee and the Indicator group often returned to the same policy issue during several consecutive meetings before they were able to reach a decision. Between meetings the Commission was asked to make the changes in the report decided on by the Committee and then at the next meeting the members discussed, negotiated and decided on the re-written text.

Nonetheless, according to the EU calendar, at the last meeting before the Council there had to be a final decision. The pressure to finalise before a certain date influenced the decision-making process. No matter how confident or insecure the members of the Indicators group or the Employment Committee felt about their report, they had to submit it to the Council. Their job as a group was to assist and give advice to the Council members. In theory, they could maintain to the Council of Ministers that it was impossible to do what they had been asked to do, but on several occasions in the Committee members stated they would not then feel that they had done their job properly. However, sometimes the members of the Employment Committee were unable to produce what the Ministers had asked for, and they therefore recommended that further work should be undertaken.

At the last Employment Committee meeting before the Council on 20-21 November 2001, the members have to make a decision before their report and opinion are sent to the next level in the hierarchy of meetings (see Table 3.1). It is evident that some of the members do not want the 'quality in work' indicators at all. Some areas are also more difficult than others when it comes to agreeing on indicators. In fact, in four out of ten classified areas the members agree that, in their opinion, further work is needed. Two of the four areas are the same areas that have been problematic from the beginning: '5. Flexibility and security' and '7. Work organisation and work-life balance'. The members decide that they need an indicator to measure social protection for part-time and fixed-term employees in relation to full-time and permanent employees, especially in relation to working time, but as before they cannot agree on how such indicators are to be formulated.

The 'new' areas that prove difficult are: '4. Health and safety at work' and '8. Social dialogue and worker involvement'. The members agree that they need an indicator on workers exposed to stress, but they cannot find a data source that will be acceptable to all of them. The data source suggested by the Commission is not thought to be trustworthy, and the members believe that they need to try and find another source. Measuring 'social dialogue and worker involvement' reveals the differences in institutional arrangements in the member states. The Indicators group has suggested to measure the 'percentage of employees covered by collective agreements' and the 'evolution of number of days lost per 1000 employees in industrial disputes'. In the member states where neither strikes nor collective agreements are a particularly common way of handling 'social dialogue and worker involvement', these indicators are not regarded as good enough. The representatives of the United Kingdom, for example, argue that they do not take into consideration all the different institutional arrangements in the member states. They want instead to measure 'works councils',[62] which is a special characteristics of British working life.

The final opinion of the Committee then, is that it needs to work further on the indicators in these four areas in the following year. This opinion together with the report is sent to the Council's Secretariat to be prepared in the Council's working groups.

Preparing for the Councils

There is a hectic stomping of feet in the entrance hall of the Council building in Brussels as the time is drawing towards 9.30. All the different meetings in the building will soon start. The security line is getting longer and longer. Once in the building, there are meeting room after meeting room in the corridors of the eight-storey building[63] and the rooms have strange names such as 50.1, 35.2, 20.4 or 70.5. Finding your meeting room the first time round is not always easy, even if each floor has a different colour, I thought ironically, wandering through the corridors and finally having to ask a guard. When I found the meeting room, some of the members were standing outside in the cramped corridor having a cigarette and a coffee from the vending machine. Others were already in the meeting room, taking their seats behind their member-state sign.

In the Employment Committee meetings everyone is seated in a circle in alphabetical order, but here, in the Council's working groups, the members are seated in order of Presidency. At one end of the table the representatives of the member state holding the Presidency are seated. On their left are the representatives of the member state which has just held the Presidency, followed by the one holding it before them, and so on until reaching the other end of the table where the Commission is seated. On the opposite side of the table the Presidencies to come are seated, with the next in line nearest to the present Presidency. This order emphasises the importance of the Presidency and the fact that the Presidency member state presides at all the

---

[62] In British labour markets, the term 'works councils' refers to enterprise-based collective bargaining (for more information see, for example, Stråth 1996:146).

[63] And at least six storeys below ground-level.

meetings in the Council. As in the Employment Committee meetings, there are interpreters' booths around the meeting room. However, in these meetings every language has to be interpreted, should the member state want it, whereas in the Employment Committee meetings there is a more limited number of languages available. In today's Social Question Working group meeting, all languages, except Swedish, are interpreted.

A President and a Secretariat support all EU committees, working groups and councils. In the meetings of the Council's working groups the Secretariat is run by the state holding the Presidency with the help of the staff of the General Secretariat. In the Employment Committee the members choose the President from among themselves for a two-year term; s/he is then assisted by four vice-presidents. Two of them are elected from the Committee and serve for two years; the remaining two consist of one representative from the member state holding the Presidency and one from the member state next in line for the Presidency. This again emphasises the importance of the holding the Presidency.

While being President in the different working groups, committees and councils in the EU, s/he has to work in the interest of all the EU member states. This is a dual role, since even if the President's perspective is to be that of the EU, s/he is still part of a member state delegation and takes part in the meetings preparing for the meeting. Nevertheless, regardless of her/his national affiliation, the President's job is to help the working group, committee or council to agree as a group. The President has to suggest a possible 'EU' opinion that is based on the national positions and s/he has to go in making suggestions until everyone can agree.

Most of the negotiations, discussions and compromises on employment issues take place in the Employment Committee, and when the Committee's report and opinion reach the Council working groups an 'EU' position is usually already formed. Nevertheless, the Council's working groups also have to make preparations for the Council of Ministers meeting to decide in the right procedural way, and in the legitimate order.

In the Social Questions Working group meeting on 26 November 2001 the 'quality in work' indicators are discussed. The Employment Committee's report and opinion have been sent to the Council's Secretariat. In addition, the Belgian Presidency has prepared 'Council conclusions' on the indicators. The Social Questions Working group usually just accepts the Employment Committee's proposals. Now, there is a lot of humming and hazing in the meeting room because the Working group members have to work on this further and be prepared to defend their national positions and the compromise 'EU' position, which their higher-level colleagues have already agreed on in the Employment Committee.

There are discussions among the members on why the Belgian Presidency has chosen to write these Council conclusions. The deduction drawn during lunch is that it probably wants to ensure that there are conclusions on this issue in the Council. It also enables the Belgian Presidency not only to determine what is to be decided on in the Council but also to influence what the decision is to be.

The members of the Working group then have to make sure that the Council conclusions are in line with what has been decided on in the Employment Committee and with the national positions of their member states. In the meeting the Commission's representative, Dimitrios, a Director in the Directorate General, also tries to make sure that the Council conclusions respect the Employment Committee's report and the Commission's position. He is accompanied by Tanja, one of the Secretaries of the Employment Committee, who is there on behalf of the Committee in order to be able to report to the President of the Committee what has happened at the meeting. Towards the end the members are able to agree on the Council conclusions on the 'quality in work' indicators, with a few reservations on the part of some member states' representatives who have not been able to consult their governments and in some cases not their Parliaments either.

The 'quality in work' indicators then move to the next level, the Coreper meetings. In the Coreper meeting on 28 November 2001 the whole discussion is very quick. The President asks the member state representatives, who have made reservations, if they can lift them.

Some changes are made in the Council conclusions but the policy issue is swept through in a hurry. The speed with which the Coreper meeting handles the different decision points is due to the fact that they have to discuss all the policy issues that are to be discussed and decided on in the Council of Ministers meetings, which means that they have a lot of different matters to consider during their meetings. When the end of the Presidency is closing in and decisions have to be made, these meetings sometimes turn into 24-hour affairs where there is not much room for discussion unless the members have not been able to agree in the previous groups. In fact, if the members have agreed and there are no reservations in the working groups preparing for the Coreper meeting, there might not be any discussion at all.

However, on this particular occasion Austria does not want to lift its reservation because it wants to add 'the revision in 2002', which several of the member states, including the next Presidency, Spain, are not too happy with. The Spanish Presidency along with others do not want to have a decision that says that the final revision of the 'quality in work' indicators has to be concluded during 2002, but wants to ensure there is an opening for it taking longer. Suddenly all those members of the Social Questions Working group, who have been seated behind their member states' representatives in the Coreper meeting, rush off into another meeting room. I am informed later by Tanja that the other members tried to persuade Austria to lift its reservation. However, Austria wants to keep it, arguing that sometimes a member state wants the decision to be made in the Council. Had the reservation been lifted in the Coreper meeting, the decision would, in fact, have already been made there. To oblige the Ministers to discuss the issue Austria wants to retain the reservation until the Council.

At the Council meeting on 3 December the Ministers ask the Employment Committee to try to develop the 'quality in work' indicators further and report back to the Council, as the Employment Committee has advised them to do. And the Prime Ministers and Presidents endorse the Ministers' decision at the European Council on 13-14 December. It is never specified whether this has to be done during 2002, but in practice it means a new sequence of meetings in relation to the 'quality in work' indicators in 2002 that will follow the same pattern as the previous year.

To sum up, this meant that, first, the Presidency together with the Commissioners, Prime Ministers and Presidents in the European Council or the Ministers in the Council determined what should be decided on, for example, developing 'quality in work' indicators in regard to employment policy. Then the Employment Committee members discussed and negotiated with the help of their working groups the Ad hoc group and the Indicators group. When they had agreed on a report and an opinion they sent them to the Council where the Social Questions Working group and then Coreper had to scrutinise and agree on the report before the Ministers in the Council could make a decision. The Prime Ministers and Presidents in the European Council then approved this decision. This was a yearly to half-yearly process affected by the Presidencies.

Thus the meeting schedule operates as an EU calendar, in which the members know that a decision has to be made in this or that meeting in order to reach a formal decision in the Council before the end of the Presidency. This meeting rhythm moves the policy-making process towards a decision, since the members know that the documents discussed in the various meetings will leave their trace and determine what the next meeting's documents will include, until the members finally have to make a decision This creates a temporal structure in EU operations. The rhythm of the meetings provides a certain beat that the member states have to follow in order to prepare, take part in and form the EU. The process of making decisions in the EU may conflict with the member states' time calendar including the time of national budget negotiations or national holidays. However, to be part of the EU means organising the work in the member states so that, if not completely adjusted, it complements the work in the EU. The EU chronology is thus formed beyond the nation state, postnationally, while simultaneously being shaped by the member states through the Presidencies.

The perception of decisions moving forward, in linear time, thereby creating an EU chronology is, however, only one side of the coin. The EU calendar may in fact appear as cyclical time[64] in which the same process is repeated over and over, with the policy issues being prepared in certain groups and committees, in a particular order. The annual meeting schedule may be compared to the circular process of farming (sowing, growing and harvesting) that is repeated every year. However, while farmers are dependent on the weather and the seasons for their deadlines during the year, the deadlines for EU policy are constructed in the EU organisation. And in organisations generally it is important to finish before the summer holidays and by the end of the year, i.e. every half a year. So it happens that this cyclical rhythm coincides with the half-year Presidencies in the EU.

The actual meeting days may also, for the bureaucrats and politicians taking part in them, appear as cyclical time in which the scheduling of meeting days and the preparations beforehand are almost the same from meeting to meeting with only (perhaps) the policy issues discussed, negotiated and decided on changing. I shall go further on this in the next section where I focus on the meeting days of the Employment Committee.

The 'two-day' meetings

The actual meeting days, usually two days for the Employment Committee, are normally scheduled to run from 10 am to 6.30 pm, with a one-and-a-half-hour lunch break from around 1 pm. Different time rationalities are in play here. There is a scheduled standard time for the meeting that pushes the decision-making process to a decision, since the members know that, especially if it is the last in the meeting cycle, they have to reach a decision, if not sooner, then at least by around 6.30 pm of the second meeting day. At the same time, the bureaucrats preparing for and taking part in the meetings have an individual personal experience of time in which they often feel stressed in preparing for the meeting since the documents that are to be discussed always seem to arrive too late. This creates stressful situations immediately

---

[64] 'Cyclical time' is usually connected with private personal life where the circle of life of birth and death is viewed in this way (Greenhouse 1996:23).

before the meetings when preparations are continued sometimes all the way to the start of the actual meeting.

The feeling in the meetings is also different depending on where in the decision-making cycle they are situated. At the beginning of the meeting sequence the members are quite relaxed and are able to push the burden of reaching a final decision into the future. However, at the last meeting when it is time to conclude, the members are much more pressed and alert, arguing intensely for their opinion while at the same time having to try to agree on a compromise decision.

Preparations at the last minute...

Before the actual meeting days of the Employment Committee different activities take place within the national governments and the EU institutions. What happens at the meetings is connected with what has been discussed, written or thought of in other places. There are the Commission's reports and the Employment Committee's opinions that will form the basis for discussion in the meeting. And there are national positions prepared in relation to the report and the opinion in the member state Ministries.

The Commission's report along with the draft opinions prepared by the Employment Committee President and the Secretariat are sent to the national governments a few days before the meeting days. The short time to prepare is a constant source of irritation among the members. It is not possible to hold the Swedish preparatory meeting earlier than two or three days, sometimes only a day, before the meeting. The member states' representatives have to decide quickly what their national position is to be and how they will argue their position. There is a general feeling among the members that they do not have enough time to prepare. They argue that they would be able to coordinate better with other Ministries and have time to really scrutinise the documents if the Commission sent them out sooner.

The national positions are also sometimes changed from one meeting to another due, according to the members, to the lack of time to obtain information. The Swedish position changed from first wanting to use the 'number of members in trade unions' as a measure of how well the 'social dialogue and worker involvement' was working, to, at the next meeting, wanting to measure the 'number of collective agreements'. At the first meeting, the Swedish members were of the opinion that the 'number of members in trade unions' would give Sweden a better score, but when they had time to check, after the Indicators group meeting, they found that 'numbers of collective agreements' would be better. One may assume that 'number of collective agreements' is also easier to 'sell' to the Indicator group since many of the member states, such as France, have a high number of collective agreements but a low number of members in trade unions.

One reason for the documents arriving late is that the meeting days are so close together. Especially at the end of the decision-making process, immediately before the end of the Presidency, the time between the different levels in the meeting hierarchy – from the Employment Committee, to the Social Questions Working group, to Coreper, to the Council of Ministers – is usually a week or only a few days. Since Miguel, the principal administrator on the 'quality in work' indicators in the Commission, and his team usually have to re-write the indicators report to find, for example, new indicators and new statistical data sources according to the discussion in the previous meetings, there are not many days left.

A second reason for the documents arriving late is, according to some of my colleagues at the Directorate General, the hierarchical system in the Commission. When Miguel and his team have written the report it has to be approved by the civil servants in higher positions in the Directorate General. First, his Head of Unit and the Head of Unit responsible for the European Employment Strategy have to agree. Secondly, the Director of these Heads of Unit has to be satisfied. Third, the deputy Director General has to give his opinion. Fourth, the Director General gives her views. And finally, the Commissioner may give her position. They usually all have something to contribute that Miguel and his team have to take into consideration. As the bureaucrats working in the Commission say, the policy proposals have to be approved by the 'hierarchy'.

When the proposal for the report on indicators is agreed on, the Employment Committee Secretariat can begin work with the President on writing a draft opinion on the report. In practice they may begin earlier if they have had meetings beforehand. The Secretariat and the President may then anticipate what the Committee members will think about the report from the Commission. However, they still have to know exactly what is in the report in order to be able to write the final draft. The draft for a Committee opinion on the Commission's report should, at best, be included with the documents sent to the member states for them to be able to prepare, but sometimes it is presented at the meeting.

In fact, the final verdict on what is to be on the agenda for the Employment Committee meeting and if there are to be any new documents presented at the meeting, is decided on the evening before the meetings by the Employment Committee's Steering group. In this way the Steering group has the opportunity to change agendas and prepare or decide to bring out new documents in the midst of the meetings, thereby changing the conditions for the pre-planned national positions. Members of the Steering group include the President of the Employment Committee plus two vice-Presidents, the Director General, the deputy Director General and a few other high-ranking officials from the Commission as well as vice-Presidents determined by the incumbent Presidency and the next Presidency. The member state holding the Presidency, and the next one, thus have the opportunity of making an input into what is to be on the Employment Committee's agenda. This structure, including the present and the next Presidency, is significant, since the Presidency has great influence on what is going to be decided on in the Council of Ministers. In the members' view, there is no point in working on policy issues that everyone knows will not be concluded in the Council of Ministers or in the European Council.

The meeting format of having to write reports, and adopting national positions and a Committee opinion before the meeting begins, pushes the policy-making process towards a decision, since the members have to try to be prepared. It can be said that, without the meetings to prepare for, there would be less incitement forcing the process to move towards a decision. However, the short preparation periods have consequences for the time the member states have to prepare. The national positions sometimes change during the course of the

decision-making process, due to the fact that new information demonstrates that another indicator would be better to use to make visible
what the member state wants to reveal to the others.

Fashioning the EU: the scheduling in meetings

The scheduling of EU time in meetings and in the preparation of
meetings gives the EU policy process a certain character. In most
organisations formal decisions are made in meetings. It is part of the
bureaucratic logic. However, what makes the EU meetings somewhat
different is the fact that they are multinational. The member states'
representatives do not share an everyday workplace but come from the
Ministries in the member states. The multinational character of the
meeting has certain organisational features that influence the time
available to make policy and take decisions. The members have their
work schedules at the national Ministries that might be competing and
have to be synchronised, with EU time. This leaves little room for
changes and delays in meeting times. Also, the fact that the interpreters
are scheduled to be in the Employment Committee meetings between
10 am and 6.30 pm means that the meeting ends, if not before, then
usually immediately after 6.30. At one meeting the President of the
Employment Committee says:

> We lose the interpreters at 6.30. Can we conclude soon so that we will
> have time for the macroeconomic dialogue?
> (Employment Committee meeting 20 November 2001)

Half an hour later he says:

> Can we continue in English? Or should I try to draft a proposal? We are
> now only in English. The interpreters have left.
> (Employment Committee meeting 20 November 2001)

The meeting ends just ten minutes later. The fact that the interpreters
have left and that the meeting day will soon be over speeded up the
decision-making process.

In addition, the member states' representatives have planes or
trains to catch and hotel rooms booked, and this contributes to ensuring that the meeting days follow the time schedule. This influences

what decisions are made at the meetings, since there is a certain time when the decision has to be made. It is not possible to continue the discussion in the corridors afterwards or to decide to meet the next day. Especially when it is the last meeting before the policy issue moves to the next level in the meeting hierarchy, the members have to decide, regardless of whether they feel 'ready' or not. There is subjective time in which there is too little time and there is 'objective' linear time following the clock.

The issue of the scheduled meeting also has other consequences. Often policies are not discussed as thoroughly at the end of the day as they would have been at the beginning. The perception of the time left at the beginning of the day is often longer than is actually the case. Bernard, one of my colleagues at the Commission, gives me an example one day when we are walking back to the Commission from an Economic and Social Committee meeting. I ask him about the Employment Committee meetings (this was before I had been to one myself). He says that they are always long because when the President opens the floor to the member state representatives they all want to state their positions. He says, with some bitterness, that last year when they were discussing the guidelines, they had eight (out of 18) guidelines left with only one hour remaining for discussion. This one hour proved enough for them to go through the remaining guidelines –and that was without the interpreters. He wonders why they cannot always be that quick! (17 September 2001).

The need for the members to express their national positions creates a climate for discussion that reflects a culture of conflict in which the member states' different positions clash with each other. At the same time, they have to agree, in this way articulating a culture of compromise, since, when the end of the day is approaching and it is the last Employment Committee meeting before the Council, a decision has to be made. Member state representatives who do not agree with the others sometimes have to 'give up' in order for a decision to be reached in the Committee. As when the Italian representative disagrees with a formulation in the opinion of the Employment Committee. Since no one else supported him he had to surrender even though he fought to the bitter end. We shall return to what he battled for in Chapter 6. If it had not been the last Employment Committee meeting before the Council, he might have been able to find allies or to come up with a new solution. As it was, he had to accept that the meeting had come to an end and that his position was not taken into consideration.

In this way the schedule of the meeting days as well as the rhythm of the meetings pushes the policy-making process towards a decision, thereby constantly creating and re-creating what we recognise as the EU.

Conclusion: forming the EU by the making of an EU chronology

If we return to the story at the beginning of this chapter, it is clear that the making of decisions is part of the everyday work of the EU. For decisions to be legitimate they have to follow a particular order in which one group discusses, negotiates and argues on a particular policy issue before it moves to the next group. There is a hierarchy here that has to be observed. The bureaucratic process of making decisions is thereby managed by time, by the rhythm of the meetings and by the changing of the Presidencies. Decisions form a chronology in EU work, in which they are identified as being made at this or that moment in this or that place.

Using the instrument of time to control individual and organisational action has mainly been connected with the nation state. It has been, and still is, part of building the nation state by forming a community among individuals through the sense of sharing a history, a present and a future (Anderson 1983:31). The notion of linear time has in this way been used as a bureaucratic and political instrument by which to form the modern state, for example, by inventing national holidays built on the past, or by having elections, in Sweden, every fourth year. However, history is also created in the EU, beyond the nation states. There are attempts in the Commission to actively build an EU history through the use of EU holidays or the notion of founding fathers such as Spaak and Spinelli (Shore 2000:56-60). These attempts have not, so far, been a serious threat to individuals' sense of community and shared history in the nation state. However, in the everyday life of the Eurocrats and politicians working in the EU (and perhaps for some of the EU citizens) an EU history has already been formed, one of its sparks being the changing of Presidencies in which the changing alone forms an EU chronology.

In addition, an EU chronology is created by the decisions made in the EU. The policy processes that take place and the policy issues decided on are what gives the EU content. The changing of Presidencies shapes the EU, since policies are pushed towards making decisions, given that member states holding the Presidency want to leave a mark on the history of the EU. The fashioning of a postnational EU is in this way encouraged by the fact that member states' representatives want to make visible the national, showing off the best side of their member state and being able to say that this or that was decided on during 'their' Presidency. The national and the postnational are complementary here, with a postnational EU being formed by the national with time as one of the driving forces. In addition, the rhythm of the meetings makes the decision-making process legitimate and thereby makes EU decisions possible.

However, the rhythm of the meetings is not the only process that makes decisions in the EU legitimate and possible. The meetings as such, as processes of negotiation, communication and decision-making, are also important for making decisions valid and for building the EU. The meetings as ritual processes of decision-making are the focus of the next chapter.

FOUR

MEETINGS: PERFORMING RITUALS OF LEGITIMATION

Introduction: meetings as ritual processes of decision-making

Much of everyday, formal, decision-making in organisations is performed in meetings. In EU employment policy-making most of the
discussions, negotiations and communications that lead up to a decision are performed in the 'first' committee, i.e. the Employment
Committee, in the series of meetings. It is here that, in practice, most
actual decisions are made even if they have formally to be passed in the
Council. To understand the meeting process in the Employment
Committee is therefore of extra significance in the study of EU employment policy. The meeting process is also the focus of this chapter.
The Employment Committee meetings may be seen as processes of
negotiation, discussion and communication of different perspectives
that are formed into decisions. The meetings may in fact be seen as
ritual processes (cf. Turner 1969) of decision-making, where the meeting
process is a repetition of formal activities, which have symbolic
authority and '...gain legitimacy for rulers...' (Kunda 1992:93).

There have been numerous attempts to define ritual (see for example de Coppet 1992; Kunda 1992; Turner 1969). Here, ritual is not only
connected with religion, moral order or myth, but also secular activities
such as meeting processes (cf. Moore and Myerhoff 1977). Relying on
Kertzer, Kunda adopts a broad definition of ritual as '...symbolic
behavior that is socially standardized and repetitive' (Kertzer in Kunda
1992:257n1). This is also the interpretation taken on ritual in this study.
In general terms, rituals may be viewed as organised processes with

formal and repetitive behaviour, in small encounters with large-scale ceremonies (Parkin 1992:13). The meeting process in the EU may in this way be seen as a ritual process. The meetings as formal, repetitive, organised processes are spatially prescribed performances with rules and regulations of where, when, and how to meet. They have ceremonial and symbolic meaning since they are perceived to provide a legitimising ground for making decisions.

Not only the definition but also the meaning and social significance of ritual have been debated in anthropology (Bell 1992). My view on the meaning of ritual in this study is to see it as a '...dramatic form that may contain both conflictual and integrative processes' (Kunda 1992:257n2). In this way ritual deals with conflict in the meeting by integrating the individuals taking part in the ritual process. The integrating character of the ritual process of meetings also has another significance here, beyond that of forming a group decision and dealing with individual conflict. The multinational character of the EU meetings highlights the fact that 'national' positions have to be transformed into a postnational EU decision. The ritual process of meetings deals with this opposition by disguising the conflict in ritualised diplomatic language, presentation practices, and ritual compromise, thereby conferring legality on the decision (Moore and Myerhoff 1977:3-4). Drawing on Power's term, *rituals of verification* in relation to audits (1999:14,138), I suggest in this context the term *rituals of legitimation*, implying that *how* a decision is made is as important for the policy outcome as is the content of what is decided on. It is not only the knowledge and the indicators produced in the committee that make the decision legitimate but the fact that the decision is made in the right way: in a meeting, with a president, through decision-making by majority, and so forth. This ritual process makes the decision-making process trustworthy and justifiable (also see Meyer and Rowan 1977:343-344).

Moving between backstage and frontstage

The meeting process as a legitimising ritual for formal decision-making is a conspicuous part of organisational life in the Western world.

However, this does not necessarily mean that decisions are actually made in the meeting, as pointed out by, for example, Boden (1994:84) and Kuper (1971:21). It may well be that the actual decision is made in relation to the meeting: when travelling as a delegation to the meeting or when making allies during lunches and dinners on the meeting days. It is useful here to turn to Goffman's ideas about backstage and front-stage (1959:109ff). Backstage, in this case before the meeting begins, the members can 'behave out of character' (Goffman 1959:116). The argument is underlined by the notion that when individuals present themselves in the public sphere they put on a front and perform 'in character'. In the EU the member states' representatives often put on the role of the civil servant representing the nation state.

However, Goffman has a particular view on the individual and the self in which all '...management [of the self] takes place inside, and the finished product is shown on the person's outside surface' (Martin 1997:249). Or, as Albrow argues, Goffman's '...stress on staged performances leaves the actor's core feelings vacant...' (1997:125). This is a view of an autonomous individual who does not interact as a whole with her/his environment but puts on different fronts in the different public spheres. Implicit in this is the idea that the individual is more her/his authentic self when being backstage. Here, Martin's (1997:247, also see Thedvall 2004:133-134) view of the self as an 'interface zone' is instead the focus. As Martin puts it: 'This world is neither inside the subject nor outside, but in the interface zone between the subject and its environment. In some ways, the line between the person and the world becomes less sharp and certain: inner self shades into interface which is already partly of the self and partly of the world' (Martin 1997:247).

This means that even if the members in the meetings are representatives of national governments or the Commission and they are there in that 'role', it is not a staged performance in the sense that they are not 'themselves'. The performance of the role in the meetings is part of who they are in that interface zone of the self and the meeting environment. Nevertheless, since meetings are staged environments, Goffman's theatre language is useful here, since the backstage behaviour of the individuals is different from the frontstage, i.e. the formal meetings. However, Goffman focuses especially on arenas where there is an 'outsider' (1959:135), such as in a restaurant where the waiters are frontstage when they are serving the customers and backstage when they are in the kitchen. In Goffman's terms a meeting, such as an Employment Committee meeting, would instead be considered backstage since the membership is privileged (cf. Law 1994:146). The public events, such as the conferences in Chapter 2, might instead be seen as frontstage, in Goffman's terms. Here, the concepts frontstage and backstage are instead used relationally. The Employment Committee meetings are backstage to the general public, but for the members at the meeting backstage is before the meeting starts, during lunches and dinners between and during meeting days, or when the meeting ends. However, it is useful to think in terms of backstage and frontstage since it demonstrates how the negotiations and discussions backstage create the staged conflict as well as hindering the integrating ritual process of making a compromise frontstage. The relationship between them will be explored further in the sections below.

Behind the scenes: making preparations

Before a meeting takes place preparations have to be made, as we have seen in Chapter 3. These preparations support the ritual process of staged conflict. At the preparatory meetings in the national ministries the national position is formed. This structures a culture of conflict in the meetings where the members' positions clash with each other. The preparatory meetings consist of the Swedish delegates as a group with a common opinion, a Swedish position, on what are good 'quality in work' indicators. A culturally intimate group is formed among a category of people who individually may very well have different opinions and who in their everyday work in the Ministry work on different policy issues, but who have to show a united front and argue for a common position.

Shaping a 'national' position

Before an Indicators group meeting in the summer of 2002 (2 July) a group of people in the Swedish Ministry of Industry met for a couple

of hours to prepare the national position for the meeting. The following day the Swedish delegation was to travel to Brussels. The Commission's report on the 'quality in work' indicators had been sent to the
member states for the delegates to consider beforehand.

It is my second preparatory meeting in the Ministry. As I wait in
the lobby of the Ministry of Industry for someone to come and get me,
a member of the Social Protection Committee Indicators group[65] walks
by. He is going to be at the meeting and he takes me with him up to
the seventh floor of the building. As we are walking along the corridor
Malin, one of the Swedish representatives in the Employment Committee,[66] approaches us. She has been asked to go and fetch me. As we
walk towards the office of Anders, a representative in the Employment
Committee, at the end of the corridor we exchange pleasantries.
Anders' room is a corner office in the old part of the Ministry. One
part of the room has a desk and a chair surrounded by bookshelves
and another part has a round table for entertaining guests and holding
meetings. Anders, Susanne and Peter, all Swedish representatives in the
Employment Committee, are already seated round the table together
with Hedda, an expert on health and safety at work.

We go through the different items on the agenda for this meeting:
'health and safety at work', 'flexibility and security', 'work organisation
and work-life balance', and finally 'social dialogue and worker involvement'. During the course of the meeting we discuss the different areas
and finally arrive at the last: 'social dialogue and worker involvement'.
There are two indicators suggested in the Commission's proposal: 'the
percentage of employees covered by collective agreements', the so-

---

65 The Social Protection Committee (SPC) is one of the Employment Committee's
sister committees, together with the Economic Policy Committee (EPC) and the
Economic and Finance Committee (EFC). These committees work in the same way as
the Employment Committee but on other questions. The Social Protection Committee
advises the Ministers of Social Affairs on issues such as social inclusion, poverty and so
on. For more information on these Committees see Jacobsson and Vifell 2005.

66 For the purpose of anonymity the personal names have been changed. They are also
all referred to as Swedish representatives of the Employment Committee regardless of
whether they are delegates or alternates or whether they are members of the
Employment Committee's subgroups: the Indicators and the Ad hoc groups.

called SD1 (short for social dialogue 1), and 'days lost in industrial disputes', the so-called SD2. Anders says, ironically, that it is going to be a fun discussing this matter in the meeting. The members have encountered problems in agreeing since the member states have different institutional systems and therefore want to measure different things. During the previous year the Employment Committee had agreed that a menu of indicators had to be worked out in this area to take into consideration all the institutional arrangements. Now, they are going to try again but the suggested indicators are almost the same as those of the year before and Anders anticipates that there is going to be a struggle.

Malin says that we [Sweden] do not like indicator, SD2 ('days lost in strikes') and that we do not want it. However, she goes on to say that it will probably not be possible to argue for this, since there are so many in the group who prefer SD2 to SD1. Instead, she thinks Sweden should argue that the only way we can agree on SD2 is if it is complemented by SD1. They have discussed this before and 'days lost in strikes' would not give Sweden a 'good' score since there are so few industrial disputes in Sweden compared with the other member states in the EU. (The logic being that a large number of 'days lost in strikes' shows 'workers' involvement'.) In addition, they also believe that SD1 is a better measure of how well the social dialogue is working. For them, as Swedes working for a Social Democratic government, workers' involvement is shown by membership of unions and collective agreements rather than by going on strike. The Swedish position is firm. If the other member states want SD2 they will also have to agree on SD1.

In this way the preparatory meetings not only form the Swedish 'positions' but also unite the Swedish delegation. In the discussions they talk about whether the indicator is in line with the political agenda of the Swedish government and/or whether it would give Sweden a good score. The preparatory meetings are part of a ritual process of forming a delegation and creating intimacy in the group, which is necessary in order to take part in the meeting process. The meetings are set up in such a way that the members need to adopt a position that is 'national' in order to create a postnational 'EU' position. Another factor which is important in forming a delegation is the nomadic relocation from the national ministries to the meeting rooms.

Going to and from the meeting: forming a 'delegation'

The periods when the members are walking or travelling to the meeting are often a time for discussing and agreeing on common ideas about what will happen in the meeting, and last-minute preparations of what 'our' delegation will say. After the meeting is also a time for forming a shared perception of what did happen in the meeting. It creates a moment where a 'we' is formed discussing what was said, or reviewing the meeting and how 'well' the member state position did.

Walking to and from the meeting

Maria, one of the Commission's representatives in the Employment Committee,[67] Mark, from the Secretariat of the Employment Committee, and I are walking to the Indicators group meeting (7 November 2001) at a conference centre fifteen minutes walking distance from the Directorate General. In thirty minutes or so, the Indicators group meeting is due to start. Mark, with the help of his secretary, has made the practical arrangements and now the documents are in place and the proposals for a report on the 'quality in work' indicators are finished, drawn up by Miguel, a principal administrator in the Directorate General, and his team.

We walk along the Rue Joseph II, through a small park, passing by the Charlemagne Commission building and the Council building at Rond Point Schuman before arriving at the conference centre. We are talking about today's meeting and predicting that it will be difficult to agree on the 'quality in work' indicators since several member states do not want them. There is a feeling of consensus in that we all agree that this is a difficult political process. Our talk about the meeting and the issues to be discussed strengthens us as a group. The people in the

---

[67] For anonymity the personal names have been changed. When mentioned by name but not role they are also all referred to as the Commission's representatives in the Employment Committee regardless of whether they are delegates, alternates, or presenters or whether they are members of the Employment Committee's subgroups: the Indicators and the Ad hoc groups.

Commission, and especially the secretaries of the Employment Committee, have contacts with the member states and often get advance
information on what the member state members may be thinking
about or how they may react on an issue. This knowledge creates an
'us', as part of the Commission. When we arrive at the meeting room,
however, the moment of intimacy between us is over. Maria and Mark
immediately begin to talk to people and to discuss the documents. I
start to prepare myself for the meeting and sit down behind the seats
reserved for the Secretariat of the Employment Committee.

When the meeting is over we return to the intimacy mode and discuss what has happened in the meeting to make sure that we have
understood the event in a similar way, or coach each other in doing so.
Another time Catherine, a representative of the Commission, Mark and
Tanja, Secretaries in the Employment Committee, and I are travelling
by car back from a meeting at which Tanja said she thought neither
Sweden nor Finland had understood what the United Kingdom meant
by 'basic skills'. She said the United Kingdom meant the ability to read
when she thought Sweden and Finland were probably thinking of skills
like computer literacy (5 October 2001). These interpretations that the
Commission employees continuously make, seeing themselves as being
knowledgeable about different member states' situations, create their
'us'.

Nonetheless, back at the Directorate General everyday duties take
over. The Secretaries of the Employment Committee prepare for
future meetings. Miguel, and his team, try to accommodate the decisions on changes made at the meeting. Maria, Catherine and the other
Commission representatives return to their other duties in the Commission, and their roles as Commission representatives are completed,
until the next meeting. The walk here signifies a 'liminal' phase (Turner
1969:95) during which the members are moving from one part of their
work, writing policy documents, to another part, being representatives
in meetings. It is a moment for concentration and focusing on another
area of their work. This is also true for the national delegations. However, they often travel from further away, like the Swedes, who have a
two-hour flight to Brussels and several nights in a hotel, which in turn
lengthens the liminal phase. This makes time not only for

concentrating on the work to be performed at the meeting, but also for discussing other issues that are on the policy agenda or getting to know each other better, which makes for greater closeness in the group as a national, Swedish, delegation.

Travelling to and from the meeting

Anders and Susanne, both Swedish representatives in the Employment Committee, and I meet at the gate at Arlanda Airport, Sweden.[68] We are going to take the last SAS plane to Brussels to make sure that we will be at the meeting at 10 o'clock the next morning. We board the plane and they take their seats in the business class while I go on towards the back of the plane to the economy class. After landing in Brussels, we meet up again and walk out of the airport to take a taxi to the hotel. Arriving at the hotel we decide to have a beer in the hotel bar. Anders and Susanne are mostly talking about procedures and issues internal to the Ministry of Industry, while I sit and listen and ask questions when I do not understand. It is evident that I am an outsider in the delegation since I have no experience of working in the Ministry. The Swedish members have a shared familiarity with Ministry matters that draws them closer together as a delegation in the context of the Employment Committee. In this way my experience is different from interacting with people in the Commission where I have actually worked.

On the morning of the first meeting day we meet in the hotel breakfast room. Anders gives last-minute coaching to Annika and Marie, two new Swedish representatives in the Employment Committee, on what they should say at the meeting. The expert on the issue of, in this case, 'gender equality' had not had time to prepare a Swedish position on the 'childcare' indicators beforehand, and now Anders informs Annika and Marie that this is an important question for Sweden, with high priority for the Swedish government. For this reason they must not only state the Swedish position but also emphasise its importance in the meeting. In this way the Swedish position is learnt in

---

[68] The story told is a typical version of all four of the travels to the meeting in Brussels that I have done with the Swedish delegation.

the group, since information about Swedish priorities is something that they as experts gain knowledge of through time.

After breakfast we walk through the Leopold Park to the meeting while Annika and Marie continue to discuss what they are to say in the meeting. During the walk they begin to concentrate on the coming meeting. When we arrive at the meeting room the moment of intimacy in the delegation is over, and Anders begins to talk to Mark, one of the secretaries in the Employment Committee, while I start to prepare myself for the meeting and sit down behind the seats reserved for Sweden.

When the meeting is over we again move from the formal to the more intimate. As Anders, Susanne and I walk back to the hotel we talk about what has happened in the meeting. Anders and Susanne wonder why the Commission is so reluctant to use a particular source on the indicators measuring 'stress'. This is an important question for Sweden and they think that this indicator is needed. Later that evening Anders, Susanne, Karin, Peter and Lars, all Swedish representatives in the Employment Committee, and I have dinner. Again, we talk about the meeting day, and reflect on what has been said. Anders thinks that Sweden is getting some of its issues across and he is quite pleased. However, they discuss further the importance of having an indicator on 'stress'. The discussion creates a joint opinion of what has been said at the meeting and what the outcome has been and whether it is in favour of 'us'.

At the end of the two meeting days, the Swedish representatives go back by plane to Stockholm. When at home the Swedish delegates have other duties and work they have to do in the Ministry and their roles as Swedish representatives are over for this occasion. The separation from the other members in the national delegation, and the separation from the meeting process as a national representative, returning to other duties, is also part of the meeting process. However, the notion of the national is also a requirement for creating the postnational EU. The national separates but also integrates the members, since the different national positions are formed into something postnational through the ritual process of meetings.

Moving in and out of meetings: separating and integrating

In meetings, the members take on the role of representatives for either the different member states or the Commission. The role of representative divides the members into different units with some as part of the Swedish delegation representing Sweden while others are, for example, part of the Italian delegation representing Italy. The fact that nationality constitutes the order in the meetings affects the meeting process of decision-making. The national is a prerequisite for the creation of the postnational EU. The ritual process of creating a conflict by constituting the national delegation, is in turn part of achieving a compromise integrating the members more and more closely decision by decision. The national differences divide the members since they speak different languages or have different bureaucratic 'cultures', but they also integrate by making it possible to achieve compromise decisions. There is an interplay between separation and integration here that becomes visible in relation to the members moving in and out of the meetings.

Engaging in Eurospeak?

The President of the Employment Committee rings the bell on the table and everyone falls silent. He puts on his microphone and welcomes everyone to the meeting. He begins by going through which languages are to be used in the meeting. He says, in English:

> You may speak in French, German, English, Italian, Spanish, Greek and Portuguese and you may listen to English, French, German, Italian and Spanish.
>
> (Employment Committee 20 November 2001).

Along the walls of the meeting room there are interpreters' booths. Language is important since the defining of concepts and the writing of opinions is the most important part of the Committee's work and also the part that is 'materialised'. Language use is, in essence, a form of power. As Bourdieu (1977:170-171) argues, the power to name things is the power to organise and give meaning to experiences. However, to name and give meaning to things in different languages creates certain problems. During the meetings at least English, French and German (in the Indicators group) and often Spanish, Portuguese,

Italian and Greek (in the Employment Committee and the Ad hoc group) are spoken, with interpreters translating directly at the meeting. The speakers of other languages have to use one of these languages.

The interpretations have consequences for understanding each other. During lunch at one of the Indicator group meetings (29 April 2002) I ask two of the Swedish delegates if they speak French. Susanne does not and Malin does a little. Susanne points out that it is sometimes difficult to understand what is said during the meeting although there are translations. The interpreters do not always know the correct term to use in the discussion, so at times they have to make their own translations of the translations, so to speak. It is also always difficult to listen to long contributions that are translated because sometimes the point is lost on the way. However, Susanne and Malin do not consider this to be a big problem, since they think they understand what the other members mean. Nevertheless, they have reflected on it in regards to their own use of English. The Swedish delegation had an informal policy of speaking in English or French even when they could demand translation (as in the Council's working groups) since they believed that their point would get across better in English or French (and because, according to them, there are not enough good Swedish interpreters in Brussels).

Nevertheless, in the Employment Committee English is the language used by most as an interim language. In fact, informally it has been agreed that English should be the only language spoken in the Committee, but this was no longer the case, as seen above. The documents in the meetings are, however, discussed in their English version. When an opinion from the Committee needs to be sent to the Council the members have to agree on its wording. The President usually guides the members by going through the document paragraph by paragraph. A good command of English is needed to understand what consequences a sentence might have. To be able to suggest new sentences, one must also know English well. The English mother tongue speakers always have a bit of an advantage since they also have the authority when new suggestions are on the table. They are trusted to have the competence to say: 'this does not mean anything in English' or 'in English it has another meaning'.

When I met the new President of the Employment Committee, six months after I finished my fieldwork, I asked him what it was like to be President. He said it was interesting but that one of the most difficult tasks was to make suggestions for new drafts since his mother tongue was not English.

The use of English by non-mother-tongue users also has other consequences. The English used in the EU context has to be made simple. Mark, a native English speaker working in the Secretariat of the Employment Committee, sometimes complained that his English had deteriorated since he had been working in the Commission. He had to write very simple English that all the members could understand. Tanja, a native Finnish speaker and a Secretary in the Employment Committee Secretariat, often had to remind him to make the language simpler because otherwise not all the members would understand. Others witnessed that it was the same in French, the other official Commission language.

This simplified multi-lingual technical expert discourse, characterised by an overabundance of Euro-acronyms such as the EES, JER, EMCO, NAP, to mention but a few with relevance to the European Employment Strategy, is sometimes referred to as 'Eurospeak' (Bellier 2000:66). As an informant of Cris Shore said: 'Ours is a language of compromise... we are creating a new language: a Euro-pidgin language' (Shore 2000:181). However, Eurospeaking by mixing English and French is a phenomenon connected with the EU institutions, in particular the Commission. For the Employment Committee members, Eurospeaking is characterised by other features, such as formality in the presentations, working with interpreters, and using interim languages, and by the use of particular concepts and acronyms that have particular meanings in the context of the Committee (such as 'quality in work'). This creates something that the members share, a form of Eurospeak that others, apart from the Committee members, might not equally easily understand.

Eurospeak was also sometimes used in the national governments. The concepts used in the meetings and the policy documents were not always translated. In the Swedish preparatory meetings Anders, Malin, Susanne, and Peter spoke Swedish but used the English concepts shared in the Committee. They spoke of 'health and safety at work' or 'social dialogue and workers' involvement' without translation when they were using them as headings or symbols for a particular set of indicators. Furthermore, the presentation of the Swedish position as well as future discussions in the Committee meeting would be in English. This meant that they had to know the language of indicators and econometrics in English to interpret what the indicators might mean. However, this did not appear to be a problem.

Ideas that had been introduced before, and had also been promoted by the Swedish Presidency, such as 'quality in work' were nonetheless translated. The Swedish term *'kvalitet i arbete indikatorer'* was frequently used instead of the English phrase 'quality in work indicators'. Except for the concepts used in the documents, the preparatory meetings were also conducted in Swedish, which made the discussions much more relaxed and natural, so to speak, since none of the delegates spoke English or any other foreign language on a day-to-day basis. In the meetings they were forced to speak English but here in the preparatory meeting their everyday language, Swedish, prevailed. The fact that it was backstage as well as in their own language allowed much more room for jokes and colloquial, spontaneous language. The use of Swedish accentuated the differences between the frontstage and backstage meetings in several ways. First, there was the use of different languages between frontstage and backstage. Second, there was the 'informal' way of discussing that had not only to do with the fact that in the meeting there were rules on how to speak, but also that they were using much more relaxed language because it was their own language.

Language, then, is part of distinguishing the delegations both backstage and frontstage, sustaining the notion of national differences between the members. Backstage the members use their own everyday language. Frontstage the use of an interim language known by all creates an integrated atmosphere. However, the mediation through interpreters make this much more difficult. To be able to form a decision, though, the members have to share a common terminology, which is where the acronyms and technical concepts come into play. National differences, however, are not only perceived to be visible in language but also in the different bureaucratic cultures. And national differences are used as explanations for why some members act in one way and others in another.

Sustaining national differences?

On one occasion (5 November 2002) Anders, Annika, Marie, all Swedish representatives, Mark and Peter, Secretaries in the Employment Committee, and I had dinner together in a restaurant in Brussels. Mark and I were talking about mutual friends from my time as a trainee at the Commission and Annika and Marie, both new as Swedish representatives, were getting to know Mark, while Anders and Peter were catching up on the latest news.

As at other times in a mixed nationality group, one of the topics discussed during the evening was national difference – a never-ending lunch and dinner topic in the EU context. I have been in numerous discussions about the differences between nationalities. Eriksen (1993:24) emphasises the need to categorise into 'us' and 'them', and that stereotypes help the individual to create order. These stereotypes are constantly re-created through the talk of differences. Stereotypification may, in this way, sometimes become a self-fulfilling prophecy (Eriksen 1993:24). As Herzfeld points out, '...people everywhere adopt rhetorical strategies on the basis of a presumed "national character". Their efficiency lies not in their recognition of some unchanging reality, but in their appeal to the conventions of collective self-representation. A German bureaucrat might feel under some pressure to demonstrate "efficiency", a Briton to show impatience with "excessive bureaucracy", a French civil servant to argue in the idiom of "rationality"' (Herzfeld 1992:72).

During lunch one day Susanne, one of the Swedish representatives, said with a smile on her face: 'If everyone was a quick as the Swedes the meetings would be over much sooner'. Malin, one of the Swedish representatives, went on to complain that the French delegate, on the other hand, never stopped talking. She said that she had difficulties concentrating during his whole contribution. Susanne and I agreed. Another time Mark, one of the Secretaries in the Employment Committee, commented that the French, Italians and Spanish always began their presentation at the meeting by thanking the people who had written the paper, while the Swedes and the Finns went straight to the point. He said with a laugh that the French, Italians and Spanish did not even have time to put their headphones on before the Swedes and the Finns had finished their contributions (15 September 2001). The Swedes and Mark seemed to have a similar view of how Swedes behaved in the meetings.

In fact, the members frequently lived up to the perceived stereotypes of different member states, as when the member states were presenting their positions on the labour market transition tables in area 6 'inclusion and access to the labour market' (transition tables 1, 2 and 3) and area 1 'intrinsic job quality' (transition tables 4, 5 and 6). The French representative argued passionately for a long time, as was expected of him by the others:

> I understand that on 2, 3 and 6 [transition tables] there are difficulties with the data. But the question we are being asked is if the tables seem reasonable. We could decide on that and then produce data that can measure this. We think the Commission's proposal is a good one. It's not all we want in France, but…. On table 5 I don't see that there's a value judgement in the table. We're supposed to see if a person a year later is in a different situation. All sorts of things have to be taken into account when analysing the data. The table doesn't say what it doesn't say! They don't make a judgement! I'm speaking at some length because we might be leaving transition tables behind that are relevant, and that's dangerous. We could say that they're relevant but that we don't have enough data?
>
> (Indicators group 15 November 2001)

The representative from the United Kingdom, on the other hand, argued efficiently on the same issue in points rather than long sentences, as was also expected and seen as distinctive to the British:

> On tables 2, 3 and 6 I've doubts about whether we should look at them at all. Training should not be in there. Is all training good? It's important with definitions. On table 4 it's not a measure of quality. On table 5 it's only the involuntary fixed-term contracts, not voluntary.
>
> (Indicators group 15 November 2001)

The representative from Sweden stated economically in short, quick sentences, as was also anticipated and considered particular to the Swedes:

> On table 1 we agree with Denmark and Belgium. Table 2 should be dropped. Table 3 needs to be developed but can maybe be used as a context. On dimension 1 we like 5 as a key, but with 'involuntary'. Table 4B is good. Table 6 could be dropped.
>
> (Indicators group 15 November 2001)

The fact that the members sometimes lived up to the stereotypes not only confirmed and sustained the idea of national differences. It also had consequences for the members' mutual understanding. It is not only the language as such that enables people to understand each other (Vandermeeren 1999:275). Non-native speakers tend to interact through those socio-cultural norms which govern their use of their first language (Vandermeeren 1999:275). Even though a majority of the members in the Employment Committee used English as an interim language, the speech styles of presenting a position often differed between the different member states.

During meetings, the different ways of presenting had different consequences. The long presentations caused some members not to listen to the whole contribution, while short presentations had the consequence, as given in the example above, that the French had not got their headphones on by the time the Swedes and the Finns had already finished. The attention spans seemed to differ. While some members thought the most important objective was to put their point across in as short a time as possible, others valued putting forward their point in long elegantly phrased sentences. This seemed to the quicker presenters to be a waste of the others' time and therefore not always worth listening to. These differences in speech styles challenged the notion of creating a European meeting at which everyone might be understood.

However, the members did not always live up to the stereotypes. But this was hardly ever noticed or discussed. The talk of national differences was also something that we, Anders, Annika, Marie, Mark, Peter and I, when having dinner between meeting days, or Tanja,

Mark, Maria and I, when having lunch in the Commission canteen, seemed to have in common. Knowledge of the perceived differences was something that we as a group of people with different nationalities were expected to have in common. As Eriksen points out in relation to the concept of 'ethnicity': 'Ethnicity is a kind of relationship that amounts to making cultural differences comparable, and thus presupposes a considerable degree of cross-ethnic cultural homogeneity; a shared cultural grammar and lexicon is required for talking about mutual differences' (1998:48). This knowledge was thus in a sense integrating by creating a shared knowledge base thereby contributing to creating a postnational community in the Committee.

However, this community was fickle. The shared knowledge of national differences may be the same but the relationships created were dependent on the individuals, regardless of their substitutability as representatives. Nevertheless, these relationships were sustained by their being representatives in the Committee. Some of them became friends, but most of the relationships were formed and continued because they met every other month according to the meeting schedule. When new members joined, the old ones were also soon forgotten. Instead, new personal alliances had to be built.

The meetings as ritual processes thus create networks and relationships between members and by extension among member states and the Commission, even if shared views on particular issues are also important in bringing members together. This networking and relationship building through the meeting days are also what makes decisions possible and in that way fashions the EU.

Meetings as processes of negotiating the EU

The meetings as ritual processes create shared ways of performing, acting and putting forward positions among the members in the Committee. These are based on rules, both written and unwritten, that determine *how* decisions may be made in a legitimate way. This in turn influences *what* decisions can be made.

The order in the meeting: a shared knowledge

At the Employment Committee meeting on 20 November 2001 the President informs us about what has happened in other meetings that may affect the work in the Committee. The Social Protection Committee's Indicators group has had a meeting on the 'Structural Indicators'.[69] One of the Commission's representatives signals that she wants to speak. The President gives her the floor and she says that the European Parliament feels that it does not have enough contact with the Employment Committee and that it would like to have an informal meeting with them. She thinks this would be useful as long as it is informal. The President responds that he supposes they could arrange an informal meeting with the European Parliament in the same way as they have done with, for example, the Social Protection Committee.

The President continues going through the agenda for the coming two days. There have been some changes. The 'quality in work' indicators are going to be the first instead of the second item on the agenda. He asks everyone if they are happy with the agenda. One of the Belgian representatives signals that he wants to speak. The President gives the floor to Belgium.

In the Committee, members are almost always referred to by their member state's name or that of the Commission. When the President gives the floor s/he usually says, for example, 'Sweden', not their personal names. This creates a sense of distance between the members. However, many of the 'old' members seem to know each other quite well, especially the Presidents of the different groups, and sometimes the members are referred to by their personal names rather than by their roles as representatives.

The Belgian representative says that he is happy with the changes in the agenda but he is worried about the 'Structural indicators' document

[69] In the preparations for the Spring Council the Commission drew up an 'Annual Synthesis Report' on the work done the previous year. Included in the Report were 'Structural indicators' in the policy areas of employment, social protection, economic reform and the environment. The Synthesis Report was the basis for discussion at the Spring European Councils as decided at the Spring European Council in Lisbon (European Council 2000a).

written by the Commission that is going to be sent to the Council for a decision. He wonders why the Employment Committee has not discussed it since the Social Protection Committee has done so, and he urges the Commission to explain this. The President gives the word to one of the Italian representatives who strongly seconds the question from the Belgians. The President asks the Commission's representative to tell us why. After an input from the Commission's representative and several other member states' representatives, who like the Belgians, want to discuss the 'Structural indicators' document, it is decided that they will put it on the agenda under 'Any other business' for it to be discussed the following day. The President returns to today's agenda:

> Now we turn to 'quality in work'. Maybe the Commission can paint in the background but first we turn to President of the Indicators group and the work done in the Indicators group. We should reach an agreement today. Then we [the Secretariat and the President] will write a draft opinion this evening and then tomorrow we should make sure that everyone agrees on the written report.
>
> (Employment Committee 20 November 2001)

The President of the Indicators group competently presents the group's opinion on the report on the 'quality in work' indicators. He also explains the changes they have made on the indicators and the problems they have encountered with some of them. The President then asks the Commission's representative to introduce the report and the discussion. This is the order of speaking at the beginning of every policy issue that is discussed in the meetings. The President gives the floor to the representatives of those who have prepared a report or an opinion, in this case the President of the Indicators group and the Commission's representative.

When the President of the Indicators group has presented the group's opinion on the report and the Commission's representative has presented the report, the member states are allowed to comment and state their national positions. They are called on to speak in the order in which they have put their member state's sign on its end. The Secretaries keep track of whose turn it is to speak and the President gives the word. When the member states ask the Commission something the President may give the floor to the Commission's representative without their asking for it, otherwise the Commission's representatives also have to ask specifically for permission to speak, since at this point they have to argue for the changes they want in the report, or for keeping it as it is.

Rules when presenting

The rules for presenting a position in the Committee have to be mastered, for the members to be able to master the arguments and influence the policy process. The members have to know when to speak, what to say and how to say it. As Schwartzman points out, a formal meeting needs, apart from rules about who starts and ends meetings, who has the right to call and so forth, '…a series of rules and conventions for ordering and regulating talk…' (1989:70). Boden continues on the same note and argues that '[m]eetings are, by the very nature, talk. Talk, talk, talk and more talk. But who talks when, to whom, and for how long is no casual matter' (1994:82). According to Richards (1971:2), a series of conventions guarding the performance in the meeting is one of the features that distinguish a council, i.e. a formal meeting, from other gatherings where people exchange views.

Some of the rules in the Committee are written down. The Employment Committee was legally created by a Council Decision based on the Treaty of Amsterdam (Council of the European Union 2000:21-22). The Council Decision specified the tasks of the Committee, the membership, how the Committee should operate, that it may establish working groups for its assistance, and how it should organise relations with other organisations and committees. The Council Decision also stated that the Committee should establish its Rules of procedure, specifying, for example, the voting system, how many are authorised to be present and so forth.[70]

Other rules are not explicitly expressed or written down but have to be learnt by the members either through learning-by-doing or by someone explaining them to them. These are the rules the members

---

[70] For a more detailed account of the Council Decision and the Rules of Procedure for the Employment Committee see Thedvall 2005.

have to know in order to be able to put forward their positions in the group, such as asking for the floor by putting the member state sign on its end or having to speak into the microphone when presenting, so that the interpreter can translate. Another one is how to begin a contribution. The contributions by the Commission and the member states in the Employment Committee often begin with thanks to either the Indicators group for doing a good job of finding indicators, the secretariat for writing a good opinion, or the like. As in one of the Employment Committee meetings, when a representative from Portugal said diplomatically:

> We would like to stress the tremendous job the Indicators group has
> done…
> (Employment Committee 20 November 2001)

In the same manner one of the representatives from Greece said:

> We would like to congratulate the Indicators group…
> (Employment Committee 20 November 2001)

The same style was used by one of the representatives from Finland:

> We would like to thank the President of the Indicators group and the
> Indicators group…
> (Employment Committee 20 November 2001)

A similar approach was used by one of the representative from Sweden, who said:

> The Indicators group has done a tremendous job…
> (Employment Committee 20 November 2001)

As Vandermeeren (1999:275) points out, a group that meets regularly is able to negotiate a 'conversation style' that is shared by all. The thanking procedure seems to be a shared conversational style. This should not be exaggerated, though. In the Employment Committee meetings there is hardly one common conversational style. Nevertheless, they do share a particular kind of Eurospeak with particular EU concepts and acronyms regarding employment policy. This shared Eurospeak is an important part of forming the Committee into a group, as part of the EU postnational community. In addition, the ways of performing in the meeting, i.e. asking for the floor, speaking into the microphone, communicating different views, making a decision by conclusions, further builds the idea of shared understandings. These ritual processes also help to make the decision-making process legitimate since the Rules of procedure have been followed according to the Council Decision.

Intermissions: having lunch, re-writing documents and re-forming positions

During a lunch break in the Employment Committee meeting I go to lunch with one of my Commission colleagues, Manfred (20 November 2001). We take the lift to the top-floor restaurant. We are almost the only ones there from the Employment Committee. Mark, one of the Secretaries in the Employment Committee, once said that when the different delegations eat somewhere other than in the conference centre, he thinks it is an indication that a difficult question is considered and that they have to discuss, in private, how to put their position across. This is certainly the case today because the discussions have been quite tough and members have encountered difficulties in agreeing.

The intermissions such as lunches and dinners on meeting-days are occasions for reflection. The members may discuss in smaller groups what has been said in the meetings and what it means for their member state. This may be seen as a liminal phase, in which the process of decision-making is, in a way, put on hold. The members are not at home in their national governments preparing a position or with easy access to the Ministry's resources to interpret what this or that brought up in the meeting might mean. Furthermore, they are not in a meeting where the policy process is being pushed towards a decision through arguments and compromises as well as through limits in the time schedule. They are, in essence, in between arenas of decision-making.

While Manfred and I are having lunch, Mark and Tanja, the Secretaries of the Employment Committee and the President have gone to write the Committee's opinion on the 'quality in work' indicators report, in which they have to try to accommodate the members' positions expressed during the morning in order to have a conclusion ready by the end of the day. The status of the policy document is 'betwixt and between' (cf. Turner 1969:95), since while Mark and Tanja and the President have a view of what the members want to include in the opinion, there is still no 'conclusion' on a final opinion and they will most likely have to re-write the document again during the evening for the next day's meeting. Sometimes breaks are also made in the middle of the meeting to re-write texts. The President of the Committee might also stop the meeting, while Tanja and Mark try to find a solution. During these breaks other members often come up to them to offer assistance with the formulations. Others again begin to talk to each other. The formal atmosphere in the meeting vanishes and the liminal phase sets in. Then the President puts on his microphone and starts up the meeting again by making a suggestion for a sentence.

After lunch Manfred leaves, and I go to the cafeteria on the ground floor to get coffee. There is still no sign of the members of the Committee. It is difficult to know if the delegations are eating by themselves to discuss their national position or if they are meeting with other delegations to form alliances. However, the assumption that members *are* at this point making alliances is understood. As the President of the Committee once pointed out in a meeting when it was time to read a draft of an opinion from the Committee:

> I'll give you five minutes to read the draft, but only five minutes be-
> cause otherwise I know there will be negotiations
> (Employment Committee 4 October 2001)

The fact that people fly in from other places in the EU to stay over in hotels in Brussels also facilitates the holding of informal meetings. The representatives of the member states and the Commission usually do not meet face-to-face other than during the meeting days. One can assume that opportunities to make alliances and draw up strategies with other representatives are much more easily available during the meetings than in the everyday work in their national governments or the EU institutions, one reason for the importance and frequency of informal meetings being that the informality of face-to-face interaction seems to create trust among individuals especially in an atmosphere where there is risk involved in revealing positions and ideas to a possible opponent (Misztal 2000:3). Nevertheless, in this context, the informal meetings, outside the meeting rooms, never included all the members, thus making it difficult to agree on decisions beforehand. Consequently, much of the negotiations took place in the actual meeting room.

Making an EU 'conclusion'

At one point in the process of forming indicators for area number 9 'diversity and non-discrimination' (more on that process in Chapter 5), the Committee members are working on indicator no. 30 that measures the 'employment rate of 55-64-year-olds'. Some of the member states think that this is not a good indicator for measuring 'diversity and non-discrimination'. A representative from Greece points out that it is almost a distraction from the main question, namely for them discrimination against ethnic minorities and immigrants (Employment Committee 20 November 2001). The French representative agrees. The Commission's representative tries to save the indicator by pointing out that the same one is in area 6 'inclusion and access to the labour market', i.e. indicator no. 21. He argues that it should be possible to retain the indicator in one or the other area. The President of the Committee tries to accommodate the members' different opinions in his 'conclusion' by saying:

> On the duplication of 21 and 30 [indicators 21 and 30]. My conclusion was to delete 21. Yes? [everyone is quiet]
>
> (Employment Committee 20 November 2001)

His suggestion is to retain the indicator on 'employment rate of 55-64-year-olds' in area 9. Even if some of the member states do not want it, there are also several who have not said anything on the subject, so he can assume that they want to keep it. By trying to conclude in this way he may be testing whether the members might agree with Greece and France in transferring it to area 6 instead. He goes on to suggest a possible 'conclusion' on the other indicators in area nine. He says:

Yes. Can we delete 'disadvantaged' [the concept] in 31.[71] I assume that's
OK? 32[72] should not be a key. We don't have a leading candidate for a
key.

(Employment Committee 20 November 2001)

One of the Italian representatives lifts its member state sign on its end
and the President gives him the floor, 'Italy':

> We are a little concerned about deleting 21 and keeping 30. I would
> have done it the other way round. I want to make a reservation for two
> reasons: one [missed] and two, to include older workers only in dimen-
> sion 9 doesn't make economic sense.
>
> (Employment Committee 20 November 2001)

The Italian representative does not agree with the 'conclusion' since he
thinks that it is important to have the indicator in area 6. In this way he
is not against retaining the indicator in area 9, but against deleting it
from area 6.

One of the Danish representatives raises its member states sign on
its end and the President gives her the floor, 'Denmark':

> We thought that '21' was included in '20',[73]
>
> (Employment Committee 20 November 2001)

The President, who is pleased with this solution from the Danes, says:

> Yes. That's a neat solution from Denmark. Is that acceptable to Italy?
> [The Italian representative nods his head.] Yes.
>
> (Employment Committee 20 November 2001)

The Secretaries of the Employment Committee, together with the
President, do their best to keep track of who wants changes and who
does not. When everyone is quiet and the members seem to have
exhausted their inputs the President tries to suggest a 'conclusion'. If

---

[71] 'The disadvantaged employment gap (difference between the overall employment
rate and the employment rate of ethnic minorities, immigrants and disabled people).'
[72] 'Employment and unemployment rate gap of non-EU foreigners compared with
average, and taking account of the distinction between low and high-level
qualifications.'
[73] 'Employment rate by main age groups and educational attainment levels.'

the members are not happy with it, the discussion continues. The President then tries again to conclude until everyone can agree. This way of deciding has been seen as consensus decision-making, where issues are discussed until everyone is satisfied and convinced that the best solution is on the table. It is possible according to the Rules of Procedures to use a system of voting, by a simple majority vote. Sometimes, if the President is unsure of how to conclude, s/he might ask all the members to give their vote: yes or no, but the common practice is consensus decision-making.

However, when I say consensus decision-making, that is not completely true. It is in fact not consensus in the sense of the members discussing and deliberating until everyone is happy. It is more of a 'majority consensus' or a compromise. This was made clear in one of the Employment Committee meetings when one of the member state delegates wanted inscribed in the opinion that only the majority of the Committee wanted the indicator, since he did not agree. Another member state delegate answered that they understood the point, but that most decisions in the Committee were decided by majority vote (21 November 2001).

Member states in a minority position have the right according to the Rules of procedures to have their position annexed to the reports, proposals or opinions, but, as the member state representative above was hinting, there is always a majority vote. However, this is usually not stated openly since the President continues to suggest 'conclusions' until everyone is able to agree. The responsibility not to argue further is then placed on the members. If they have an opinion that is not shared by other members there might be no point in going on arguing. This system is not visible in the reports, proposals and opinions. If everyone can agree on the 'conclusion', that is what ends up in the documents. In this way the documents are almost always written as if they were preceded by a consensus decision.

In relation to the 'conclusion' document of the Committee, the negotiations and compromises in the meetings are performed backstage resulting in policy documents that in public, frontstage, are presented as the outcomes of a consensus decision. It is only the people present at the meetings who know what discussions, negotiations and argu-

edge and therefore used as a legitimising ground for 'fair' politics. This will in turn make policies and policy-making 'transparent'. The next chapter is about trust in the science of statistics and how the fact that indicators are culturally biased is handled by the members by distinguishing between the 'political' and the 'technical'. Timing is important here since the knowledge produced is dependent on the meetings schedule and the knowledge available at that particular time.

FIVE

'QUANTIFYING THE QUALITATIVE': TURNING POLITICS INTO NUMBERS

Introduction: making the ambiguous precise

'We must work to quantify the qualitative. With indicators that measure the real impact of our various policies and our basic goals of improving the everyday lives of our citizens. [...] Qualitative factors are not fundamentally different from quantitative ones. They may be more difficult to measure accurately. But we will succeed. There was a time when you could only judge the quality of water by whether you died after drinking it. But we can now measure air and water quality with the same precision as temperature. [...] To ensure real value from public money, we will need to be much more efficient in measuring the full costs and benefits of different actions and policies. Taking account of so-called "qualitative" benefits and costs as well as the "quantitative"'.
(Commissioner Anna Diamantopoulou, February 2001.)

The speech was given by the Commissioner Anna Diamantopoulou at a conference, 'Investing in Quality', in Brussels in February 2001. It reflected the work that was taking place in the Directorate General. It also reflected what had been agreed on by the Prime Ministers and Presidents at the European Council in Nice in December 2000. The Commission had then been asked to suggest classifications and potential indicators for 'quality in work'. To recapitulate, a few months after the Commissioner's speech, in the Commission's Communication, ten areas and possible indicators for measuring 'quality in work' were suggested. The speech revealed the difficulties the Commission had encountered in finding measurable indicators for 'quality in work'. However, the Commissioner was convinced that it would be possible to measure 'quality in work' as accurately as temperature, as long as they tried hard enough. It was a question of making the ambiguous precise so that policies could be evaluated in a politically neutral way. This was based on a view of the 'political' as ambiguous and open to interpretation, and the 'technical' in the form of indicators as precise and objective. By her trust in numbers Commissioner Diamantopoulou joined a growing trend of making policies auditable through numbers. This trend was based on the idea that the effectiveness of policies had to be 'managed by results' in the form of indicators in order to be able to make the policies transparent and the bureaucrats and politicians accountable.

Empirically this chapter follows the process of developing indicators in area 9, 'diversity and non-discrimination', of the 'quality in work' indicators. When the Commission and the member states were trying to think of what they wanted 'Social Europe' to be about in the area of employment, they expressed the notion of producing not just 'more jobs' but also 'better jobs'. As we have seen above, 'more and better jobs' was soon translated into 'quality of work'. 'Quality in work' was then divided into ten different areas, as shown in Chapter 2 and 3. However, the ten classified areas were not measurable in themselves. They were seen as too vague, too ambiguous. They had to be made precise in order to be measurable. This task of developing indicators, to make the ambiguous precise, brought to the surface conflicting interpretations and political ideas of what 'diversity and non-discrimination' meant in relation to 'quality in work'.

The policy-making process illustrates the political considerations that have to be taken into account when developing indicators in the EU, making the vision of objective, politically neutral indicators problematic. As Petryna points out '...the processes of making scientific knowledge are inextricable from the forms of power those processes legitimate and even provide solutions for' (2002:10). The politics of numbers ultimately calls in question the notion of numbers' ability to make policies transparent and bureaucrats and politicians accountable.

The bureaucratic logic of quantification

To turn people, things and ideas into numbers is part of the bureaucratic logic of quantification of the Western world. As Cohen points out '[w]e live in a world of numbers' (2005:17). Numbers in the form of statistics and indicators are seen as a guarantee of objectivity. Through statistics and indicators political decisions become legitimate, based on scientific 'facts' rather than political values (Porter 2001:746). As pointed out in Chapter 1, this calculative idealism dominates a general view on numbers and indicators. It forms an epistemic culture of numbers that is difficult to attack.

However, the Employment Committee members were often faced with the fact that the 'one-best-indicator' (cf. Radaelli 1999:28) was not to be found, which they frequently explained by lack of time or lack of available data. The cultural boundedness of the 'one-best-indicator' was seldom explored. Nevertheless, this awareness of the missing 'one-best-indicator' alerted the Committee members to the fact that indicators do have political meaning and may have purpose.

As the 'development' apparatus in Ferguson's Lesotho becomes '...a machine for reinforcing and expanding the exercise of bureaucratic power...' (1990:255), the work with developing euro-statistics is a way expanding EU bureaucratic and political power in the member states. This makes the definition of indicators imperative for the members since it will determine what is measured, and thereby what it is possible to compare, finally influencing what direction EU employment policy will take.

Nevertheless, the transforming of politics into indicators instrumentalises politics. In Standish's words, this may be called a 'fetishisation of instrumentality' (Standish 2000:159), fetishism in the sense that, by instrumentalising politics, in other words by turning politics into numbers, it appeals to our understanding of statistics not as something politically created in our own culture but something beyond reach and not contaminated by people's values and beliefs (cf. Miller 2003:360). The methodology of indicators then becomes a way of performing politics. Regardless of whether indicators are perceived as representing reality as it really is, or as mere 'attention-directing devices', they make policy-making possible in the first place, by framing the scope of how policy may be made by creating a shared knowledge among the members.

In this bureaucratic culture of policy-making the arguments used by the members to claim the rightfulness of their position is based on distinguishing between what is seen as the political goals and the way in which these can be made technical by the science of statistics. These two perspectives are described by the members of the Employment Committee as the 'political' and the 'technical'.

Knowledge of the 'political' and the 'technical'

The concepts of 'technical' and 'political' and the ideas behind them are used as tools for arguing in favour of or against an area or an indicator in the EU meetings. To be able to make good arguments, both 'political' and 'technical', the representatives of member states and the Commission have to know what can be used as such. In this context, the 'political' arguments are based on the knowledge of what has been decided previously in the relevant Councils and what the Prime Ministers and Presidents had in mind when they concluded that 'quality in work' indicators needed to be developed. The knowledge of what is written in the Council Decisions and European Council Conclusions is of particular importance, since these constitute what the EU should ideally be about and in this case what EU employment policy should really be about. These decisions are, of course, open to interpretation, but there is still a text, in the form of a decision, that the members have to relate to and could also use when making their case.

The members' 'technical' arguments have to be based on knowledge about statistics in general, and EU statistics in particular. As mentioned above, they need to have a good overview of the available statistical databases. The EU statistical databases are mainly developed in Eurostat,[74] which is a General Services institution in the Commission. There are other data sources used when developing euro-statistics, such as national databases or databases from the Dublin

---

[74] For more information on Eurostat see, for example, Franchet 1999.

Foundation[75] or the OECD,[76] but the EU's own databases are developed at Eurostat. They are also the data the Commission members prefer and trust when they suggest sources for indicators. One may assume that the trust is in part based on the fact that Eurostat is part of the Commission and thus under its control.

Two statistical databases from Eurostat were widely used in relation to the 'quality in work' indicators: the Labour Force Survey (LFS) and the European Community Household Panel (ECHP). The LFS data are based on data from the national statistical institutes. The latter are responsible for collecting the data according to a common coding scheme developed by Eurostat, where the data are collated. The LFS data are individual data, which means that questions are asked of individuals, and not necessarily the same individuals every year. The LFS data are available three months after the end of the reference period, i.e. the time of asking. Data are renewed every year and the survey has been carried out since 1983.

As opposed to the LFS data, the ECHP data[77] were based on a common questionnaire provided by Eurostat. The ECHP data-gathering procedure also differed from that of the LFS in that the sample was based on a pure panel, which means that the same people taking part in

---

75 The full name of the Dublin Foundation is: 'The European Foundation for the Improvement of Living and Working Conditions'. It is generally referred to as the Dublin Foundation since it is located in Dublin. The Dublin Foundation is a European Agency set up by the European Council to contribute to the planning and design of better living and working conditions in Europe. For more information visit its website: http://www.eurofound.eu.int/ Last visited 2005-12-09.

76 There are three dominant international/postnational organisations that develop European statistics: Eurostat, the Organisation for Economic Co-operation and Development (OECD), and the United Nation (UN) organisation; the Economic Commission for Europe. In addition, there are other organisations that have an impact on European statistics such as the International Labour Organisation (ILO), the United Nations Educational, Scientific and Cultural Organisation (UNESCO), the World Trade Organisation, the International Statistical Institute, the International Monetary Fund (IMF), the World Bank and so forth (Franchet 1999:241). However, Eurostat is the organisation responsible for developing EU statistics.

77 The ECHP database was replaced by the EU-SILC database in July 2003. For more information on the similarities and differences between these databases see CEC 2005.

the first survey were followed up in subsequent surveys. This gave the ECHP an advantage according to the member states and the Commission's representatives, because the same people were asked several times, which provided continuity in the answers. However, a drawback with the ECHP, according to the Committee members, was 'timeliness': both how often the questions were asked, which was every five years, and the discrepancy between when the questions were asked and when they were presented as statistics, which was sometimes years afterwards. This could mean that governments might change between the time of asking and the time of presenting, so that what was measured would be partly the result of another government's politics, as was sometimes argued. The ECHP also used a smaller sample than the LFS, which was not considered good. The larger the group of respondents, the more legitimacy the result would give, since it was understood that there would be a greater degree of representativeness. Most of the time the member states preferred LFS data. One of the reasons could have been that the LFS data are based on national data, while the ECHP was more of a 'European' database.

'Political' or 'technical': choosing your arguments

The notions of the 'technical' and the 'political' were thus used to give weight to the arguments of the member states and the Commission. They had to choose their arguments according to this logic.

In the Employment Committee meeting on 4 October 2001, the German delegate says that it is 'technically' impossible to measure job quality. He goes on to argue that, even if it is 'politically' possible, it is not a question for the political leaders but for the social partners. He says:

> I'd like to look at the political issues and statistics. Statistically it's impossible to measure job quality. Wages can only say so much. This area cannot be quantified. Politically this is the main task of the social partners. We reject having indicators on something we don't have a hand in. (Employment Committee 4 October 2001)

One of the Belgian delegates gets somewhat upset and says that this is a changing process and that the members must not hide behind 'technical' excuses and imply that it is impossible to measure 'quality in work'. He argues:

> This is a changing process. We will not be ready until Christmas. But we have to continue and not hide behind technical excuses.
>
> (Employment Committee 4 October 2001)

In the following Indicators group meeting the French delegate also argues for setting the 'technical' problems aside and looking at the 'political' question to hand. He states:

> We have to situate this in the political situation. We have to deal with the subject, but at the same time we know that we don't have the right tools. I think that everyone will agree with that. But that should not stop us from making a decision on what kind of indicators we want. We then have to deal with the data.
>
> (Indicators group 7 November 2001)

If a member state, such as Belgium in this case, wanted to push for 'quality in work' indicators, it might use the 'political' argument as it was agreed in the European Council in Nice. Member states that did not want the suggested indicator might instead use 'technical' arguments, implying that it is impossible to measure what is agreed upon or that the data sources are all wrong. It might also be the other way round. Members sometimes argued for rejecting an indicator by saying that it did not reflect EU politics. Other members who wanted to keep the indicator might use 'technical' arguments, such as maintaining that the data are 'robust'.[78]

However, the actual national politics and preferences were seldom put into words, other than, for example, when a member state's representative pointed to a particular issue as being important to them. The different national, political and ideational visions were thus in a way hidden. To interpret why this or that member state put forward a particular argument, the members instead tried to get updated on the

---

[78] As a reminder the concept of 'robust' is part of the language of statistics and econometrics. In a general sense and for the bureaucrats in the EU an indicator is perceived as 'robust' when it is statistically reliable and valid.

different national, political and ideational contexts in all the member states.

Nevertheless, notions of the 'political' and the 'technical', where the 'political' is seen as ambiguous and the 'technical' is believed to be precise, permeate the policy-making process in the EU.

Defining the indicators

When I began work as a trainee in the Commission, the Communication on 'quality in work' had been published a few months earlier. The Communication had been discussed in the Employment Committee during the summer of 2001 and now in the autumn the Indicators group was given the assignment for developing indicators so that they would be ready for the last Employment Committee meeting in November (2001). The first Indicators group meeting discussing 'quality in work' indicators took place at the end of September.

This was my first real encounter with the language of statistics and indicators, and I showed my novice status by asking two of my colleagues at the Commission what they actually meant when they said: 'defining the indicator'. They replied that it meant defining how to measure the indicator. Maria explained that there are, for example, different ways of measuring 'gender equality'. The indicator then has to be 'defined' to measure, for example, women's wages as compared with men's by inventing an indicator that measures the 'ratio of women's hourly earnings index to men's for paid employees at work 15+hours', as in the case of the 'quality in work' indicators. Robert also pointed out that it included taking into consideration the statistical source in order to determine that it is possible to obtain data (26 September 2001).

In the following sections the process of 'defining' area number 9, 'diversity and non-discrimination' of the 'quality in work' indicators, will be followed. The political vision stated was '[t]o ensure that all workers are treated equally without discrimination in terms of age, ethnic origin, religion, sexual orientation' (CEC 2001:13). This was then translated into 'diversity and non-discrimination'. There are reasons to believe that discrimination is a highly charged topic in the member states, and this showed in the difficulties in making it measurable. As put bluntly at the meeting, the document had to be 'watered-down' to make possible a multitude of interpretations.

The visible conflict in this particular area is helpful here, since it brings out the members' capacity to argue for their viewpoint. The study follows the process of defining 'diversity and non-discrimination' from the Indicators group meeting on 24-25 September 2001 to the last Employment Committee meeting of the year in 2002, 21-22 November 2002. The process of making the ambiguous precise is here characterised by a clash between different national and political interests and how these are handled by the idea of separating the political and the technical.

Making the indicator on 'ethnic minorities' precise

One way for the Commission to try to find indicators to suggest measuring 'diversity and non-discrimination' was to focus on different groups that it believed were discriminated against in the labour market. The Commission classified these groups into: 'ethnic minorities', 'immigrants', 'disabled people' and 'older workers'. In this chapter, the focus is placed on defining 'ethnic minorities'. 'Ethnic minorities' came to be a difficult area for which to find measurable indicators. The concept had different political connotations that the members were not able to come to terms with. The cultural and political context in which the indicator was suggested gave political signals that some member states did not want. Secondly, there were no statistical sources to measure what the members wanted to measure. This example shows the difficulties in first, finding indicators that are politically neutral and secondly, if they have ideas about a 'good' indicator there might not be technical statistical data that support that definition.

In the meeting on 24 September 2001, at 10:15 am the President of the Indicators group rings the bell on the table as a sign that the meeting is about to start, the people around stop talking and begin to focus. The first item on the agenda is the 'quality in work' indicators. The President gives the floor to one of the Commission's representatives to introduce the Commission's work area by area. The hours pass and after lunch we arrive at area number 9 'diversity and non-discrimination'.

We turn to page 9 in the document from the Commission (Nonpaper IND/12/01/EN). Table 5.1 includes one column on how the Commission, in its Communication, had initially defined 'diversity and non-discrimination'. In the second column there are suggested indicators that measure this definition. The indicator no. 45 is in bold print to signal that it is a suggested 'key' indicator. The concepts of 'key' and 'context' indicators will be discussed further in Chapter 6. In brief, the idea of a key indicator refers to an indicator that may be used to measure between member states for comparative purposes, while a context indicator may only be used to measure within member states. Based on context indicators, it is thus only possible to measure if a member state does better or worse from one year to another and to compare progress with the other member states. The members refer to this as measuring 'trends'.

In the third column is stated what statistical source could be used, and the fourth column informs us of what had been said before on the indicator in other contexts. The Commission's representative introduces the indicators in the table, which reads as follow:

Table 5.1: *Table from the 'draft report' on indicators for 'diversity and non-discrimination'*

Dimension as stated in the Communication	Proposed indicator	Statistical source	Previous uses and comments
Employment rates and pay gaps of older workers compared with average	44. Employment rate of 55-64-year-olds. [No information available for pay gap]	LFS	Agreed by EMCO[a] and used in the JER[b] 2000 and Synthesis Report[c]
Employment rates and pay gaps of persons with disabilities, and persons from ethnic minorities – compared with	**45. Share of low-skill, low-paid jobs in total working age population of disadvantaged groups**		To be developed. Includes immigrants, people with disabilities and ethnic minorities in 'DDD' jobs

average			
	46. The difference between the overall employment rates of the disadvantaged group in question. [No information available on pay gap for these groups]	National data	EMCO has agreed on the 'disadvantage employment gap', for use in the JER 2001. Need to be developed
	47. Employment rate gap of foreigners non-EU compared with average	LFS	Included in Belgian paper
	48. Employment rate gap of persons with disabilities compared with the average	National sources	Included in Belgian paper
Information on the existence of labour market complaints procedures, and of successful outcomes			

Notes: a) EMCO = Employment Committee b) JER = Joint Employment Report in the European Employment Strategy. c) The Synthesis Report is the report the Commission prepares before every Spring European Council in March, devoted to employment, social and economic issues.

(The table is from the Commission's report presented at the Indicators group meeting on 24 September 2001)

As we can see in the table the Commission had suggested one indicator (indicator no. 47 in the table) to measure discrimination against 'ethnic minorities'. This indicator was named: 'employment rate gap of foreigners non-EU compared with average'. The thought behind it was that if the employment rate, in general, was compared with the employment rate of non-EU foreigners it would show whether 'ethnic minorities' were discriminated against and the extent to which the member states' labour markets can be said to show diversity. The fact that 'ethnic minorities' is defined as 'non-EU foreigners' became a source of disagreement in the group during the following months. The discussions revealed that member states had different political priorities and social challenges that made some definitions more relevant than others.

In the meeting, the Portuguese delegate does not agree at all with the notion of measuring 'ethnic minorities'. He questions the very idea of an 'ethnic minority'. This issue is irrelevant in his country. In the second Indicators group meeting on 'quality in work' indicators he points out that:

> We don't know what 'ethnic minorities' are.
>
> (Indicators group 8 November 2001)

The question is expressed in the form of what is perceived as a technical argument since the categorisation of 'ethnic minorities' is needed in order to have an indicator measuring it. It also reveals the political opinion of the Portuguese, since for their representative it is discrimination even to single out 'ethnic minorities'. This reveals different perceptions of what can be measured in the EU. Other member states' delegates think it is possible to define groups of people as 'ethnic minorities'. However, they question the idea of measuring discrimination against 'ethnic minorities' in the labour market by comparing 'non-EU foreigners' with citizens in the member states, the argument being that 'non-EU foreigners' might also be US citizens and they do not believe it can be argued that they are discriminated against.

In the first Indicators group meeting the Dutch delegate emphasises:

> Non-EU may not measure what you want to measure. Non-EU is also,
> for example, Americans and they're not discriminated against.
>
> (Indicators group 24 September 2001)

The Dutch delegate continues with persistence:

> Many disadvantaged people are considered Dutch, for example third-generation Turks.
>
> (Indicators group 24 September 2001)

These arguments are seen as political since the Dutch argument for their viewpoint points out that discrimination against US citizens is not what the EU wants to measure. The Dutch, along with the British and the Italians, who were against most of the indicators in the first place, were thus able to argue against this indicator. However, political arguments are not always believed to be as persuasive as technical ones. In the same meeting the Italian delegate uses what is understood to be a technical argument:

> Foreigners are not always included in labour market surveys.
>
> (Indicators group 24 September 2001)

The fact that there are no statistical sources is a powerful argument for omitting an indicator. On the other hand, if there is a statistical source for an indicator this is a valid argument for retaining it. As when one of the British delegates goes on to question the indicator on 'non-EU foreigners:

> We also wonder about the indicator on diversity and discrimination. People not from the EU might be discriminated against but does that also go for people from the US, for example?
>
> (Employment Committee 4 October 2001)

The President of the Indicators group then informs the group that it is the only indicator with an EU statistical source available on 'ethnic minorities'. He says:

> In the guidelines there is mention of disadvantaged groups like ethnic minorities but we don't have the statistics. The only ones that exist are for non-EU members.
>
> (Employment Committee 4 October 2001)

However, at the next meeting, the second Indicators group meeting, the Italian delegate repeats what the Dutch and the British have said earlier. He continues, in his view, the political argument, stressing that:

We can't have a key. It's not only a question of US nationals on [indicator] 19, but also what it doesn't take into account. People may be nationals but still be discriminated against, for example third generation immigrants.

(Indicators group 8 November 2001)

At the same meeting the French, who were in favour of having indicators on 'quality in work', try to give the member states the possibility of choosing what to measure. The French representative suggests:

The non-EU is not a good measure if we want to look at discrimination. Every country could decide on what they think is the group that should be targeted? France would like to compare salaries and use the same methodology as for gender pay gaps.

(Indicators group 8 November 2001)

They thus tried to save the possibility of having an indicator in this area in the first place by making room for different interpretations of the area. The members went on to argue their national positions. However, at the last Employment Committee meeting of 2001, the Committee had to finish the report and the opinion of the report on the indicators, which were then to be sent to the Council.

As discussed in Chapter 3, there was considerable time pressure here. Since the Ministers had asked the Employment Committee members to agree on an opinion before a certain date, they had to try to do so. There were also some member states that had more of an interest in agreeing than others. During the autumn of 2001, Belgium held the Presidency. As explained in Chapter 3 the 'quality in work' indicators were an important question for Belgium and it wanted an agreement before its Presidency ended in December. Together with the two former Presidencies, France and Sweden, and the Commission, Belgium had invested a great deal of time and energy in promoting the idea of 'quality in work' in the employment policy area of the EU. They were not all in agreement on how it should be achieved, but they had an interest in reaching a 'conclusion'.

There was also a group of member states that were pushing for the document to have as few 'conclusions' as possible, most obviously the United Kingdom, the Netherlands and Italy. There are reasons to believe that they did not think 'quality in work' was a suitable topic for the EU, but rather a national question. This also puts the arguments they used in another light. The member states' representatives knew how to argue in the meeting by the use of political and technical arguments, but there was a more likely hidden agenda, namely that some of the member states, for different reasons, thought the indicators were important and others did not. However, it was the Presidency, in this case Belgium, that decided on the agenda for the Council and therefore in practice decided which areas were open for decisions to be taken in the Council. With the Belgians in favour of the indicators, the work continued.

Keeping it ambiguous?

In the last Employment Committee meeting of 2001 we all turn to page 11 in the report. The Commission has re-written the indicators since the last Indicators group meeting, and the following indicator (indicator no. 32 in Table 5.2) is suggested for measuring discrimination against 'ethnic minorities': 'Employment rate gap of non-EU foreigners compared with average, and taking account of the distinction between low- and high-level qualifications'. For the members, the intention to include low- and high-level qualification is a way of dealing with the problem of defining US citizens as a discriminated-against 'ethnic minority'. It is believed that US citizens working in the EU will have a high level of qualifications. The argument behind it is that people with high-level qualifications will not be as discriminated against as those with low-level qualifications.

As mentioned above, there are four columns in the table in the report. The first column contains the political ideas behind using the indicators. In the second column we find the suggested indicators. The third column lists the statistical databases that include data on the suggested indicators, and in the last column there are comments on whether the definition of the indicators has been used in other contexts and what has been said about it there. In the Commission's report the table reads as follows:

Table 5.2: *Table from the 'draft report' on indicators for 'diversity and non-discrimination'*

Dimension as stated in the Communication	Proposed indicator	Statistical source	Comments and previous uses
Employment rates of older workers compared with average	30. Employment rate of 55-64-year-olds (from EMP 3)	LFS	Agreed by EMCO and used in the JER 2000 and Synthesis report
Employment rates of persons with disabilities, and persons from ethnic minorities compared with average	31. The disadvantaged employment gap (difference between the overall employment rate and the employment rate of ethnic minorities, immigrants and disabled people)	National sources	Agreed by the EMCO for use in the JER. Further work is needed to develop this indicator. Only national data sources are currently available. Member states might highlight the most relevant disadvantaged groups within their own national labour markets.
	32. Employment rate gap of non-EU foreigners compared with average, and taking account of the distinction between low- and high-level qualifications	LFS	Although this indicator is proposed as a context indicator for the moment, it could become a key indicator once better quality data are available from the LFS (expected end 2002). Further work will be

			needed to include information on the pay gap.

(Table from the Commission's report presented at the Employment Committee meeting on 20 November 2001)

As seen in the table, the notion of 'non-EU foreigners' still remained an indicator in this area (indicator no. 32), despite the earlier protests. However, the group against it was not prepared to give up. There was still time to change the indicator even if this was the last meeting. One of the Dutch delegates, as well as one of the British, immediately put their member state sign on their ends.

The President gives the floor to the Netherlands. The Dutch delegate says somewhat irritatedly:

> We have problems with 32 [see above]. Discrimination is not only between non-EU foreigners and EU members. The point of discrimination runs along other lines than passports!
> (Employment Committee 20 November 2001)

Next, the British delegate is given the floor. She emphasises:

> In the UK we have ethnic minorities that are not immigrants. They've lived in the country for 200 years and are still discriminated against.
> (Employment Committee 20 November 2001)

The Commission's representative explains why they have used 'non-EU foreigners'. He establishes:

> On 31 and 32 we have to look at all dimensions of discrimination. But it's difficult to define ethnic minorities. In some countries it's forbidden to do so. Therefore we came up with the idea of non-EU foreigners. That was the logic. But more work needs to be done.
> (Employment Committee 20 November 2001)

As the Commission's representative points out, the use of 'non-EU foreigners' as a definition for 'ethnic minorities' has to do with the availability of data, but also the concept 'ethnic minorities' is not included in some member states and even forbidden in others. The technical work of finding a robust indicator with a good source clashes with the political problems of what the indicator might imply. An indicator might be robust and objective from a statistical perspective, but the member states have and continue to have problems with what the indicator may point to in the political and cultural context.

However, most member states do not seem to mind about the indicator on 'non-EU foreigners', and the indicator is retained with a minor change to include the unemployment rate as well. The idea is that if both the employment rate and the unemployment rate of 'non-EU foreigner' are compared with overall employment and unemployment rate, then it is possible to compare both the employment rate and the unemployment rate gaps. To use the unemployment rate gap as well will show 'diversity and non-discrimination' by disclosing whether there are more 'non-EU foreigners' looking for work than in the population at large.

The following day, 21 November, the document with the Employment Committee's opinion and the report with the proposed indicators are discussed again. The report has been re-written, based on the discussion of the day before, by Miguel, a principal administrator in the Directorate General, and his team working on the indicators in the Commission. The Secretariat and the President of the Employment Committee have also written an opinion on the report. These are the documents that will be sent to the Council, which is also why they have been designed somewhat differently, as we shall see in Table 5.3. The Ministers have asked for differentiation between 'key' and 'context' indicators.

In Table 5.3 the first column should include recommended key indicators – though there are none suggested in this area any longer. In the second column are suggested context indicators and the third column contains indicators that are perceived to be in need of further work. The indicator on 'ethnic minorities' (no. 28 in the table) now reads: 'Employment and unemployment rate gap of non-EU foreigners compared with average, and taking account of the distinction between low and high-level qualifications'.

Table 5.3: *Table from the final report on the 'diversity and non-discrimination' indicators to the Council – first draft*

Recommended key indicators	Recommended context indicators	Indicators requiring further work
	26. Employment rate of 55-64-year-olds (source LFS).	
	27. The employment gap (difference between the overall employment rate and the employment rate of ethnic minorities, immigrants and disabled people) (source: national sources)	
	28. Employment and unemployment rate gap of non-EU foreigners compared with average, and taking account of the distinction between low- and high-level qualifications (source: LFS)	

(Table from the Commission's report presented at the Employment Committee meeting 21 November 2001)

As soon as the Commission's presenter has introduced the re-written report on the indicators, one of the Dutch delegates puts its member state sign on its end. The President gives him the floor: 'Netherlands'. He comments on different indicators and ends his contribution by asking:

Why do we still have 28 [see above]?
(Employment Committee 21 November 2001)

The mood in the Committee is one of intense concentration. The members are concerned about the outcome of the discussions since this is the last meeting. One of the French delegates argues, with the use of a technical argument, against deleting indicator no. 28 on non-EU foreigners. He has a different reason for doing so from the Dutch and the British delegates. He deduces that this is the only indicator in which the unemployment rate of discriminated groups is included. He thinks it is important to have one indicator in the area of 'diversity and non-discrimination' that measures the unemployment rate. He says that if 'non-EU foreigners' (no. 28) is deleted, then he would like instead to include the unemployment rate in indicator no. 27, now reading: 'The employment gap (difference between the overall employment rate and the employment rate of ethnic minorities, immigrants and disabled people)'. He reasons as follows:

> We would like to react to the Netherlands proposal to delete 28. Then we wouldn't have anything on unemployment. It's a bit late in the day to discuss this, but can we include unemployment in 27?
>
> (Employment Committee 21 November 2001)

The Dutch delegate is pleased with this suggestion and agrees that this can be a solution on condition that indicator no. 28 is deleted. This makes one of the German delegates put its member state sign on its end and one of the Commission's representatives puts the Commission sign on its end straight away. The President gives the floor to Germany first. The German delegate says the proposal to include unemployment rates in 27 is a good suggestion, but he does not want to delete 28.

The Commission's representative wants to keep the report as it is. He comments on the French suggestion seconded by the Netherlands. He is somewhat disturbed and reminds the group that there is another dimension in 28 that should not be forgotten. He points out that indicator 28 also includes 'low- and high-level qualifications'.

> The only problem we had yesterday was that 28 should not become a key. Why can't we keep it? There's another element in 28 and that is on qualifications. We should make a reference to the need for further work.
>
> (Employment Committee 21 November 2001)

The arguments go back and forth and finally the President of the Committee states that the indicators will have to be re-drafted during lunch.

The people most passionate about it must meet with the Support team [the Secretariat of the Employment Committee] during lunch and draft something.
(Employment Committee 21 November 2001)

It was not unusual for lunches during the meetings to be used to re-draft opinions. Especially when the final opinion and report had to be sent to the Council, as noted in Chapter 3 and 4. The members then had to agree and they wanted to see the final text before they could do so.

The people most passionate about the final result met during lunch and the document was re-drafted. Apart from the Secretariat of the Employment Committee, the President of the Committee and the President of the Indicators group, some of the member state delegates (France, and most probably Belgium, the Netherlands and the United Kingdom) were also in the re-drafting group. When we came back from lunch the document was distributed and the members were given a few minutes to go through the changes.

In the new table (Table 5.4) the additions have been underlined and the words which are no longer relevant have been crossed out. Now indicator no. 28 is instead about low- and high-level qualifications and disabled people, and the definition of 'ethnic minorities' has now been included in indicator no. 27. It has also become more ambiguous, not clearly stating that it pinpoints 'ethnic minorities' or 'immigrants', but instead reading: 'ethnic minorities, immigrants and other target groups'. After all the discussions, 'non-EU foreigners' has now been deleted, which is a victory for the British, Dutch and Italians. On the other hand, 'ethnic minorities' is still included among the indicators, which can be considered a victory for those who want to retain it. However, the precision of 'non-EU foreigner' is lost. The whole indicator (no. 27) now reads: 'The employment and unemployment gaps, taking into account the distinction between low- and high-level qualifications (difference between the overall employment rate and the employment rate of ethnic minorities, immigrants and other target groups disabled people'. In the Commission's report the table now reads accordingly:

Table 5.4: *Table from the final report on the 'diversity and non-discrimination' indicators to the Council – second draft*

Recommended key indicators	Recommended context indicators	Indicators requiring further work
	26. Employment rate gaps of 55-64-year-olds (source LFS) In addition, the Committee believes that there need to be additional context indicators covering the following areas:	
	27. The employment and unemployment gaps, taking into account the distinction between low- and high-level qualifications (difference between the overall employment rate and the employment rate of ethnic minorities, immigrants and other target groups ~~disabled people~~) (source: national sources)	Further work is needed to extend these indicators to include the pay gap
	28. The employment and unemployment rate gaps, taking into account the distinction between low and high level qualifications (difference between the overall employment rate and the employment rate of disabled people) (source: national sources). ~~Employment and unemployment rate gap of non-EU foreigners compared with average, and~~	

| | ~~taking account of the distinc-~~
~~tion between low and high-~~
~~level qualifications (source:~~
~~LFS).~~ | |

(Table from the Commission's report presented at the Employment Committee meeting on 21 November 2001).

Immediately a discussion starts on why 'non-EU foreigners' has been deleted. It is suggested (by France) that 'non-EU foreigners' can be an example of 'other target groups' in indicator 27 (see table 5.4). Then the indicator will read: 'other groups such as non-EU foreigners'. The Commission's representative is not pleased with this and instead wants: 'Other groups that experience difficulties in the labour market'. She points out that such a definition will also include discrimination by sexual orientation. However, in the end it is concluded that 'non-EU foreigners' shall be included, since 'ethnic minorities' and 'immigrants' are mentioned in the indicator. 'Other target groups' is also deleted, since 'ethnic minorities' and 'immigrants' are believed to include the target groups that they want to measure.

However, the indicator that was approved (indicator no. 27) was to be based on national sources, i.e. sources from the national statistical institutions. The use of national sources usually means that the data are not considered to be comparable across member states, since the member states often have different definitions. This was not satisfactory and the Employment Committee therefore recommended in its opinion that the Council should ask the Committee to go back and improve the statistical sources of the indicators on 'diversity and non-discrimination' during 2002.

The Employment Committee members had managed to define the indicator to make it more precise, while still keeping it somewhat ambiguous. The concept of 'ethnic minorities' had shifted from being defined as 'non-EU foreigners' to not being defined at all. This final wording gave scope for different interpretations in different member states and left room for politics. The members were very particular about the wording of opinions and papers produced by the Committee. The negotiations were coloured by the understanding that as soon as a definition was made it tended to guide forthcoming discussions. Definitions of indicators might be changed, but further work would be based on what had been decided on at one moment in time.

The meeting on 21 November 2001 ended at about 6 pm. Everyone seemed tired and glad to be leaving after two days of intense negotiations. The discussions had come to an end and the atmosphere in the room suggested that now that the discussions were over the disagreements had also vanished. Until the next series of meetings...

The defining process continues

After the meeting the opinion and the report were re-drafted by the Secretariat and the President of the Employment Committee and then sent to the Council. The indicator which had started by defining 'ethnic minorities' as 'non-EU foreigners' had now become less precise and read: 'The gap between the employment and unemployment rates for ethnic minorities and immigrants, taking into account the distinction between low and high-level qualifications, as compared with the overall rates'.

In the Council, the reports and opinions go through the Council's working groups, the Social Questions Working group and Coreper, before the Ministers in the Council make the final decision. However, as mentioned in Chapter 3, the only document discussed was the 'Council conclusions' prepared by the Belgian Presidency. The Employment Committee's opinion and the report with the proposed indicators were sent directly to the Secretariat of the actual Council meeting. The members, both the member states' and the Commission's representatives, in the Council's working groups, as well as one of the Secretaries of the Employment Committee, tried instead to make sure that the Employment Committee opinion was 'respected', i.e. concluding on a decision along the same lines as in the 'Council conclusions'.

In the Council meeting on 3 December 2001, the Ministers presented carefully prepared speeches on the theme of the 'quality in work' indicators.[79] Several (Germany, Greece, Italy, the Netherlands, Portugal, Spain) said that the 'quality in work' indicators were important, but that the Employment Committee needed to be allocated enough time to develop good indicators that were comparable and linked to the European Employment Strategy. It was pointed out that it was the Ministers, not the Commission, who decided how the indicators should be used (the United Kingdom). Furthermore, several of the member states (Germany, Greece, Italy, the Netherlands, Spain, and Sweden) plus the Commission said that it was an evolutionary process and that the Employment Committee had to go back to the meeting room and continue its work. The Council adopted the 'Council conclusions', the Employment Committee's work so far on the indicators[80] and its opinion where it was stated that the work had to be continued following year. The documents were then sent to the European Council in Laeken, and duly endorsed by the member states' Prime Ministers and Presidents and the President of the Commission (European Council 2001c). The work then continued during 2002.

Finding statistical sources

In 2002 the indicators in the area of 'diversity and non-discrimination' were discussed only in the last Indicators group meeting of the year (4-5 November 2002). The members were satisfied with the way the indicators had been defined. They agreed that they should be defined as they had been in 2001. As a reminder, the indicator no. 27 read: 'The gap between the employment and unemployment rates for ethnic minorities and immigrants, taking into account the distinction between low and high level qualifications, as compared with overall'. However, it had also been concluded that the statistical sources used on the indicators needed to be worked on, since there were only national sources. In Sweden this would be the statistics developed by, for

---

[79] I was not able to attend the Council meeting but through one of the Secretaries in the Employment Committee I was informed about the general outcome of the speeches.

[80] Indicators had been developed and agreed in all ten areas but the Council asked the Employment Committee to work further to improve four areas: '4. health and safety at work'; '5. flexibility and security'; '7. work organisation and work-life balance'; and '8. social dialogue and worker involvement' (IND/32/290402/EN).

example, Statistics Sweden[81] or the Swedish National Labour Market Board.[82] As discussed above, this was not considered ideal, the reason being that member states have different ways of defining and measuring, which means that it is not possible to make a comparison between member states other than through trends.

During the year, Miguel and Wilhelm, principal administrators in the Directorate General, had worked to try to find an EU source, but this proved impossible. Now it turned out that the use of national sources would be difficult as well. The Commission had asked the member states to send in their data, but most of them had failed to do so.

At the Indicators group meeting on 4 November 2001, the Commission's representative emphasised that the Council had asked the Committee to provide data, but that the political interest also had to apply when the Ministers returned to their member states. She argued that lack of technical data should not be an excuse for not having the indicator. Instead the member states should have the political interest to develop new EU databases if data were missing. She said:

> This is an area for which the Council has said that it wants an indicator, but member states have not yet been able to provide data. I think we should point that out. That member states have to establish that they want figures and find them!
>
> (Indicators group 4 November 2002)

However, the members showed little interest in launching a political crusade to develop new EU statistical databases. They only commented on whether they could provide data or not. The atmosphere in the group was calm and the hectic feeling of the year before had gone. The technical arguments are also much more difficult for the members to argue against, except when arguing for the development of more EU statistical databases, as the Commission had done.

The Danish delegate declares that Denmark can provide the data but that it has its own definition of 'immigrants'. She says:

---

[81] In Swedish: *Statistiska Central Byrån (SCB).*
[82] In Swedish: *Arbetsmarknadsstyrelsen (AMS)*

We have our own definition of 'immigrant', which is based on citizenship, birthplace and birthplace of parents. But we can use the LFS data
[their own national LFS not the EU]. We can provide data.

(Indicators group 4 November 2002)

The Italian delegate establishes that their data on 'migrant workers' are
underestimated and that Italy does not have any data on 'immigrants'
and 'disabled'. He points out:

We don't have the unemployment rate on the number of migrant workers. There's an underestimation. We can't provide data on immigrants
and disabled.

(Indicators group 4 November 2002)

The difference in the availability of national statistical sources made it
difficult to find a source even to measure trends. Finally, it was decided
that the opinion of the group should indicate that some member states,
but not all, have the data in their National Action Plans, and further
work is therefore needed.

Even if some member states did not have any national data, no attempts were made to try to find a new indicator to measure 'ethnic
minorities'. Instead, member states' representatives informed the
Commission as to whether they had data or not. There had been an
agreement in the Council that these were the right indicators, and the
work the Employment Committee and the Indicators group had to do
was to find the sources. If they could not find a statistical source, that
in itself was considered a legitimate reason for not pressing the matter
further. Building a new statistical database that included the data that
were needed was not the Committee members' decision to make; it
was up to the politicians.

Ending the policy-making process

The last Employment Committee meeting of 2002 (21-22 November)
had to complete the report for it to be sent to the Council meeting that
was to be held at the beginning of December. In the draft report to the
Employment Committee meeting, the Indicators group had pointed
out the difficulty in finding data and that in a number of member states

data were not available for all the groups in the area of 'diversity and non-discrimination'.

At the meeting, the members turned to the 'quality in work' indicators on the agenda. One of the Danish delegates asked to speak and said that Denmark, now as holding the Presidency, did not insist on having the 'quality in work' indicators on the agenda for the Council. Member states that had not really argued for having them in the first place jumped at the chance to bury the report. After some discussion it was decided that the report, as prepared by the Indicators group, and accompanied by a letter from the President of the Committee, would be sent to the Secretariat of the Council meeting for information. The Presidency would then decide whether it should be on the agenda. This meant in practice that the report would not be discussed and decided on. In fact, the report was not sent until after the Council meeting in December.

I discussed the stopping of the report a month later with the President of the Indicators group, who revealed that the Presidency's action in the Employment Committee meeting had come as a complete surprise to many of them. In the Steering Group the day before, the Presidency had not said anything about it, and the last thing that was said was that it was very important that the report should go to the Council. He speculated about what had happened, saying that the Presidency might have made a pact with some of the member states. Or maybe, when the Presidency gave the opportunity, the member states which did not like the report leaped at the chance to get rid of it. According to him, the Commission wanted the Employment Committee to go through the report a third time but not many member states were keen on this. He did not really know what would happen, but his member state's view was that this was an important area, but since nothing had changed in terms of the availability of statistical sources, there was no point in going through the document again.

Since there was no Council Decision in 2002, the indicators decided on in the Council of 2001 were those that were valid. In the area of 'diversity and non-discrimination' this meant that the final proposal on the indicator on 'ethnic minorities' read: 'The gap between the employment and unemployment rates for ethnic minorities and immigrants, taking into account the distinction between low and high level qualifications, as compared with the overall rates'. This also meant that the source was still national, even if not all member states had national sources, as had become clear in 2002. While the 'conclusion' from the Employment Committee in 2002 might very well have said that there were no sources for the indicator, this meant that the Council Decision of 2001 stood as it was and it appeared as if there were national sources – a consequence that the member states opposed to the indicator might not have been aware of at the time.

Decisions made: the ambiguous becomes precise

When a political decision is made on an indicator and the indicator is put into print it is ready to be used. The members might still think that the data were not, in their view, robust, but since they had been politically decided, the bureaucrats' mission was completed. During the different meetings that I have taken part in, I have only once heard a member question a Council Decision. One of the members thought that the definition of one of the indicators did not describe what it was intended to describe. He did not think that the Ministers had understood the definition of the indicator properly and therefore had not understood the mistake they had made. The President of the Indicators group immediately responded that the Council had endorsed it and therefore it was no longer on the table. The President seemed surprised that anyone would waste time discussing something that had already been decided on, even if the definition was not seen as robust. There is an overall belief that as soon as the right data are found and the definitions are precise, there will be objective, politically neutral indicators, but in the meantime compromises have to be made for the sake of policy-making.

When the indicators are decided on, they are published in EU documents. The indicators are used as arguments for reviewing policies or as grounds for new policies, and the conflicts and political compromises involved in trying to develop them are forgotten. The indicators become *black-boxed*, i.e. the conflicts and negotiations involved in producing them become invisible (Latour and Woolgar

1986[1979]:242). Instead they become independent factors with their own life. The differences in the definitions of 'ethnic minorities' in the member states are no longer visible. According to the bureaucratic logic, the indicators become objective and politically neutral. In a way they may be seen as artefacts in Miller's terms, as embodying '...the organisational principles of human categorisation processes' (1985:1). Indicators are in this way object-like, not in a physical form but rather as 'text' (Woolgar and Cooper 1999:435), where the bureaucratic logic of quantification is imbued in the object, i.e. the indicator. In this way, the indicators, shaped in the precise language of numbers, disguise the ambiguity in the definitions and statistical sources.

Conclusion: the apparent neutrality of indicators

If we return to Commissioner Diamantopoulou's speech, and the extract cited at the beginning of this chapter, she advocated the need to measure the qualitative as accurately as the quantitative in order to be able to evaluate policy and the use of public money. Implicit in her speech is the belief that it is possible to measure everything precisely, i.e. in a politically neutral way. It is simply a matter of finding the right definition and robust data sources. This idea, and the fact that political values are drawn into the negotiating process, would seem difficult to reconcile. The Committee members constantly have to balance the ideal of numbers being able to fully represent reality with the fuzziness of reality. Policy decisions are to be based on and evaluated by objective facts, but at the same time the objective facts are produced in the context of the policy-making process.

However, at the same time we live in an epistemic culture of numbers where statistics and indicators are treated as neutral and easy to read. In this culture the division between the political and the technical is much easier to make. When a decision on an indicator is made it is perceived as purely technical and therefore politically neutral and objective. The underlying conflicts are hidden and instead the indicators are black-boxed and treated as precise. Statistics, as 'attention-directing devices', are useful instruments for pointing out and making visible social phenomena in society (see, for example, Cohen 2005).

However, there is nothing neutral about them, regardless of how statistical data are treated. The idea of transparency, built on the neutrality of statistics, is thus as political as it is instrumental.

Making the distinction between the technical and the political is thus an ideal but also a practice, a practice of transparency, that enables the quest for openness and visibility in EU policy to live on, even if the separation between the two is not in any real sense viable. The bureaucratic culture of policy-making is thus characterised by mutual dependence between the political and the technical, where in the end everything is political.

In the next chapter, the study goes on to focus on practices of transparency. The use of key and context indicators is explored and how these are used to handle the conflict between the national positions, thus enabling a compromise postnational EU decision. The expected comparisons between member states are placed in focus here when the Swedish members try to influence the Committee's 'EU' position towards their perspective, in order to ensure having a good outcome in the benchmarks and perhaps even becoming a 'good example'.

SIX

COMPARISON IN ACTION: MAKING
POST(INTER)NATIONAL DECISIONS

Introduction: comparing statistical tables

'They all want good numbers', Thom said with a smile on his face. Abigail responded that we should have put the table in the Supporting document of the Joint Employment Report[83] instead, and then no one would have noticed it. They laughed as if this was joke, but at the same time there was some seriousness in the remark. It was the afternoon of 15 October 2001 in Abigail's office in the Directorate General. One of her colleagues, Thom, had come to speak to Abigail, both of them civil servants in the Commission. She had drawn up a table in the Joint Employment Report that some of the member states were not happy about. They believed that their score was not accurate.

A month earlier the Commission had launched the proposal for this year's European Employment Strategy. Now the complaints about the proposal were coming in from the member states, especially about the tables in the Joint Employment Report where a comparison be-tween the member states was most visible. The member states hardly

---

[83] As mentioned earlier, the Joint Employment Report is an analysis of the member states' National Action Plans. Annexed to the Joint Employment Report is the Supporting document, which includes most of the statistical comparisons in tables and diagrams. For more information and to study the Joint Employment Reports see web-site
http://europa.eu.int/comm/employment_social/employment_strategy/employ_en.ht
m Last visited: 2005-12-09.

ever wanted to 'look bad' in these comparisons. They were 'bench-marked' against each other to find 'best practices' and 'good examples', and there was prestige in being such an example. It was also not pref-erable to be considered a 'bad example', receiving too many Recom-mendations for change put forward by the Commission.

The idea behind the work with EU indicators was that when a good definition and the right source were found, the comparisons would be impartial. However, member states had difficulties in agree-ing on what a good definition and the right source were, as we have seen in Chapter 5. The present chapter focuses on the strategising in the preparation of the national positions before the Employment Committee meeting and how this is transformed into arguments in the Committee. During the course of the meetings the member states conflicting ideas are turned into compromises. This brings to the surface the politics of transparency and how the making of nation states transparent is guided by the expected comparisons trying to ensure that the definitions of the indicators are in their favour.

Manoeuvring national and EU interests

Concepts such as 'conflict', 'strategise', and 'compromise' suggest that there is competition between the member states, and that members bargain and make alliances with each other in order to 'win'. The effort to form decisions in the EU committees, working groups and councils has also been described by concepts such as 'strategic bargaining', 'interstate bargaining' or 'intergovernmentalism' (see, for example, Jupille 1999:410; Moravcsik 1993:480). The notion of strategic bar-gaining implies that decisions are the result of member states trading different national positions. Implicit here is also that member state representatives are able to be 'rational' actors who make 'rational choices,' i.e. who know what they want, who are able to do cost-bene-fit calculations and who have fixed national interests (Moravcsik 1993:481). This corresponds to the Weberian (Weber 1958:196) ideal form of the bureaucrat.

However, the notion that individuals and organisations have clear preferences and are knowledgeable about which technologies support which preferences has been criticised by a number of writers (see Cohen et al. 1982[1976]:24; Douglas 1986:8; March 1978; Perrow 1986[1972]:123; Simon 1961[1957]:xxiv). The bureaucratic culture of policy-making in the EU is based on the idea of rational decision-making, in which the member states are supposed to have clear preferences and to argue and negotiate their positions. Yet, this is a different kind of rationality from what is presumed in rational-choice theory. Simon suggests the notion of 'limited' or 'bounded rationality' (1961:xxiv) in which rational choices are specific to a particular context, i.e. in a particular context particular choices are considered rational (also see Malinowski 1984[1922]:156-157). To be rational here is thus to act in accordance with what is expected by the bureaucratic logic. The member states should adopt a solid national position, and form alliances and arguments that they think will persuade the other members to think like them.

In practice, however, positions can be revised and changed during the course of the meetings and the meeting days, because new information is brought forward or they are persuaded by other member states' arguments. However, what we see in the Employment Committee is rarely consensus decision-making, in the sense that the members in a meeting discuss and deliberate until they find the best solution. As pointed out in Chapter 4, it is more of a 'majority consensus' or a compromise, in which some members give up their position if they do not win support or fail to find persuasive arguments (also see Lewis 1998). In addition, as also seen in Chapter 4, the fact that the members speak different languages and come from different bureaucratic cultures, exposes different perspectives on what it means to make persuasive arguments or to put forward a position. What it entails to be rational is thus culturally biased.

Nevertheless, the members are able to come to an 'EU' decision in the meetings. This chapter shows how member states, in this case Sweden, try to push for their positions in the meetings and how the conflict between the member states' national positions is then turned into a postnational EU compromise. The conflicts in the meetings are partly based on the anticipated comparisons between the member states. However, with the help of tools such as 'key' and 'context' indicators, but also by member states attracting supporters for their positions, they are able to agree. This is also supported by the temporal organisation of the meeting, as seen in Chapter 3, as well as the ritualised form of meetings, as seen in Chapter 4, pushing policy-making towards a decision.

'Key' and 'context' indicators: facilitating compromises

At the beginning of July 2001, the Ministers met at the informal Council in Liège[84] to discuss the different indicators suggested in the Communication on 'quality in work'. The Ministers had problems with some of the indicators and someone came up with the idea of dividing them into indicators that are comparable between member states and indicators that are not. The idea was that indicators not comparable between member states, i.e. indicators with different definitions and sources often from national statistical databases, could be used to provide the context for the indicators which were comparable.

In the informal Employment Committee meeting that took place in Genval a few days later, it was suggested that the indicators that were 'comparable between' member states should be called 'key' or 'headline' indicators and the indicators 'comparable within' member states should be called 'context' or 'supporting' indicators. Later on the concepts 'key' and 'context' indicators prevailed.

The notion of key and context indicators is interesting as a policy-making tool in several ways. To get some progress made in some of the areas it was now possible to use context indicators. This arrangement suited the Committee members who wanted to develop more indicators, and it also suited those who did not want to develop additional ones. For those who wanted the indicators, the division between key and context made it possible to agree on context indicators in areas that might not otherwise have had an indicator at all. For the members who did not want the indicators, the division between key and context opened up the possibility of arguing for the context indicator alternative whenever possible. Otherwise they might be forced to agree on key indicators in more areas, since the Ministers had asked them to

---

[84] As Belgium held the Presidency the informal Council was held in Belgium, in Liège.

find them. For these members, it also meant that, since the context indicators were based on national data, they would have greater control over the data since they were produced within the member states. The context indicators column in the tables often became a light column, where the indicators that could almost be agreed on were put in order to achieve some progress in the decision-making process.

During the negotiations in the meetings many of the proposed key indicators were also transformed into context indicators. At the first meeting there was one key indicator suggested in all areas, and with two key indicators being suggested in three of the ten areas.[85] At the last meeting in 2001 one key indicator was suggested in eight[86] out of the ten areas. This reveals the conflict between retaining the national control over the indicators and transferring some of it to the EU. It also makes the fear of comparability explicit and efforts to avoid making comparisons between the member states possible.

Before these tools could be used, however, the members had to agree on what they actually meant and how they would be used in practice. The concepts key and context indicators were not in themselves unproblematic. In fact, the idea of key and context was discussed at several meetings during the autumn of 2001.

At the second Employment Committee meeting on the 'quality in work' indicators in October 2001, the members are wondering what the difference between the two different indicators actually is, and they are clearly concerned about how they are going to be used. One of the Spanish delegates asks if both of them are obligatory for member states. She wonders if the member states have to report in the National Action Plans on both the key and context indicators, implying that, even if the indicators are divided into key and context, it would not make much difference to the member states since both of them can be used in the Commission's Joint Employment Report. The delegates from the United Kingdom and the Netherlands quickly follow the

---

[85] In '5. Flexibility and security'; '6 Inclusion and access to the labour market'; and '7. Work organisation and work-life balance.'

[86] No 'key' indicators were suggested in area '8. Social dialogue and worker involvement'; and '9. Diversity and non-discrimination.'

Spanish delegate's argument. The Dutch delegate wonders if the context indicators will be voluntary. If they are only to be used to give context to the key indicators, both the British and the Dutch delegates argue, their use should be voluntary for the member states. The delegates from France and Belgium, both of whom have an interest in making progress (as we have seen in the previous chapter), try to explain. They both emphasise that the context indicators are only used to measure trends within states, not the national results. One of the Belgian delegates says:

> Context indicators are meant to take into account the national differences. The context indicators allow us to adjust the key indicators to the national level. This is how I understand it. We agree with France. Trends should be evaluated, not the national results, otherwise we might judge member states that are good at reporting, for example, accidents at work.
>
> (Employment Committee 4 October 2001)

Member states are worried about how the context indicators will be used and what they will have to report. The understanding is that context indicators are to be used when the members cannot find data and definitions that are considered objective or, to put it another way, not politically possible to agree on. Context indicators may in that sense become even more politically sensitive than key indicators, not only because they are used in politically sensitive areas, but also because the member states' national trends will still be compared.

One of the Commission's representatives tries to calm down the member state delegates by pointing out that the context indicators are only embellishments and that member states can pick and choose among them. She says:

> Regarding the differences between key and context. Key indicators are references to principles we have agreed on. It's on them that we make joint analysis so that we have something to make policy on. Context indicators are enrichments. Member states can pick and choose from the context indicators. They're domestic indicators.
>
> (Employment Committee 4 October 2001)

However, at the next Employment Committee meeting in November 2001, the Commission's representative is a little more specific on how the context indicators should be used. They are not, in practice, for member states to pick and choose. The context indicators are to be used in the National Action Plans. She emphasises this sturdily:

> On the key indicators - they should be included in the NAPs [National Action Plans]. The context indicators should also be included in the NAPs. They will not have the same value as the key, but will show the context in which the NAPs are produced.
>
> (Employment Committee 20 November 2001)

Context indicators used in this way will push forward policy-making for its own sake, since the indicators, though seen as not robust enough, will still enable comparisons between the member states in the Joint Employment Report since they have to be included in the National Action Plans. This continues to concern several of the member state delegates, especially Ireland, Italy, the Netherlands, Spain and the United Kingdom. One of the Dutch delegates asks for a document in which the key and context indicators are explicitly explained. He demands:

> We would like to produce a document where the key and context indicators are explicitly explained. We want to know how they are going to be presented in the NAPs [National Action Plans] and the JER [Joint Employment Report]. We have to be clear!
>
> (Employment Committee 20 November 2001)

The Irish, British, Spanish, Finnish, German, Danish and Dutch delegates continue the discussion. They argue that the key indicators should be the only ones to be discussed and decided on at the meeting. They believe that since the Employment Committee has to send the final opinion to the Council after the meeting, they should not cover context indicators if they are not sure of how exactly they are to be used.

One of the Belgian delegates (Belgium holds the Presidency), tries to save the situation. He says:

The Commission has tried to clarify the different states of key and context. We thought it was quite clear. We should not confine ourselves to key indicators only. Our Ministers would like as broad a view as possible. We have to show the progress that has been made with the clear distinction.

(Employment Committee 20 November 2001)

The representatives of France and the Commission respectively, agree that both key and context indicators have to be discussed and be part of the opinion. The Commission's representative points out that if only the key indicators are discussed, there will not be much progress. One of the Spanish delegates suggests using some of the context indicators for which the members have agreed on the data source, to show progress. She says:

Let's take some context indicators where we agree on the source to show progress, but we have to be cautious.

(Employment Committee 20 November 2001)

Finally, the President of the Committee states that the Committee has to arrive at a clear standpoint, and that the Ministers prefer not to have the discussion on the difference between key and context indicators take place in the Council. He says that so far a majority is in favour of discussing only the key indicators. One of the delegates from France immediately responds. He is upset and argues convincingly that it will be impossible to find key indicators in all ten areas and that the Ministers have asked them to find indicators, key or context, in all ten areas. He says:

We can't find all ten key indicators today! That's impossible! We don't have a key for all ten areas! All ten areas should be covered for the Ministers. In the compromise from the Indicators group the context indicators were included, not only key indicators since we don't have key indicators for all ten areas.

(Employment Committee 20 November 2001)

As this is an important political argument, this becomes the end of the discussion. Both key and context indicators in the ten classified areas of 'quality in work' have been discussed. The member state representatives have to ignore the different opinions on the key and context indicators in order to produce a report and an opinion to be sent to the Council.

The debate on the use of key and context indicators is part of the bureaucratic logic of classifications where words and concepts have to be scrutinised and defined in detail to have a clear meaning. Regardless of whether the member states are in favour of or against having 'quality in work' indicators, the key indicators are still the ideal, since they are comparable across member states. The context indicators, on the other hand, are perceived as a compromise. They are used as tools to enable agreements to be made on the indicators in the first place. The fact that there are context indicators exposes the conflicts between the member states on what ought to be measured, since their use supports the division between the member states rather than encouraging a postnational EU.

A culture of conflict: forming a national position

The conflict, then, is visible in several ways. The member states' representatives have to form and adopt national positions to enable decision-making. The differentiation between member states is also encouraged by the use of key and context indicators. This creates a 'culture of conflict' in the meeting, where the positions of the different member states clash with each other. In essence, they have divergent ideas on what employment politics in the EU should be.

This section focuses on how member states, in this case Sweden, tried to press for their national position, and how this supported the culture of conflict. It is important to have robust indicators, but the member states' representatives also have in mind where in the tables and diagrams 'their' member state will end up, as seen in the preceding chapter. Future comparisons between member states are always lurking in the background when the members construct their arguments. In addition, they have to argue in line with the government politics of their member state. The member states try to persuade the others that 'their' national politics is the right one for the EU, one reason being that they actually want to 'win' and are prepared to make compromises for it. It might also be that they just want to make a point and in this way gradually influence the other members in line with 'their' views. Here the use of context indicators becomes a way of handling the conflicts.

Forming a 'Swedish' position: to 'win'

In the Indicators group meeting on 4 July 2002, the first item on the agenda is the 'quality in work' indicators. The President of the Indicators group announces that we shall begin with area 4, 'health and safety at work'. He gives the floor to the Commission's representative for him to introduce the indicators in this area. From last year, 2001, there was one agreed key indicator, 'accidents at work', and one agreed context indicator, 'days lost due to accidents at work', but the Employment Committee has been asked to find new indicators in the area of 'occupational disease rates including new risk, for example repetitive strain' and 'percentage of workers exposed to stress'.

On 'stress' Wilhelm, a principal administrator at the Directorate General, and his team have found two possible indicators. The first is 'percentage of workers exposed to stress', but here the Commission has no data and the Commission's representative wonders whether there are national data in this area. The second indicator they suggest is based on EU data from the European Foundation for the Improvement of Living and Working Conditions,[87] or the Dublin Foundation, which has data on an indicator that reads 'workers reporting stress'. The Commission's presenter says that the Commission would like to use national sources and then use the Dublin Foundation's data as complementary, since they are based on the subjective feelings of workers. However, he says, the Commission would like to know if there are national data available.

A few days earlier, in the Swedish preparatory meeting, Malin points out that indicator no. 2 ['workers reporting stress'] is new. The data are from the Dublin Foundation but are old, from 1990 and 1995, she continues. The indicator is difficult to understand, says Susanne.

---

[87] For more information see the Foundation's web site: http://www.eurofound.eu.int/ Last visited 2005-12-09.

Malin wonders if, since there is data from all the member states, they should be seen as comparable between them. Anders, however, concludes that we (Sweden) can accept the Dublin Foundation indicator, but only if it measures 'trends', i.e. a context indicator. Can we agree on both? Malin asks. We can if Hedda (an expert on health and safety at work statistics present at the meeting) does not object, Susanne suggests. Hedda replies that she has to check the Dublin Foundation data and come back to them. Malin also informs us that she has asked Statistics Sweden if Sweden has national data, and it turns out that we do. The national data on 'stress' are not much better, though, since they are also based on subjective feelings, Tage objects. Malin and Anders both agree on this, but Anders points out that this is an important question for Sweden. It has been put forward in the speech of Mona Sahlin (one of the Ministers in the Ministry of Industry at the time) in the Council. However, he concludes the discussion by saying that they should try to persuade the Indicator group to choose one or the other, since they do not want to have too many indicators.

In this case politics preceded the methodological difficulties of finding a robust indicator. The Swedish representatives may not think that the indicator has the right source or is robust, but they argue for the indicator anyway because the matter is an important political issue for the Swedish government. When member states argue for keeping or rejecting an indicator it may be because, as mentioned earlier, they are concerned about where in the diagram the member state will end up, and what the implications of this may be. However, by taking into account the political importance of an issue, a 'good score' may very well be having any score at all. The members of the Committee have a double role to play here: they are experts in an expert committee, but they also have to act as politicians in accordance with their governments.

To return to the Indicators group meeting. The Italian, British and Swedish delegates put their member state signs on their ends during the Commission's presentation of the indicators in the area of 'health and safety at work'. When the Commission's representative finishes, the President gives the floor to Italy. The Italian representative says:

> We don't see any problem to measuring stress, but we want to under-
> line that it's the subjective feeling of the worker.
> (Indicators group 4 July 2002)

The British delegate wonders if the Dublin Foundation data are only
produced every five years. He says:

> The Dublin Foundation [a representative] is not here, but is it going to
> give data only every five years? [One of the Commission's representa-
> tive nods]. Yes. Then it is better to use national data.
> (Indicators group 4 July 2002)

The Swedish delegate gives the Swedish contribution on the 'stress'
indicator:

> And turning to the stress indicator. Stress is estimated by the individual.
> We think we should choose one of them [the two different sources],
> but Sweden is in favour of measuring stress. If we choose one of them
> we prefer national data, but if the other member states don't have na-
> tional data then we can use the Dublin Foundation data.
> (Indicators group 4 July 2002)

Since this is important to Sweden she emphasises the need to measure
'stress'. She gives the other members the opportunity to choose between the data sources in order to have an indicator in this area. She
points out that even if the data are based on subjective feelings, this is
not necessarily a problem. However, the Finnish, Spanish and Portuguese delegates think it is important that the indicator is not based on
the subjective feelings of the workers. For this reason they think
national data are the best to use, but the Spanish delegate wonders if
they are really comparable. The French delegate seconds the Spanish
question and thinks that we should use national data sources, but that
we have to make sure that they are comparable. He says that the
Dublin information could be useful as complementary information,
but he prefers national data. Comparability is an issue here, since it
would determine whether it is possible to use the indicator as a key
indicator. To use the technical argument of non-comparability may be
a way of ensuring that it will not become a key indicator.

However, the Greek, Belgian, Austrian, and Danish delegates all say that they do not have sufficient national data on 'stress'. But, the Greek and Belgian delegates point out that they still think it is important to measure 'stress' and that they think the Dublin Foundation data could be used. The President of the Indicators group tries to reach a 'conclusion' by stating that the Dublin Foundation data should be used to measure 'stress'. The Commission's representative puts its sign on its end. The President gives the Commission the floor: 'Commission'. The Commission's representative says:

> Concerning the Dublin data on occupational disease and stress there is a problem of periodicity. We can only use the Dublin data as background for occupational disease and stress.
>
> (Indicators group 4 July 2002)

The Commission's representative tries to argue for retaining both indicators as the Commission had suggested in the beginning. The President says, somewhat irritatedly, that it is possible to have both but there would then be four indicators on this area: two on 'occupational disease' and two on 'stress'. He thinks this is too many. He concludes:

> You heard the Commission's and my proposal.
>
> (Indicators group 4 July 2002)

The Austrian and British delegates immediately signals their wish to speak. The President calls on Austria. The Austrian delegate says:

> We prefer the second suggestion where we only have two: national data on occupational disease and Dublin data on stress.
>
> (Indicators group 4 July 2002)

The British delegate seconds this proposal. The 'conclusion' at this meeting is therefore to use the Dublin Foundation data on 'stress'.

At the next preparatory meeting on 31 October 2002 in the Swedish Ministry the indicator on 'stress' is discussed again. Gudrun, from Statistics Sweden, is at the meeting and she says that it is possible for Sweden to agree on the data from the Dublin Foundation, but that we should be aware that we shall have a very high score, since we have good statistics that actually measure this. Anders asks if they are better than the Swedish national data. He points out that previously we have said in the Indicators group that we prefer national data. Gudrun says that in the national data it has only been measured once, and that the Dublin data are more regular. Anders says that the 'conclusion' must therefore be that the Dublin Foundation data are the best at the moment, but that it cannot be a key indicator but only a context indicator and can only measure trends. In this way, it will not be so important that Sweden is good on reporting because the comparison 'between' member states will only be on the difference between measurements 'within' member states.

At the Indicators group meeting on 5 November 2002 a representative from the Dublin Foundation is present. He is asked to explain the indicator on 'stress'. He says that it is based on self-reporting, but that the Foundation can make changes if the Indicators group would like it to do so. However, most of the other member states' delegates do not mind using the Dublin Foundation data on 'stress' and in the end it is possible for the President of the group to conclude that the indicator may be used as a context indicator. This is also the final 'conclusion' in the Employment Committee.

Sweden thus won support from other members, and in the 'conclusions' there was an indicator on measuring 'the percentage of workers exposed to stress' using the Dublin Foundation 'workers reporting stress' data. In this case, the fact that Sweden would have a high score on this indicator did not determine whether it should argue against having the indicator. This was also solved by suggesting it as a context indicator simply measuring trends. Since 'stress' was an important Swedish political issue, it was better to use the Dublin Foundation data rather than having no indicator on 'stress' at all.

The need to have the support of others to ensure that one's position will 'win' is important here. It is possible to fight hard and put forward good arguments, but in the end if no one else supports the position it is difficult to succeed, as we shall see in the section below.

To make a point

Other areas that were important to the Swedish government and the Swedish representatives were indicators that had to do with equality between men and women. This was an area where the Swedish representatives often failed to get backing. In the Indicators group meeting on 5 July 2002, an adaptability index, constructed to be included in the area of 'work organisation and work-life balance', was presented by a research centre that had worked on the index. In its report, one of the variables for adaptability was labour mobility. Here measurements had been made of transitions between different jobs as well as transitions to a job among people who had been studying or had not been working the year before. The text read: '...of those in education and women "fulfilling domestic responsibilities" the year before' (Scientific report presented by a research centre in the Indicators group, 5 July 2002).

The Swedish delegate signals her wish to speak and the President of the Indicators group gives her the floor. She says:

> There seems to be a mistake in the study. It only says 'women fulfilling domestic responsibilities'.
> (Indicators group 5 July 2002)

The representative from the research centre replies:

> No, men are not in the graph. Men make up only 1% so it makes no difference.
> (Indicators group 5 July 2002)

The Swedish delegate continues:

> Surely it varies between member states?
> (Indicators group 5 July 2002)

The representative from the research centre answers, smiling:

> Yes, I agree that it is higher in the Nordic member states. It could have been in but the graphs would not be different.
> (Indicators group 5 July 2002)

Many of the (male) members smile as if they are thinking: 'Ok, we expect this from Sweden but we really do not take it seriously'. This also, in a way, was a self-assumed role of the Swedish representatives – always to point out where there were gender-biased passages in the text.

At the same meeting, as well as at the meeting before, the member
states are asked to fill in how secure employees working part-time and
fixed-term really are. The table includes 'pensions', 'accidents at work'
and 'occupational disease, health and unemployment', The Swedish
delegate tries to press for including 'parental leave', arguing that this is
as important as other benefits and social security schemes in the list.
However, this is not supported by anyone else, which means that in the
end it is not included. The Swedes certainly knew that Sweden would
get a beneficial score if this was measured, but they also saw it as their
responsibility to point out the omission whenever possible.

Another issue stressed by the Swedish delegates is the indicator on
'childcare'. The indicator includes all kinds of childcare from day-care
centres to grandparents. At the Indicators group meeting on 6
November 2002 the Swedish delegate states:

> I start by agreeing with my colleagues from the UK. The number of
> hours is not important but the fact that it enables people to work. We
> should ask if they have enough childcare. The goal of 90% is very good
> but we have some areas we think are important. It's important that par-
> ents are able to foresee the childcare in advance. The question of LFS
> 'lack of childcare…' captures an important issue. While I'm speaking I
> want to go on. I think 'care facilities' should not have too broad a defi-
> nition. We don't want to capture last-minute solutions. We should only
> take into account planned-for-in-advance solutions. We should not in-
> clude last-minute solutions.
>
> (Indicators group 6 November 2002)

The Swedish delegate emphasises the importance of being able to plan
childcare, which means that, for example, grandparents should not be
included in such an indicator. Sweden gets support from, for example,
Austria, but the position is not taken into consideration since there are
a number of member states, for example Greece and Italy, which
believe that a broad definition is the best. The Greek delegate says:

> Contrary to other speakers I think that a broad definition is good since
> it will make it possible to compare between member states since it is
> very different in different countries.
>
> (Indicators group 6 November 2002)

Greece and Italy would not get as high a score on available day-care centres as, for example, Sweden. On the other hand, using grandparents for childcare might not be as much of a last-minute solution as the Swedish delegate had argued. However, the Swedish delegates, especially the women, feel passionately about this issue, and they think that childcare should be available for all, not just for people whose parents are still alive and not working. They believe that if there is no childcare in the form of day-care centres, it will be impossible to plan one's working life, and this will disadvantage the women's possibilities of entering the workforce. The passions and interests of the bureaucrats may in this way colour their efforts in making an argument.

In this way the conflicting ideas about employment politics in the member states became visible. The member states have different institutional arrangements, reflecting different perceptions of gender roles and the responsibilities of men and women respectively. However, the Swedes often did not expect to 'win' on this question, but rather to make a point and maybe 'win' in the long run.

Shown here is the need for the support of other members if one wants to press a particular question. One does not necessarily have to be in the majority, but to have support. In addition, the members in the Committee have to believe that the question is of some importance, even if they do not agree with it. This was often not the case in reference to men's responsibilities for children and childcare.

A culture of compromise: making a group decision

Regardless of the underlying conflicts, the opinions and reports produced in the Committee are something more than the sum of the different national positions of the Committee members. The finished opinion or report is the result of hours of negotiations and compromises. If the discussions and negotiations demonstrate a culture of conflict, then the actual process of reaching a decision and producing reports and opinions at the end of the series of meetings illustrates that conflict and compromise are two sides of the same coin, so to speak, and that there is, to some extent, also a culture of compromise in the EU meetings. However, compromises are made in different ways.

Chapter six

There are different ways of making sure that decisions offer room for competing national interpretations. The process of *engrenage*, i.e. the '...steady "meshing together" of national civil servants and Commission officials in the various Brussels-based committees and institution' (Shore 2000:147) in the name of European integration thus becomes limited. One way, as expressed in one of the meetings, is to 'water down' the decisions in the 'drafting sessions'. The drafting sessions often take place when the Employment Committee members have to send the report and their opinion of the report to the Council. The opinions are usually the more important political documents, since it is in them that future work or future interpretation may be included or excluded. It is also very likely that the opinions are the only documents that Ministers will have time to read.

In the drafting sessions, the report and especially the opinions of the Committee are reviewed word by word until the member states agree. The drafting sessions are often edgy in the sense that the members have to be on their toes. On the 'quality in work' indicators the drafting sessions' sometimes lasted almost a whole day, with the Secretariat and the President of the Employment Committee re-writing the text during the lunch break.

The first drafting session on the 'quality in work' indicators in the Employment Committee took place on 4 October 2001, just a few days before the Council meeting on 8 October. The President of the Employment Committee was going to make an 'oral statement'[88] in the Council on the progress made on the 'quality in work' indicators, see also Chapter 3. When the members became aware of this at the Employment Committee meeting on 4-5 October 2001, they insisted that the oral statement should be drafted in the Committee. This showed how politically sensitive the 'quality in work' indicators were. When issues were not so sensitive, the President was sometimes trusted to write an opinion by himself, but this time he was not even trusted to write an oral statement. The Secretariat, together with the President,

---

[88] As a reminder the 'oral statement' would be submitted to the Council in written form but it would not be included as an official document since it was only a progress report, not a written opinion of the Employment Committee.

had to draft a proposal in the evening of 4 October to be discussed the following day.

At the meeting on 5 October the President of the Committee distributes the proposal for the oral statement one and half hours before lunch, hoping that the Committee will be able to reach an agreement on it before lunch. He says with a touch of irony:

> Now, we return to quality in work. We have prepared a draft statement. It would be nice if we could conclude this before lunch so that we can go home, but I'm prepared to sit here all day to reach an agreement. I want to have a full agreement.
>
> (Employment Committee 5 October 2001)

The members are given a few minutes to read the statement. The room is quiet for a while and then the members start to talk to one another and there is a mumbling sound all over the meeting room. After a while the President resumes the meeting and goes through the document paragraph by paragraph. The members are invited to give their comments on each paragraph. They have suggestions for changes in almost every paragraph. For example, paragraph 6 reads:

> 'Turning to the other dimensions of quality, the Committee recommends that the Indicators Group explores the possibility of a composite indicator which would measure progress from unemployment to low paid work and from low paid work into higher paid work. The possibility should also be explored of extending this concept to cover progression from unemployment into part-time and fixed-term work and from there into full-time and permanent work'.
>
> (Employment Committee, draft on oral statement 5 October 2001)

Some of the member states (Germany, the Netherlands, and Spain) are not happy with the idea of mentioning a 'composite indicator', which they think will be too complicated since it will include too many variables. They want to delete 'explores the possibility of a composite' and replace it with 'present an'. In addition, as mentioned in Chapter 3, the Dutch delegate does not want the last sentence on the '…progression from unemployment into part-time and fixed-term work and from there into full-time and permanent work', since he believes it is biased, suggesting that full-time and permanent work is better. The Dutch delegation also wants to delete 'progress' in the previous sentence and replace it with 'transition'. The Irish delegate agrees with the Netherlands and says that the indicators will have to be contextualised in the member states. The Belgian delegate tries to solve the problem by suggesting making a distinction between voluntary and involuntary part-time and fixed-term work, but he does not get any response from the opposing member states.

Finally, they have to break for lunch and they are far from finished. Instead, the Secretariat together with the President have to re-write the statement during lunch. After lunch the new draft is distributed and gone through paragraph by paragraph again. Once more, they stop at almost every paragraph to change the wording. Paragraph 6 now reads:

> 'The Committee recommends that its indicators group explores the possibility of indicators to measure transition from unemployment and inactivity into work. Some Members of the Committee would like to include transition from low pay into higher paid work. Others believe that this aspect should be excluded'.
>
> (Employment Committee, draft oral statement, revision one, 5 October 2001)

One of the delegates suggests putting a comma after 'inactivity to work' and including 'and also progression in pay and work statutes (for example part-time and fixed-term work)' and then deleting the two sentences that follow. One of the British delegates puts its member state sign on its end. The President gives her the word. The British delegate says:

> I have a problem with the word: 'work statutes'.
>
> (Employment Committee 5 October 2001)

The President of the Committee answers:

> May I have two minutes to consult with the Support team [the Secretariat of the Employment Committee]?
>
> (Employment Committee 5 October 2001)

There is a short break and the Commission's representative and one of the Italian delegates join the Secretaries and the President to help with the formulation. The President resumes the meeting and reads a new suggestion for the paragraph: 'inactivity into work, and the transition within employment'. One of the German delegates objects. He wants to have a reference to 'pay' here as well as retaining 'the progression in the employment statutes'. One of the Dutch delegates protests against the use of the wording 'progression in employment statutes'. He says:

> We should be clear on what progress and statutes mean. Progress means to go to something better. I don't want it to appear that it is better with full-time work. 'Employment statutes' gives this idea.
>
> (Employment Committee 5 October 2001)

The Commission's representative tries to solve the problem by using the wording: 'transitions in employment'. She also suggests, supporting Germany, having a new sentence on pay. She puts forward: 'In this context the Committee will give further consideration to other issues such as pay'. The President asks the German delegate if he is happy. He is not happy with the use of 'other issues'. The President tries to suggest 'other aspects'. The German delegate says that he wants there to be a clear connection with the sentence above, i.e. the sentence on 'transitions in employment'. He says that he thinks the Commission understands. One of the Commission's representative says that his point is that it should read 'specific aspects'. In the end, the President reads, before the Council, the following sentences:

> 'The Committee recommends that its Indicators group explores the possibility of indicators to measure the transition from unemployment and inactivity into work and the transition within employment. In this context, the Committee will give further consideration to specific aspects, such as pay'.
>
> (Non-paper[89]. Oral statement at the Employment and Social Policy Council 8 October 2001)

The members in this way suggest different solutions to what, for some members, are problematic formulations until everyone can agree on a compromise.

---

[89] A 'Non-paper' is an unofficial paper. It is, if you will, a working paper that will not be registered.

The next drafting session took place in the last Employment
Committee of the year 2001 (20-21 November 2001), when the Committee had to send the final report and opinion to the Council. This
time the drafting session lasted much longer, most likely because this
was the last chance to influence the documents. The report on the
indicators had three columns: 'recommended key indicators', 'recommended context indicators', and 'indicators requiring further work'.
When the discussion came to area 8, 'social dialogue and worker
involvement' there were two indicators suggested: 'number of days lost
in strikes' and 'percentage of workers covered by collective agreements'. These indicators had been put in the column headed 'indicators
requiring further work' and the other columns were empty.

At the meeting, the Commission's representative is concerned
about this and wonders if it is possible to move the indicators to the
column 'recommended context indicators'. The President of the
Committee replies that it is what they concluded the day before,
namely that the indicators do need further work. One of the Belgian
delegates thinks that at least 'number of days lost in strikes' can possi-
bly be moved to the 'context indicators' column. The President of the
Employment Committee says:

> I ask each delegation if you can accept this?
>
> (Employment Committee 21 November 2001)

One of the British delegates quickly puts its member state sign on its
end and the President gives her the floor. The British delegate says:

> We can accept it. But what we discussed was that we needed wider
> definitions. That we need to do further work with a menu of indicators.
>
> (Employment Committee 21 November 2001)

The President of the Committee suggests:

> We could have a reference that further work is needed and that we need
> a menu of indicators.
>
> (Employment Committee 21 November 2001)

One of the French delegates signals his wish to speak and the President gives him the floor. Somewhat upset, the French delegate reminds
the Committee members that it is only a question of putting it in the

'context indicators' column, not in the 'key indicators' column. He says:

> We agree that it is difficult to find a key, but it's a context indicator!
>
> (Employment Committee 21 November 2001)

The President of the Committee is growing somewhat weary:

> I don't know what to suggest now.
>
> (Employment Committee 21 November 2001)

One of the German delegates gives the signal and then speaks his mind:

> The whole question of social dialogue is a central question for Germany. If we only talk of strike days and judge the quality of work on that... We still need to do a lot of work. This is far more important than the question of strikes. It's better to have them all in the third column.
>
> (Employment Committee 21 November 2001)

However, the President responds:

> We'll try to come up with something in the middle column during lunch.
>
> (Employment Committee 21 November 2001)

The compromises made sometimes do not suit all members. Some may want to open up the discussion to press for, perhaps, a more precise decision. In this case the representatives of the Commission, France and Belgium are trying to press for agreeing on, at a minimum, context indicators in this area.

After lunch the President asks the Committee to look especially at the indicators on 'social dialogue and worker involvement'. He points out that they have tried to give the table a more positive appearance. The text is now moved to the middle column on 'recommended context indicators' but the text is different now. Instead of suggesting the two indicators: 'number of days lost in strikes' and 'number of employees covered by collective agreements', the text indicates that a menu of indicators should be identified that take into consideration the differences in arrangements, practices and traditions between member states. In the text, possible arrangements are suggested, such as 'number of days lost in strikes' and 'number of employees covered by collective agreements', but now only as two possible indicators out of many. So, instead of becoming more precise, the report turns out to be even more ambiguous, even if the text is moved to the middle column.

The Commission's representative is not completely happy and wants to include the words key and context in the text. He suggests:

> When we talk of a menu of indicators are we talking about key or context? Should we add 'menu of key and context indicators' instead?
> (Employment Committee 21 November 2001)

The President responds that this is impossible for the Committee to know and that the wording has been left deliberately ambiguous to allow some space for different interpretations. One of the Finnish delegates points out that it is important to show progress, but that the indicators are still in need of further work. The President then again points out that the text is clear on the fact that it is work in progress and he urges them to agree. This is also the 'conclusion' in the end. In the process of making compromises, decisions and conclusions may open and close until all the different angles are exhausted or the end of day is closing in, so that a decision has to be made.

When the report has been scrutinised, the Committee turns to the written opinion on the report for review. After having had to re-write the opinion twice, the second revision of the draft is distributed to the meeting. One of the Italian delegates puts its member state sign on its end. The President gives him the floor. He wants to change the paragraph where a definition of context indicator is given. He is not happy with the reference to the context indicators being used in the Joint Employment Report in the analysis of the member states' National Action Plans. The text reads:

> 'Context indicators will be used to support the analysis in the Joint Employment Report of the National Action Plans for Employment...'
> (Employment Committee, draft opinion revision 2, 21 November 2001).

Other members support him. One of the Spanish delegates says that it is important to make a sharp distinction between the two indicators. However, one of the Belgian delegates is strongly opposed to this. He points out that the work on developing the 'quality in work' indicators is part of the European Employment Strategy and should therefore be included in the National Action Plans as well as the Joint Employment Report.

One of the German delegates points out that the Italian representative will achieve the opposite of what he wants. The German delegate also, does not want the indicators to be used in the National Action Plans. He thinks that as the text is now formulated it means that they should only be used to analyse the National Action Plans, not be used in them. However, the Italian delegate does not agree with this. The President tries to accommodate him by suggesting dropping the reference to the National Action Plans altogether, but then the Commission's representative protests, saying that he prefers the opposite since the Joint Employment Report is an analysis of the National Action Plans. The Italian delegate still insists on dropping the paragraph on the National Action Plans. The President tries again to persuade him that the paragraph does not say that the indicators will be used in the National Action Plans. He says:

> There is not a suggestion that they should be used in the NAPs [National Action Plans], only in the JER [Joint Employment Report].
> (Employment Committee 21 November 2001)

The Italian delegate insists:

> I don't agree that it doesn't say that here.
> (Employment Committee 21 November 2001)

The President raises his voice:

> That's not what the paragraph says! The paragraph is not committing the member states. It points to the use of the context indicators in the analysis, not in the drawing up of the NAPs.
> (Employment Committee 21 November 2001)

The Italian delegate is still not happy. He says:

We shall have to come back to this in February 2002. I still have a problem.
(Employment Committee 21 November 2001)

In the end the text remained as it was written, but, as the Commission's representative pointed out, the Joint Employment Report is used to analyse the member states' National Action Plans. The context indicators, most of which relied only on national data sources, would thus have to be delivered to the Commission for them to be used in the Joint Employment Report. It could mean that if the Employment Committee agreed that the context indicators were to be used in the analysis of the Joint Employment Report, they might also have to be included in the National Action Plans.

However, since it did not actually state that the context indicators were to be included in the National Action Plans, any suggestion that they should be included, could be rejected by the member states on the grounds that this was not the agreement. It was a question of interpretation. Nevertheless, the Italian delegate did not obtain support from the other members even if there were members who in principle agreed with him. Since he was isolated, and the suggested changes to accommodate Italy were rejected by the other members, he was forced to agree for the sake of reaching a decision. In this way compromises are made either by being outvoted or by being able to find a solution that can be accepted by everyone.

Conclusion: post(inter)national transparency

Different practices of transparency, such as dividing the indicators into key and context indicators, reveal the national order of the EU. The member states are concerned with where in the statistical diagrams and tables they will end up and how their score will in comparison with other member states in the 'benchmarks'. Through the comparisons in EU documents the moulding of national positions in 'their' member state's favour is cultivated. The idea of transparency and the view of indicators as objective and politically neutral reinforce this notion.

The culture of conflict is thus part of the system, in which member states should have national positions and argue their case. However, at the end of the series of meetings, the members have to come to a compromise. This culture of compromise is based on the notion that the members should exhaust their arguments in order to be able to agree on the 'best' decision, preferably based on a consensus. However, more often than not, other factors such as the timing or the ritual process of the meetings determine when a decision is to be made. The decisions are also generally based on 'majority consensus' or compromises rather than consensus, since the member states that fail to get support usually drop 'their' case, if not earlier, then at the end of the series of meetings.

The need for support from the other member states in the form of alliances and like-minded thinking in the Committee, is thus important for member states if they want to put forward their national position as the EU position. The other member states have to see the relevance of a policy issue for it to become a decision. As seen in the area of 'gender equality', the absence of perceived relevance makes it impossible to 'win' an argument. The forming of national positions is, thus, part of making the member states aware of their interests in different policy areas. Putting forward these national positions in the meetings may also be a way of learning what the other member states think is important, such as, again, on the area of 'gender equality'.

At the same time, the formation of national positions is a condition for making EU indicators, since the discussions and negotiations feed on the conflict. In this way postnational transparency is partly achieved through the national order of things and is thereby part of constructing the EU. In the concluding chapter I summarise and visualise how the bureaucratic culture of policy-making in the EU is formed in a constant pendulum movement between different ideas and practices. It is not only the meetings that have a specific rhythm but also the repeated movement between, for example, conflict and compromise. These movements outline a structure, in progressive form, that signifies the bureaucratic culture of policy-making in the EU.

SEVEN

CONCLUSION

MAKING THE NATION STATE TRANSPARENT

Introduction: policy-making in the EU

The European Union as a social construct is constantly changing and being re-formulated through the everyday practices of making policies and putting forward decisions. These decisions and policy-making processes are part of forming an EU chronology, making EU history, a history that may not be known very well by the general public in the EU but is very much part of the Eurocrats', if not everyday life, at least everyday working life.

The EU and EU policy-making have in recent years become the focus of anthropological studies. Shore (2000), for example, paid special attention to the study of EU cultural policy-making. Here, my aim has been to show the process of making employment policy and how policy decisions on the subject are taken in the EU. Particular focus has been placed on *how* decisions are made, what practices and ideas are in play, and the actors involved. The policy-making processes performed and the decisions made by bureaucrats and politicians are an important subject for scrutiny since they fashion that which is identified as the EU. The centre of attention has been the Eurocrats working to develop 'quality in work' indicators for the EU, illustrating the notion of making the nation states transparent, and thus moving the member states of the EU into the postnational era. The idea of transparency, bringing with it a constant stream of EU indicators that should make visible that which previously has been unseen, constitutes the grounds for a postnational European community.

Visibility and technicisation creating tensions

The notion of transparency carries ideas of making organisations and their policy-making processes and policy outcomes visible to a general public and therefore trustworthy. This way of managing policy-making has been discussed in terms of 'regulation by revelation' (Florini 2003:34). Transparency has to do with trust or the lack of trust in policy-makers' abilities to make the 'right' decisions (cf. Power 1999:2-3). The bureaucratic culture of policy-making in the EU is in this way guided by the idea of transparency in which policies and policy-making processes should be opened up so that EU citizens will be able to evaluate them and hold the politicians accountable.

Thus, the indicators are part of a political project fashioning the EU. The measurements of the level of 'quality in work' in the EU are creating Euro-numbers so that EU citizens can make comparisons transcending the nation state. This can be the basis for social transformations which make the member states' employment policies more similar. Here, the political vision of establishing a 'Social Europe' could be seen as a root metaphor for the EU, guiding employment and social policy in the Community as well as forming views of what the EU should be about. By the use of specific key concepts that capture the political vision and clarify the political direction, policies can be made understandable and shared knowledge among bureaucrats and politicians.

This shared meaning is, however, to a large extent a chimera. The member states' views on employment and social policy are connected to different welfare models that are sometimes in conflict with the EU ideal. The member states have different views on what 'Social Europe' should be about. This conflict is hidden or latent as long as the vision is kept ambiguous and broadly defined, so that many different ideas can be accommodated. It is when the vision is to be made more precise in order to make policy transparent that the conflicts between the member states spring to the surface. The indicators are utilised to benchmark the member states in reference to an ideal of what EU employment policy should be about. The 'results' of the comparisons in tables and diagrams are often the object of controversy. Thus, through the comparisons the tensions between the member states and the national and the postnational are further enhanced.

Hence, to have a say in and ultimately to gain control over how concepts are classified and indicators are defined is highly important. This study has been about what remains unseen beneath the 'veil of transparency' (Sanders and West 2003:26), i.e. the conflicts, negotiations and compromises that operate to produce transparency. Thus, whilst it may seem that policy-making in the case of EU labour markets is a process based on visible, clearly defined and solid indicators, these indicators are themselves the result of a process of negotiation and compromise. They appear as proxies for the ideal, and as compromises between representatives of nation states, political interests, and situational judgements. And while they may reveal a number of relevant aspects of the targeted phenomena, they also hide a number of significant aspects.

This brings to the surface the political dimension of transparency, in particular how transparent the member states want to be and what they want to be accountable for (also see Garsten and Lindh de Montoya 2006; Thedvall 2006). Transparency instead becomes a way of organising accountability, shaping the bureaucratic culture of policy-making in the EU, thereby making decisions in the EU legitimate.

The bureaucratic culture of policy-making in the EU

To sum up: the bureaucratic culture of policy-making in the EU has been at the centre of this study. The study illustrates how the Eurocrats operate to formulate policy by following the policy-making process of developing 'quality in work' indicators in the EU. This work is heavily influenced by the national logic of the member states and their reluctance to make what is culturally intimate transparent to a general public as well as to the politicians and bureaucrats of the other member states.

The political goal of establishing a common employment and social policy across the member states has particular significance as 'society-creating', in that it aspires to make the welfare of others the concern of all citizens of the EU. It plays an important role in forming a postnational EU in which the primacy of the nation state is, in certain respects, overridden through the fashioning of common EU policy. The three-party couplings of the national and the postnational, transparency and cultural intimacy, and 'Social Europe' have characterised the elaboration of 'quality in work' indicators and influenced the decision-making process. This gives the bureaucratic culture of policy-making in the EU certain characteristic features.

'Instances of bureaucracy' setting policy-making in motion

Civil servants and administrators in the national governments and EU institutions work closely with their political leaders. In the different member states' governments as well as in the EU institutions political views are formed and explored not necessarily in sync with one another. This is manifested when the member states and the Commission come together to make common decisions on employment policy. The different national perspectives formed in the domestic bureaucracies often clash in these encounters. The bureaucrats and politicians move between the pre-scheduled EU committee, group and council meetings and the domestic bureaucracy preparing their arguments at national level and presenting and defending them at the meetings.

The meetings, as arenas for negotiations, may in this way be seen as 'instances of bureaucracy' that exist and are manifested at regular intervals in the sequence of everyday working life. They provide a punctuated rhythm to the regular flow of events in the EU bureaucracy and the bureaucracies at home. The policy-making process is set in motion by this temporal organisation of the work through the changing of Presidencies and the rhythm of the meetings. Policies move towards decisions through the need to reach 'conclusions' at the end of every Presidency. The rhythm of the meetings is thus determined by these changes of Presidencies and the priorities that are set up to be decided on during a Presidency period. A policy issue moves between the different EU committees, working groups and councils before a final 'conclusion' can be made in the European Council at the end of a Presidency.

In these meetings, the decision-making process is moved along not only by time but also by the observance of rules that guide the process. These rituals of legitimation, i.e. rules and procedures that make decisions legitimate, constitute an elaborate network of regulations. The members also have an obligation to represent 'their' member states, or the Commission, in trying to negotiate in 'their' best interest. The work in the EU committees, working groups and councils is in this way shaped by the notion of the national, forming and presenting national positions and opinions. The members move in and out of the meetings preparing their national positions backstage, as it were, and presenting them frontstage, at the committee, working group and council meetings.

This conflicting atmosphere of different national positions is at the same time a prerequisite for being able to form an EU decision. It is partly the tension between the national and the postnational that transforms policy discussions into an EU decision. The Presidents of the EU working groups, councils and committees formulate and re-formulate compromises based on the notion of different national positions until the members are able to reach agreement. These compromises are affected both by the ritualised sequence of meetings and the regulations surrounding them as well as by the tensions between the national and postnational, making a culture of conflict more evident at the beginning of the meeting days while a culture of compromise prevails at the end, especially as the deadline approaches when a 'conclusion' has to be reached.

The temporal organisation of the process and the regulation of the meetings set the process in motion, moving between backstage and frontstage and between a culture of conflict and a culture of compromise, making it ultimately possible to reach a common decision. However, it is not only the time scheduling and the rules and regulations of the meetings that create a rhythm moving the policy process towards a decision. The constant pendulum movement between different ideas such as the ambiguous and the precise, the political and the technical, or key and context indicators, sets the policy-making in motion. Such pendulum couplings may appear as opposites but should rather be seen as paired and intertwined in the policy-making process. These dynamics, the tensions and movements between positions, provide a certain structure to policy-making and contribute to the formation of a *particular* bureaucratic culture of policy-making in the EU.

Transparency at work

The fact that the member states have national and political interests when trying, according to in their understanding, to make EU employment policy transparent gives birth to strategies to cope with the different interests. These strategies are referred to here as practices of transparency, signalling that they have to do with the quest for making EU policies transparent. Here, making a distinction between the political and technical may be seen as such a practice. The conflict between the member states is partly handled by the technification of politics into indicators and statistics that makes politics appear neutral. Such a transformation would remove all need for compromise and negotiations between the members since the one-best-way would have been found.

However, the notion of the political and the technical is an ideal. In practice, the political and technical are used as tools for arguing and making claims. The Eurocrats and politicians often see the indicators as 'attention-directing devices' (Power 2003a:14) imbued with political conflict and compromise. Thus, fed at the same time by an epistemic culture of numbers, the technical indicators are often treated as objective and neutral. It is therefore essential for the members to have knowledge about what is seen as political and technical in order to be able to form and argue their national positions in line with these notions. It is in a way a shared method for discussing and negotiating in the meetings that both encourages the conflict as well as making it possible for the members to agree on a compromise.

The member states' conflicting perspectives are also handled by making a distinction between key and context indicators. The idea of key and context indicators makes especially evident the divide between the national and the postnational. If key indicators could be seen as indicators transcending member states' borders and creating postnational statistical knowledge, the context indicators are used when this is not possible, either for political or for technical reasons. The context indicators are favoured by the member states that want to make as few comparisons between member states as possible. Hence, the context indicators are only to be used to provide national context, not to compare between member states other than by trends. Context indicators are also more often based on national databases, in this way leaving more control over the data produced for the indicators in the hands of the member states. This makes the clash between the member states' perspectives visible, while at the same time making it possible for them to agree on a greater number of 'quality in work' indicators, thereby at least giving the impression of being 'more' transparent.

By shifting between key and context indicators and between political and technical arguments the member states and the Commission can arrive at compromises on what should be seen and what should remain veiled. Transparency at work is thus a delicate balancing act between divergent perspectives and interests. Nevertheless, postnational ideals and perspectives are formulated through these practices keeping the conflicts out of sight.

Towards a postnational community?

So, is the EU moving towards a 'postnational community' taking over the nation state's role as principal community builder, and forming EU citizens and identities beyond the nation state? As put forward in Chapter 1, the notion of the 'postnational' is connected with the decoupling between the nation and the state, and citizenship and nationality (Appadurai 1996:168-169; Delanty and O'Mahony 2002:169). In the EU today, the nation or nationality is no longer the master discourse of either statehood (Delanty and O'Mahony 2002:173; Delanty and Rumford 2005:190) or citizenship (cf. Koopmans and Statham 1999:655-656; Soysal 1994:1). The member states, by the meddling in each others' domestic affairs, are breaking up the idea of the

Westphalian state and moving into this postnational, or in Cooper's terms postmodern,[90] era (Cooper 2003:27).

This postnational (or postmodern) age is signified by transparency and openness among nation states, rather than by the balance of power and secrecy (Cooper 2003:26). Cooper points out that today the EU member states have left the battlefields of war and moved into diplomacy in the corridors and meeting rooms of the EU. To make this possible, he (2003:28, 36-37) argues, the member states have to reveal, and are revealing, their innermost secrets and making their nation state policies and their outcomes transparent to each other. This is understood to creating trust between them. In fact, the name of the procedure used in the EU to co-ordinate the member states' employment policy signals this idea of transparency and openness, i.e. the *open* method of co-ordination. As Haahr points out, '[b]y entering into a system of open co-ordination, member states, their bureaucracies, their agencies and civil servants, have also subjected themselves to the surveillance, scrutiny and evaluation of others in new domains, with a view to arriving at certain common objectives' (2004:220). In the fashioning of a postnational European community, 'transparentisation' of the nation states is therefore needed.

However, as we have seen, the notion of transparency is problematic. The member states have no interest in revealing everything, leaving nothing hidden. Instead, they keep parts of the 'nation' out of sight, while other parts are made visible. There are different political and national interests at stake and policy areas or results that are sources of embarrassment or idiosyncrasies are often kept culturally intimate. Instead, the member states compete with each other in trying to influence the definition of the indicators so that they will obtain, in their opinion, a 'good' score compared with the others. The fact that the member states are benchmarked against each other fuels this competition. Consequently, one reason for a postnational European

---

[90] This study is more about the efforts to build a postnational order of things than a postmodern, the national and nationality being an integral part of building the EU and the national continually communicating and negotiating with the postnational.

community not to be realised to the full is the failure to make nation states transparent.

Nevertheless, there are seeds of postnationality (cf. Jacobsson 2004b:363). Through the process of developing indicators in the EU the member states are creating euro-statistics that make possible to formulate EU averages and targets in the EU labour market. A possible postnational European community would then be based on a particular kind of formation where the mappable and the measurable constitute the ground for its existence. The indicators form a 'grid of visibilities' (Haahr 2004:220). However, it is, as Haahr (ibid.) points out, a dense grid including only parts of society, the *calculable society* (cf. Johannisson 1988 in Swedish: *det mätbara samhället*), and excluding what is non-quantifiable.

The indicators thus visualise EU problems and objectives as a common concern for the member states. EU categorisations and labels make possible other forms of identification among the EU inhabitants. However, it is a shaky ground for creating a sense of belonging and a feeling of solidarity among people beyond the nation states. Techniques of governmentality such as the census, mapping or surveillance are part of creating 'full attachment', i.e. people's passion for defending the rights and values of an entity such as the nation state (Appadurai 2000:131-132). However, to achieve 'full attachment' something more is needed. What that is, is difficult to pinpoint, as Appadurai (ibid.) points out. Habermas (2000:112) puts forward the need for a cosmopolitan consciousness and solidarity, which may be spurred on by creating a 'Social Europe'. There have been and are ongoing attempts, by Eurocrats and politicians in the EU, to create a feeling of 'full attachment' to the EU in the peoples of the Union, by the use of cultural symbols (Shore 2000). The use of technologies such as 'transparentisation' of the nation states is part of this project (Shore 2000:31; Walters and Haahr 2005:74).

Transparency may be more about rituals of legitimation than about openness – a mechanism for organising accountability and making the

EU project legitimate (cf. Walters and Haahr 2005:75). However, through the creation and the calculations of euro-statistics, the seeds are planted of a postnational European community. Whether these seeds will germinate and eventually bloom, only time will tell.

EPILOGUE

EU employment policy in the mid-'00s

Three years have passed since I left the field. Many new papers, reports and policy documents have been written since and many more decisions have been prepared and decided on. During this period I have continued to follow EU employment and social policy-making from a distance. In a way, one never really leaves the field. I have become more attentive both professionally and personally to EU employment and social policy issues than to other fields, both in the news and in research. I have glanced at the Commission's website now and then, gone through new policy documents on a regular basis, kept in touch with people from the field and carried out a few interviews.

EU employment and social policy-making is an ever-changing field (like any field). Since I did my fieldwork ten new members have joined the EU, a possible Constitution for the EU has been discussed and the organisation of the European Employment Strategy has changed twice, first in 2003, after the five-year evaluation, in which the EU employment guidelines were reduced from eighteen to ten (Council of the European Union 2003), and again in 2005, when they became integrated with the broad economic policy guidelines in relation to the new label for EU employment policy – 'growth and jobs'. In the EU as in any other organisation new ideas are adopted and structures change continuously. As Brunsson and Olsen (1997:34) argue, organisational reforms are a sign of organisational stability rather than change.

Through these integrated guidelines the process of the European Employment Strategy has also moved from being an annual process to a three-year process, in which the guidelines, instead of being reviewed every year, remain the same for three years, 2005-2008. This timetable of the 'new' European Employment Strategy changes the timing of EU employment policy decisions. The employment guidelines are therefore to be followed up in the 'National Reform Programmes' (NRP), earlier referred to as National Action Plans (NAP), in the member states every year. The Council then writes a progress report to the European Council. As before, the Commission, together with the Council, also evaluates the National Reform Programmes in the Joint Employment Report and the Commission makes suggestions as 'Recommendations' to the member states which are then decided on by the Council.

More members, more meetings...

With the change from fifteen to twenty-five member states[91] in the EU there have also been logistical changes that may affect what we identify as the EU. The Presidencies still move between the member states every six months, but the European Council meetings are since the end of 2003 held in Brussels. The bureaucrats and politicians in the EU can no longer refer to a decision as 'concluded in Nice' or 'in Lisbon'. Whereas the EU decisions were previously connected with different locations where the Prime Ministers and Presidents met and decided on a specific issue, the EU chronology is now tied less to locations and more to content.

Since the EU became a union of twenty-five member states the number of members in the meetings has also inevitably increased. This gives rise to new ways of organising decision-making. When I was talking to one of the Swedish delegates in the Employment Committee in April 2004, she said that the meeting room and its table are much bigger now (at least in one of the meeting rooms), which means that it is sometimes difficult to see the expressions on people's faces. And as she pointed out, one of the reasons for meeting is that the members of the Committee want to have the face-to-face contact.

In addition, she explained that the members are now often organised in smaller groups in preparation for the Employment Committee, thus adding a new layer of meetings to the decision-making process.

---

[91] The ten new members that joined in the summer of 2004 are Cyprus, the Czech Republic, Estonia, Hungary, Latvia, Lithuania, Malta, Poland, Slovakia and Slovenia.

This arrangement makes possible alliance-building in a more organised way. It may also result in decision-making being prepared increasingly outside of the meeting rooms so that conflicts of interest are negotiated towards a compromise before the meeting takes place.

Bailey (1965:2) argued a long time ago that actual decision-making in meetings demands a smaller number than fifteen members in the meeting room. If there are additional members, decisions tend to be made elsewhere. Bailey seems to have a point. With twenty-five members in the EU, the committee, working group and council meetings become less intimate and the division into smaller groups suggests that it is difficult to handle too many members. It may also be a question of time making it impossible to hold meetings at which all twenty-five members should have their say at least once and maybe several times, since the meeting would last too long. There are many factors involved. However, it is safe to say that changes have occurred due to the shift from the 'EU-15' to 'EU-25'.

Moving away from the 'social'?

In 2005, the 'integrated' EU employment and broad economic policy guidelines were divided into 'macroeconomic guidelines' (1-6), 'microeconomic guidelines' (7-16) and the 'employment guidelines' (17-24) (Council of the European Union 2005a, 2005b). The process is now described as the 'Lisbon Strategy', emphasising the economic, social and the environment, at which the European Employment Strategy is a part instead of being a more independent strategy. It is relevant to ask here where 'Social Europe' is moving.[92] If the assumption is that the economic and the social are opposites, even though interlinked, it is possible to argue that since the EU employment guidelines are integrated with the broad economic policy guidelines, employment and social policies lose authority in relation to the economic. However, it is also possible to argue that through this integrated approach the EU employment guidelines gain in status in relation to the economic. In

---

[92] In the social sciences there is an ongoing debate on which direction 'Social Europe' should be moving. For such a debate see, for example, Salais and Villeneuve's edited volume *Europe and the Politics of Capabilities* (2004).

either case the idea of 'Social Europe' now appears in a slightly different conceptual context.

The main focus on 'more and better jobs' or 'quality in work' has changed in the Lisbon Strategy to 'growth and jobs'. Instead 'more and better jobs' and 'quality in work' are part of, are defining, 'growth and jobs'. However, the notion and the use of 'quality in work' have changed during this period. In 2001 and 2002 it was one of the 'horizontal objectives' of all guidelines. In 2003 and 2005 it continues to be one of three 'overarching and interrelated objectives' (Council of the European Union 2003, 2005a). However, the centre of attention is now 'improving quality and productivity at work' (ibid.), which signals a shift in focus from emphasis on 'quality *in* work' to 'quality *and* productivity *at* work'. The notion of 'in' and 'at' was also discussed during 2001 and most members then agreed that the correct preposition would be 'in' since it accentuated the 'quality' in people's individual work situations. 'Quality at work', on the other hand, stresses the quality of the actual workplace, i.e. wage levels, contracts and so on as one member state put it (Employment Committee meeting on 4 October 2001).

There is a certain recycling of ideas that manifest the EU as an organisation. However, the meaning of these ideas may shift, and be discursively transformed. What the member states then choose to measure in indicators may give a sign of what is on the political agenda at the time.

The indicators for 'quality in work' have been scattered into different policy areas, becoming part of the European Employment Strategy monitoring the EU employment guidelines in general rather than just 'quality in work'. The indicators have since then been revised in 2004 in reference to the guidelines of 2003 and then updated on 15 April 2005.[93] However, whether the last update will be the indicators

---

[93] The reports on the indicators may be found at the Employment Committee's website at
http://europa.eu.int/comm/employment_social/employment_strategy/docindic_en.htm The 'quality in work' indicators are referred to as 'Q' in the column: 'other uses of the indicators' in the report. Last visited 2005-12-09. Print-out in author's possession.

monitoring the new guidelines for 2005-2008 is too soon to tell. As pointed out in Chapter 5, the different political views among member states as well as the conflict between the political and the technical are hidden from view, are being 'black-boxed', when there is a formal decision on indicators that may be used. The indicators instead take on a life of their own and are treated as 'objective'. This view makes it possible to disconnect the indicators from the political visions that once gave birth to them. The numbers are treated as detached, being used in other contexts, which confirms the belief in the political neutrality and objectivity of numbers.

A post(inter)national European community?

These changes, both in the policy-making process and in the accession of the new member states, have relevance for my overarching argument about the pendulum movements between the idea of transparency and opacity and the national and postnational in the field of 'Social Europe'.

As argued in Chapter 2, the EU chronology is closely connected to the idea of the nation state. An EU history is created through the changes in Presidencies and decision-making through the rhythms of the meetings. Now, having the European Council meetings in Brussels makes decision-making less connected to the nation state, adding seeds of postnationality to the EU project. In the same fashion, the decoupling of nation and state, with state apparatuses promoting diversity and multiculturalism, is prevalent. However, this is truer of most of the 'old' member states, the 'EU-15'. Several of the 'new' member states are instead relatively new *nation* states, i.e. states built on perceived nations, such as the Czech Republic, Estonia, Latvia, Lithuania, Slovakia, and Slovenia, manifesting the continued and maybe even furthered importance of the nation state in the EU.

The technology of the open method of co-ordination continues to be emphasised promoting soft law and transparency as instruments for building a postnational community of the EU. However, it is safe to assume that as long as the member states are measured and compared with each other they will also want to keep the embarrassing and/or the idiosyncratic culturally intimate. The continued use of key and context indicators supports this. To have unifying power, the hierarchical classifications system should instead focus on other categories at the top of the system such as unemployed people, regardless of their national origin. However, the tables and diagrams in the Joint Employment Report are still categorised in member states.

Nevertheless, the indicators are important in the EU since they may, in a way, be one of the few materialised features that have the potential to form a uniting symbol for the EU. This would, as argued in the Conclusion, make the postnational European community one based on ideals of calculability more than on a sense of postnational belonging.

REFERENCES

Abélès, Marc. 1993. Political Anthropology of the Transnational Institution: The European Parliament. *French Politics & Society*, 11(1):1-19.

___. 2000. Virtual Europe. In *An Anthropology of the European Union. Building, Imagining and Experiencing the New Europe*, edited by Irène Bellier & Thomas M. Wilson. Oxford: Berg.

Abram, Simone. 2003. Anthropologies in Policies, Anthropologies in Places: Reflections of Fieldwork 'in' Documents and Policies. In *Globalisation. Studies in Anthropology*, edited by Thomas Hylland Eriksen. London: Pluto Press.

Ahrne, Göran. 1989. *Byråkratin och statens inre gränser*. Stockholm: Rabén & Sjögren.

Albrow, Martin. 1970. *Bureaucracy*. London: Macmillan.

___. 1997. *Do Organizations have Feelings?*. London: Routledge.

Alonso, William & Paul Starr (eds.). 1987. *The Politics of Numbers*. New York: Russell Sage Foundation.

Anderson, Benedict. 1983. *Imagined Community: Reflections on the Origin and Spread of Nationalism*. London: Verso.

Andersson, Jenny. 2004. A Productive Social Citizenship? Reflections on the Concept of Productive Social Policies in the European Tradition. In *A European Social Citizenship? Preconditions for Future Policies from a Historical Perspective*, edited by Lars Magnusson & Bo Stråth. Brussels: P.I.E. Peter Lang.

Appadurai, Arjun. 1993. Patriotism and Its Futures. *Public Culture*, 5(3):411-429.

___. 1996. *Modernity at Large*. London: University of Minnesota Press.

___. 2000. The Grounds of the Nation-State. Identity, Violence and Territory. In *Nationalism and Internationalism in the Post-Cold War Era*, edited by Kjell Goldman, Ulf Hannerz & Charles Westin. London: Routledge.

Asad, Talal. 1994. Ethnographic Representation, Statistics and Modern Power. *Social Research*, 61(1):55-87.

Bailey, Frederick G. 1965. Decisions by Consensus in Councils and Committees: with special Reference to Village and Local Government in India. In *Political*

214 References

214
References

Systems and the Distribution of Power, edited by Michael Banton. London: Tavistock Publications, A.S.A. Monographs 2.

Bean, Charles, Samuel Bentolila, Giuseppe Bertola & Juan Dolado. 1998. *Social Europe: One for All?* London: Centre for Economic Policy Research.

Beetham, David. 1996. *Bureaucracy. Second edition.* Minneapolis: University of Minnesota Press.

Behning, Ute & Amparo Serrano Pascual (eds.). 2001. *Gender Mainstreaming in the European Employment Strategy.* Brussels: ETUI.

Bell, Catherine. 1992. *Ritual Theory, Ritual Practice.* Oxford: Oxford University Press.

Bellier, Irène. 1997. The Commission as an Actor: An Anthropologist's View. In *Participation and Policy-Making in the European Union*, edited by Helen Wallace & Alasdair R. Young. Oxford: Oxford University Press.

___. 2000. The European Union, Identity Politics and the Logic of Interests' Representation. In *An Anthropology of the European Union. Building, Imagining and Experiencing the New Europe*, edited by Irène Bellier & Thomas M. Wilson. Oxford: Berg.

Bellier, Irène & Thomas M. Wilson (eds). 2000. *An Anthropology of the European Union. Building, Imagining and Experiencing the New Europe.* Oxford: Berg.

Ben-Ari, Eyal & Efrat Elron. 2001. Blue Helmets and White Armor: Multi-Nationalism and Multi-Culturalism among UN Peacekeeping Forces. *City & Society*, 8(2):275-306.

von Benda-Beckmann, Keebet & Maykel Verkuyten. 1995. *Nationalism, Ethnicity and Cultural Identity in Europe.* Utrecht: European Research Centre on Migration and Ethnic Relations.

Bercusson, Brian, Simon Deakin, Pertti Koistinen, Yota Kravaritou, Ulrich Mückenberger, Alain Supiot & Bruno Veneziani. 1997. A Manifesto for Social Europe. *European Law Journal*, 3(2):189-205.

Bergström, Carl Fredrik. 2003. *Comitology. Delegation of Power in the European Union and the Committee System.* Stockholm University: Department of Political Science, Dissertation.

Biagi, Marco. 2000. The Impact of the European Employment Strategy on the Role of Labour Law and Industrial Relations. *The International Journal of Comparative Labour Law and Industrial Relations*, 16(2):155-173.

Blau, Peter M. & Marshall W. Meyer. 1956. *Bureaucracy in Modern Society.* New York: Random House.

Bloch, Maurice. 1971. Decision-Making in Councils among the Merina of Madagascar. In *Councils in Action*, edited by Audrey Richards & Adam Kuper. Cambridge: Cambridge University Press.

Boden, Deirdre. 1994. *The Business of Talk. Organizations in Action*. Cambridge: Polity Press.

Borneman, John & Nick Fowler. 1997. Europeanization. *Annual Review of Anthropology*, 26:487-514.

Bourdieu, Pierre. 1977. *Outline of a Theory of Practice*. Cambridge: Cambridge University Press

___. 1994. Rethinking the State: Genesis and Structure of the Bureaucratic Field. *Sociological Theory*, 12(1):1-18.

Britan, Gerald M. & Ronald Cohen (eds.). 1980. *Hierarchy and Society. Anthropological Perspectives on Bureaucracy*. Philadelphia: Institute of the Study of Human Issues.

Brunsson, Nils & Johan P. Olsen. 1997 [1993]. *The Reforming Organization*. Bergen: Fagbokforlaget.

Le Cacheux, Jacques & Éloi Laurent. 2003. *The 'New Social Europe' and the Capability Approach*. Paper presented at the EUROCAP workshop: Grounds for a New Approach to Social Policies in Europe, Florence 6-7 June 2003.

Carson, Marcus. 2004. *From Common Market to Social Europe? Paradigm Shift and Institutional Change in European Union Policy on Food, Asbestos and Chemicals, and Gender Equality*. Stockholm: Acta Universitatis Stockholmiensis. Stockholm Studies in Sociology. N.S. 22. Dissertation.

Castells, Manuel. 1998. *End of Millennium*. Oxford: Blackwell Publishers.

CEC. 1986. *Social Europe, no1/86*. Luxembourg: Office for Official Publications of the European Communities.

___. 1993a. *Green Paper: European Social Policy – Options for the Union*. Luxembourg: Office for Official Publications of the European Communities COM (93) 551.

___. 1993b. *White Paper: Growth, Competitiveness, Employment – The Challenges and Ways Forward into the 21st century*. Luxembourg: Office for Official Publications of the European Communities.

___. 1994. *White Paper: European Social Policy – A Way Forward for the Union*. Luxembourg: Office for Official Publications of the European Communities COM(94) 333.

___. 2000. *European Social Policy Agenda 2000-2005*. Luxembourg: Office for Official Publications of the European Communities. COM(2000)379.

___. 2001. *Employment and Social Policies: a Framework for Investing in Quality*. COM(2001) 313 final.

___. 2005. *The Continuity of Indicators during the Transition between ECHP and EU-SILC*. Working papers and studies at Eurostat: population and social condition. Luxembourg: Office for Official Publications of the European Communities.

Christiansen, Thomas & Emil Kirchner (eds.). 2000. *Committee Governance in the European Union*. Manchester: Manchester University Press.

Cohen, I Bernard. 2005. *The Triumph of Numbers. How Counting Shaped Modern Life*. London: W.W. Norton & Company.

Cohen, Michael D, James G. March & Johan P. Olsen. 1982 [1976]. People, Problems, Solutions and the Ambiguity of Relevance. In *Ambiguity and Choice in Organizations*, edited by James G. March & Johan P Olsen. Bergen: Universitetsforlaget.

Cohen, Rosalie A. 1969. Conceptual Styles, Culture Conflict, and Nonverbal Tests of Intelligence. *American Anthropologist*, 71(5):828-856.

Cohn, Bernard S. 1968. Notes on the History of the Study of Indian Society and Culture. In *Structure and Change in Indian Society*, edited by Milton Singer & Bernard S. Cohn. Chicago: Aldine Publishing Company.

Cooper, Robert. 2003. *The Breaking of Nations. Order and Chaos in the Twenty-First Century*. London: Atlantic Books.

de Coppet, Daniel (ed.). 1992. *Understanding Rituals*. London: Routledge.

Council of the European Union. 1996. *Regeringskonferensen. 1996 – Reflektionsgruppens rapport och dokumenthänvisningar*. Luxembourg: Office for Official Publications of the European Communities.

___. 1999. *Council Resolution on the 1999 Employment Guidelines 1999/C 69/02*. Official Journal of the European Communities

___. 2000. *Council Decision 2000/98/EC*. Official Journal of the European Communities.

___. 2001. *Council Decision on the Guidelines for Member States' Employment Policies for the Year 2001 2001/63/EC*. Official Journal of the European Communities.

___. 2003. *Council Decision on Guidelines for the Employment Policies of the Member States 2003/578/EC*. Official Journal of the European Union.

___. 2005a. *Council Decision on Guidelines for the Employment Policies of the Member States 2005/600/EC*. Official Journal of the European Union.

___. 2005b. *Council Recommendation on the Broad Guidelines for the Economic Policies of the Member States and the Community (2005 to 2008) 2005/601/EC.* Official Journal of the European Union.

Cowles, Maria Green, James Caporaso & Thomas Risse (eds.). 2001. *Transforming Europe: Europeanization and Domestic Change.* London: Cornell University Press.

Cram, Laura. 1997. *Policy-Making in the European Union. Conceptual Lenses and the Integration Process.* London: Routledge.

Davis, Charlotte Aull. 1999. *Reflexive Ethnography. A Guide to Researching Selves and Others.* London: Routledge.

De la Porte, Caroline. 2002. Is the Open Method of Coordination Appropriate for Organising Activities at the European Level in Sensitive Policy Areas?'. *European Law Journal,* 8(1):38-58.

De la Porte, Caroline & Philippe Pochet (eds.). 2002. *Building Social Europe Through the Open Method of Coordination.* Brussels: PIE Peter Lang.

Delanty, Gerard & Patrick O'Mahony. 2002. *Nationalism and Social Theory. Modernity and the Recalcitrance of the Nation.* London: Sage Publications.

Delanty, Gerhard & Chris Rumford. 2005. *Rethinking Europe. Social Theory and the Implications of Europeanization.* London: Routledge.

Douglas, Mary. 1986. *How Institutions Think.* Syracuse: Syracuse University Press.

Eriksen, Thomas Hylland. 1993. *Ethnicity and Nationalism. Anthropological Perspectives.* London: Pluto Press.

___. 1998. *Common Denominators. Ethnicity, Nation-Building and Compromise in Mauritius.* Oxford: Berg.

European Council. 1997. *Presidency Conclusions: European Council in Luxembourg, Nov 1997.* http://ue.eu.int/ueDocs/cms_Data/docs/pressData/en/ec/00300.htm Last visited 2005-12-09. Print-out in the author's possession.

___. 1998. *Presidency Conclusions: European Council in Cardiff, June 1998.* http://ue.eu.int/cms3_applications/Applications/newsRoom/LoadDocume nt.asp?directory=en/ec/&filename=54315.pdf Last visited 2005-12-09. Print-out in the author's possession.

___. 2000a. *Presidency Conclusion: European Council in Lisbon, March 2000.* http://ue.eu.int/ueDocs/cms_Data/docs/pressData/en/ec/00100-r1.en0.htm Last visited 2005-12-09. Print-out in the author's possession.

___. 2000b. *Presidency Conclusion: European Council in Nice, December 2000.* http://ue.eu.int/ueDocs/cms_Data/docs/pressData/en/ec/00400-r1.%20ann.en0.htm Last visited 2005-12-09. Print-out in the author's possession.

___. 2001a *Presidency Conclusions: European Council in Stockholm, March 2001.*
http://ue.eu.int/ueDocs/cms_Data/docs/pressData/en/ec/00100-
r1.%20ann-r1.en1.html Last visited 2005-12-09. Print-out in the author's
possession.

___. 2001b. *Presidency Conclusions: European Council in Gothenburg, June 2001.*
http://ue.eu.int/cms3_applications/Applications/newsRoom/loadBook.asp
?target=2001&bid=76&lang=1&cmsId=347 Last visited 2005-12-09. Print-
out in the author's possession.

___. 2001c. *Presidency Conclusions: European Council in Laeken, December 2001.*
http://ue.eu.int/cms3_applications/Applications/newsRoom/LoadDocume
nt.asp?directory=en/ec/&filename=68827.pdf Last visited 2005-12-09.
Print-out in the author's possession.

Featherstone, Kevin & Claudio M. Radaelli (eds.). 2003. *The Politics of
Europeanization.* Oxford: Oxford University Press.

Ferguson, James. 1990. *The Anti-Politics Machine. 'Development', Depolitization, and
Bureaucratic Power in Lesotho.* Cambridge: Cambridge University Press.

Florini, Ann. 1998. The End of Secrecy. *Foreign Policy,* 111:50-64.

___. 2003. *The Coming Democracy. New Rules for Running a New World.* London: Island
Press.

Foden, David & Lars Magnusson (eds.). 1999. *Entrepreneurship in the European
Employment Strategy.* Brussels: ETUI.

___ (eds.). 2000. *Contested Territory. Entrepreneurship in the European Employment
Strategy.* SALTSA Brussels: ETUI.

Foucault, Michel. 1988. The Political Technology of Individuals. In *Technologies of
the Self. A Seminar with Michel Foucault,* edited by Luther H. Martin, Huch
Gutman & Patrick H. Hutton. Massachusetts: The University of
Massachusetts Press.

___. 1991. Governmentality. In *The Foucault Effect,* edited by Graham Burchell,
Colin Gordon & Peter Miller. London: Harvester Wheatsheaf.

Franchet, Yves. 1999. Performance Indicators for International Statistical
Organisations. *Statistical Journal of the United Nation ECE,* 16 (4):241-250

Gallie, Walter. B. 1956. Essentially Contested Concepts. *Proceedings of the
Aristotelian Society, New Series,* 56:167-198.

García, Soledad (ed.). 1993. *European Identity and the Search for Legitimacy.* London:
Pinter Publishers.

Garsten, Christina. 1994. *Apple World. Core and Periphery in a Transnational
Organizational Culture.* Stockholm Studies in Social Anthropology, 33.
Stockholm: Almqvist & Wiksell International.

Garsten, Christina & Kerstin Jacobsson (eds.). 2004. *Learning to be employable. New agendas on work, responsibility and learning in a globalizing world*. Houndsmill, Basingstokes: Palgrave Macmillan.

Garsten, Christina & Monica Lindh de Montoya. 2004. *The Politics of Transparency: Accountability through Visibility*. Paper presented at the 20th EGOS Colloquium in Ljubljana University, Slovenia 1-3 July, 2004.

Garsten, Christina & Monica Lindh de Montoya (eds.). 2006. *The Politics of Transparency: Unveiling Organizational Visions for a New Global Order*. London: Edward Elgar Publishing.

du Gay, Paul. 2000. *In Praise of Bureaucracy. Weber, Organization, Ethics*. London: Sage Publications

Gell, Alfred. 1992. *The Anthropology of Time. Cultural Construction of Temporal Maps and Images*. Oxford: Berg.

Goddard, Victoria A., Josep R. Llobera & Cris Shore (eds.). 1994. *The Anthropology of Europe. Identity and Boundaries in Conflict*. Oxford: Berg.

Goetschy, Janine. 1999. The European Employment Strategy. Genesis and Development. *European Journal of Industrial Relation*, 5 (2):117-137.

___. 2003 The European Employment Strategy and the Open Method of Coordination: Lessons and Perspectives. *Transfer* 9(2):281-301 .

Goetschy, Janine & Philippe Pochet. 1997. The Treaty of Amsterdam: A New Approach to Employment and Social Affairs?. *Transfer*, 3(3):607-625

Goffman, Erving. 1959. *Presentation of Self in Everyday Life*. London: Penguin Books.

___. 1963. *Behavior in Public Places. Notes on the Social Organization of Gatherings*. New York: The Free Press.

___. 1983. The Interaction Order: American Sociological Association, 1982 Presidential Address. *American Sociological Review*, 48(1):1-17.

Graham, Mark. 1999. *Classification, Persons and Policies: Refugees and Swedish Welfare Bureaucracy*. Stockholm University: Department of Social Anthropology, Dissertation.

Greenhouse, Carol J. 1996. *A Moment's Notice. Time Politics across Cultures*. London: Cornell University Press.

Grillo, Ralph D. 1980. Introduction. In *"Nation" and "State" in Europe. Anthropological Perspectives*, edited by Ralph D. Grillo. London: Academic Press.

Gustafsson, Claes. 1994. *Produktion av allvar. Om det ekonomiska förnuftets metafysik*. Stockholm: Nerenius & Santérus Förlag.

Haahr, Jens Henrik. 2004. Open Co-ordination as Advanced Liberal Government. *Journal of European Public Policy*, 11(2):209-230.

Habermas, Jürgen. 2001. *The Postnational Constellation. Political Essays.* Cambridge: Polity Press.

Hacking, Ian. 1986. Making up people. In *Reconstructing Individualism. Autonomy, Individuality, and the Self in Western Thought,* edited by Thomas C. Heller, Morton Sosna & David E. Wellbery. Stanford: Stanford University Press.

___. 1990. *The Taming of Chance.* Cambridge: Cambridge University Press.

Handelman, Don. 1981 Introduction. The Idea of Bureaucratic Organization. *Social Analysis,* 9:5-23.

___. 1990. *Models and mirrors: towards and anthropology of public events.* Cambridge: Cambridge University Press.

___. 1995. Comment to Josiah McC. Heyman Putting Power in the Anthropology of Bureaucracy. The Immigration and Naturalization Service at the Mexico-United States Boarder. *Current Anthropology,* 36(2):261-287.

___. 2004. *Nationalism and the Israeli State: Bureaucratic Logic in Public Events.* Oxford: Berg.

Hannerz, Ulf. 1992. *Cultural Complexitity. Studies in the Social Organization of Meaning.* New York: Columbia University Press.

___. 1996. *Transnational Connections. Culture People Places.* London: Routledge.

___. 2003. Several Sites in One. In *Globalisation. Studies in Anthropology,* edited by Thomas Hylland Eriksen. London: Pluto Press.

Harlow, Carol. 2002. *Accountability in the European Union.* Oxford: Oxford University Press.

Herzfeld, Michel. 1987. *Anthropology through the Looking-Glass. Critical Ethnography in the Margins of Europe.* Cambridge: Cambridge University Press.

___. 1992. *The Social Production of Indifference. Exploring the Symbolic Roots of Western Bureaucracy.* London: The University of Chicago Press.

___. 1997. *Cultural Intimacy. Social Poetics in the Nation-State.* London: Routledge.

Heyman, Josiah McC. 1995. Putting Power in the Anthropology of Bureaucracy. The Immigration and Naturalization Service at the Mexico-United States Boarder. *Current Anthropology,* 36(2):261-287.

Hood, Christopher. 1991. A Public Management for all Seasons?. *Public Administration,* 69(1):3-19.

Hoskyns, Catherine. 1996. *Integrating Gender. Women, Law and Politics in the European Union.* London: Verso.

Huzzard, Tony. 2003. *The Convergence of the Quality of Working Life and Competitiveness. A Current Swedish Literature Review.* National Institute for Working Life: Worklife in Transition 2003:6.

Jacobsson, Bengt. 1987. *Kraftsamlingen. Politik och företagande i parallella processer.* Lund: Studentlitteratur.

Jacobsson, Bengt & Ulrika Mörth. 1998. Europeiseringen och den svenska staten. In *Stater som organisationer*, edited by Göran Ahrne. Stockholm: Nerenius & Santérus Förlag.

Jacobsson, Bengt, Per Lægreid & Ove K. Pedersen. 2004. *Europeanization and Transnational States. Comparing Nordic Central Governments.* London: Routledge.

Jacobsson, Kerstin. 1999. *Employment Policy in Europe: A New System of European Governance?.* Score working paper series 1999:11.

___. 2001 *Innovations in EU Governance – The Case of Employment Policy Co-ordination.* Score working paper series 2001:12.

___. 2004a. Between Deliberation and Discipline: Soft Governance in EU Employment Policy. In *Soft Law in Governance and Regulation. An Interdisciplinary Analysis*, edited by Ulrika Mörth. Cheltenham: Edward Elgar Publishing.

___. 2004b. Soft Regulation and the Subtle Transformation of the State: The Case of EU Employment Policy. *Journal of European Social Policy*, 14(4):355-370.

Jacobsson, Kerstin & Karl-Magnus Johansson. 2001. Väfärdspolitik och nya samarbetsformer i EU. In *Mot en europeisk välfärdspolitik? Ny politik och nya samarbetsformer i EU*, edited by Kerstin Jacobsson, Karl Magnus Johansson & Magnus Ekengren. Stockholm: SNS Förlag.

Jacobsson, Kerstin, Karl Magnus Johansson & Magnus Ekengren. 2001 *Mot en europeisk välfärdspolitik? Ny politik och nya samarbetsformer i EU.* Stockholm: SNS Förlag.

Jacobsson, Kerstin & Åsa Vifell. 2005. Soft Governance, Employment Policy and Committee Deliberation. In *Making the European Polity. Reflexive integration in the EU*, edited by Erik Oddvar Eriksen. London: Routledge.

Johannisson, Karin. 1988. *Det mätbara samhället. Statistik och samhällsdröm i 1700-talets Europa.* Stockholm: Norstedts Förlag.

Jupille, Joseph. 1999. The European Union and International Outcomes. *International Organization*, 53(2):409-425.

Keller, Berndt. 2000. The New European Employment Policy or: Is the Glass Half-Full or Half-Empty?. In *Transnational Industrial Relations in Europe*, edited by Reiner Hoffman, Otto Jacobi, Berndt Keller & Manfred Weiss. Düsseldorf: Hans Böckler Foundation.

Kenner, Jeff. 1995. EC Labour Law: The Softly, Softly Approach. *International Journal of Comparative Labour Law in Industrial Relations*, 11(4):307-326.

___. 1999. The EC Employment Title and the 'Third Way': Making Soft Law Work?. *International Journal of Comparative Labour Law and Industrial Relations*, 15(1):33-60.

Kern, Stephen. 1983. *The Culture of Time and Space 1880-1918*. Cambridge, Massachusetts: Harvard University Press.

Knorr Cetina, Karin. 1999. *Epistemic Cultures. How the Sciences Make Knowledge*. London: Harvard University Press.

Kockel, Ullrich. 1999. *Borderline Cases. The Ethnic Frontiers of European Integration*. Liverpool: Liverpool University Press.

Koopmans, Ruud & Paul Statham. 1999. Challenging the Liberal Nation-State? Postnationalism, Multiculturalism, and the Collective Claims of Making of Migrants and Ethnic Minorities in Britain and Germany. *The American Journal of Sociology*, 105(3):652-696.

Kunda, Gideon. 1992. *Engineering Culture. Control and Commitment in a High-Tech Corporation*. Philadelphia: Temple University Press.

Kuper, Adam. 1971. Council Structure and Decision-Making. In *Councils in Action*, edited by Audrey Richards & Adam Kuper. Cambridge: Cambridge University Press.

Lafoucrière, Céline. 2000. *The European Employment Strategy. The Third Pillar: Adaptability*. ETUI working paper DWP 2000.01.03.

Landelius, Ann-Charlotte. 2001. *Om soft law på det social skyddsområdet – en EG-rättslig studie*. Stockholm: Norstedts Juridik.

Langley, Ann, Henry Mintzberg, Patricia Pitcher, Elizabeth Posada & Jan Saint-Macary. 1995. Opening up Decision Making: The view from the Black Stool. *Organization Science*, 6(3):260-279.

Larsson, Torbjörn. 2003. *Precooking in the European Union. The World of Expert Groups*. Government Offices of Sweden: Ministry Publications Series, Ds 2003:16.

Latour, Bruno and Steven Woolgar. 1986 [1979]. *Laboratory Life. The Construction of Scientific Facts*. Princeton, New Jersey: Princeton University Press.

Law, John. 1994. *Organizing Modernity*. Oxford: Blackwell Publishers.

Lewis, Jeffrey. 1998. Is the 'Hard Bargaining' Image of the Council Misleading? The Committee of Permanent Representatives and the Local Election Directive. *Journal of the Common Market Studies*, 36(4):479-504.

Liebfried, Stephan & Paul Pierson. 2000. Social Policy. In *Policy-Making in the European Union*, edited by Helen Wallace & William Wallace. Oxford: Oxford University Press.

Lindblom, Charles E. 1959. The Science of Muddling Through. *Public Administration Review*, 19(2):155-169.

Lipsky, Micheal. 1980. *Street-Level Bureaucracy*. New York: Russel Sage Foundation.

Macdonald, Sharon (ed.). 1993. *Inside European Identities. Ethnography in Western Europe*. Oxford: Berg Publishers.

Malinowski, Bronislaw. 1984 [1922]. *Argonauts of the Western Pacific*. Prospect Heights, Illinois: Waveland Press Inc.

___. 1927. Lunar and Seasonal Calendar in the Trobriands. *The Journal of the Royal Anthropological Institute of Great Britain and Ireland*, 57(1):203-215.

Malkki, Liisa H. 1999[1997]. National Geographic: The Rooting of Peoples and the Territorialization of National Identity among Scholars and Refugees. In *Culture Power Place. Explorations in Critical Anthropology*, edited by Akhil Gupta & James Ferguson. London: Duke University Press.

Mallard, Alexandre. 1998. Compare, Standardize and Settle Agreement: On some Usual Metrological Problems. *Social Studies of Science*, 28(4):571-601

March, James G. 1978. Bounded Rationality, Ambiguity, and the Engineering of Choice. *Bell Journal of Economics*, 9(2):587-608.

Marcus, George E. 1986. Contemporary Problems of Ethnography in the Modern World System. In *Writing Culture. Poetics and Politics of Ethnography*, edited by James Clifford & George E. Marcus. Berkeley: University of California Press.

___. 1995. Ethnography in/of the World System: The Emergence of Multi-Sited Ethnography. *Annual Review in Anthropology*, 24:95-117.

Martin, Emily. 1997. Managing Americans – Policy and changes in the meanings of work and the self. In *Anthropology of Policy. Critical perspectives on governance and power*, edited by Cris Shore & Susan Wright. London: Routledge.

McDonald, Maryon. 1997. Identities in the European Commission. In *At the Heart of the Union. Studies of the European Commission*, edited by Neill Nugent. London: Macmillan Press Ltd.

___. 2000. Accountability, Anthropology and the European Commission. In *Audit Culture. Anthropological Studies in Accountability, Ethics and the Academy*, edited by Marilyn Strathern. London: Routledge.

Meyer, John W & Brian Rowan. 1977. Institutional Organizations: Formal Structure as Myth and Ceremony. *The American Journal of Sociology*, 83(2):340-363.

Meyer, John W, Richard W. Scott, David Strang & Andrew L. Creighton. 1994. Bureaucratisation Without Centralization: Changes in the Organizational System of U.S. Public Education, 1940-1980. In *Institutional Environments and Organizations. Structural Complexity and Individualism*, edited by Richard W. Scott & John W. Meyer. London: Sage Publications.

Miller, Daniel. 1985. *Artefacts as Categories. A Study of Ceramic Variability in Central India*. Cambridge: Cambridge University Press.

___. 2003. Could the Internet Defetishise the Commodity?. *Environmental and Planning D: Society and Space*, 21(3):359-372.

Miller, Peter. 2001. Governing by Numbers: Why Calculative Practices Matter. *Social Research*, 68(2):379-395.

Miller, Peter & Nikolas Rose. 1995. Production, Identity, and Democracy. *Theory and Society*, 24(3):427-467.

Misztal, Barbara A. 2000. *Informality. Social Theory and Contemporary Practice*. London: Routledge.

Moore, Sally F & Barbara Myerhoff (eds.). 1977. *Secular Ritual*. Assen/Amsterdam: Van Gorcum.

Moravcsik, Andrew. 1993. Preferences and Power in the European Community: A Liberal Intergovernmentalist Approach. *Journal of Common Market Studies*, 31(4):473-524.

Munn, Nancy D. 1992. The Cultural Anthropology of Time: A Critical Essay. *Annual Review of Anthropology*, 21(1):93-123.

Mörth, Ulrika. 1996. *Vardagsintegration – La vie quotidienne – i Europa. Sverige i EUREKA och EUREKA i Sverige*. Stockholm University: Department of Political Science, Dissertation.

Mörth, Ulrika (ed). 2004. *Soft Law in Governance and Regulation. An Interdisciplinary Analysis*. Cheltenham: Edward Elgar Publishing.

Nader, Laura. 1972. Up the Anthropologist—Perspectives Gained from Studying Up. *Reinventing Anthropology*, edited by Dell Hymes. New York: Random House, Pantheon Books.

Noon, Mike & Paul Blyton. 1997. *The Realities of Work*. London: Macmillan Press.

Ortner, Sherry B. 1973. On Key Symbols. *American Anthropologist, New Series*, 75(5):1338-1346.

___. 1997. Fieldwork in the Postcommunity. *Anthropology and Humanism*, 22(1):61-80.

Paley, Julia. 2001. Making Democracy Count: Opinion Polls and Market Surveys in the Chilean Political Transition. *Cultural Anthropology*, 16(2):135-164.

Parkin, David. 1992. Ritual as Spatial Direction and Bodily Division. In *Understanding Rituals*, edited by Daniel de Coppet. London: Routledge.

Perrow, Charles. 1986[1972]. *Complex Organizations. A Critical Essay 3rd edition*. London: McGraw-Hill.

Peters, Guy B. 2001. *The Politics of Bureaucracy 5th edition*. London: Routledge.

Petryna, Adriana. 2002. *Life Exposed. Biological Citizens after Chernobyl*. Princeton: Princeton University Press.

Pochet, Philippe. 2005. The Open Method of Co-ordination and the Construction of Social Europe. A Historical Perspective. In *The Open Method of Co-ordination in Action. The European Employment and Social Inclusion Strategies*, edited by Jonathan Zeitlin & Philippe Pochet with Lars Magnusson. Brussels: P.I.E. Peter Lang.

Porter; Theodore M. 1995. *Trust in Numbers. The Pursuit of Objectivity in Science and Public Life*. Princeton: Princeton University Press.

___. 2001. On the Virtues and Disadvantage of Quantification for Democratic Life. *Studies in History and Philosophy of Science part A*, 32(4):739-747.

Portnoy, Stephen & Xuming He. 2002. A Robust Journey in the New Millennium. In *Statistics in the 21st Century*, edited by Adrian E. Raftery, Martin A. Tanner & Martin T. Wells. London: Chapman and Hall/CRC.

Power, Michael. 1999[1997]. *The Audit Society. Rituals of Verification*. Oxford: Oxford University Press.

___. 2003a. *The Invention of Operational Risk*. Discussion paper no: 16. Centre for Analysis of Risk and Regulation (CARR).

___. 2003b. Auditing and the Production of Legitimacy. *Accounting, Organizations and Society*, 28(4):379-394.

Premfors, Rune, Peter Ehn, Eva Haldén & Göran Sundström. 2003. *Democrati & Byråkrati*. Lund: Studentlitteratur.

Protocol on social policy. 1992. Annex to the Treaty of the European Union. http://www.europa.eu.int/eurlex/en/treaties/dat/EU treaty.html#0090000 015. Last visited 2005-12-09. Print-out in author's possession.

Radaelli, Claudio M. 1999. *Technocracy in the European Union*. London: Longman.

Reich, Robert B. 1992. *The Work of Nations. Preparing Ourselves for 21st Century Capitalism*. New York: Vintage Books.

Richards, Audrey & Adam Kuper (eds.). 1971. *Councils in Action*. Cambridge: Cambridge University Press.

Richards, Audrey. 1971. The Nature of the Problem. In *Councils in Action*, edited by Audrey Richards & Adam Kuper. Cambridge: Cambridge University Press.

Rose, Nikolas. 1991. Governing by Numbers: Figuring Out Democracy. *Accounting, Organizations and Society*, 16(7):673-692.

___. 1999. *Powers of Freedom. Reframing Political Thought.* Cambridge: Cambridge University Press.

Ross, Marc Howard. 1993. *The Culture of Conflict. Interpretations and Interests in Comparative Perspective.* New Haven: Yale University Press.

Sahlin-Andersson, Kerstin. 2000a. *National, International and Transnational Construction of New Public Management.* Score working paper series 2000:4.

___. 2000b. *Transnationell reglering och statens omvandling. Granskningsamhällets framväxt.* Score working paper series 2000:14

Salais, Robert. 2004. La Politique des Indicateurs. Du tuax de Chômage au taux d'Emploi dans la Stratégie Européenne pour l'Emploi. In *Les Sciences Sociales à l'Épreuve de l'Action. Le Savant, le Politique et l'Europe*, edited by Bénédicte Zimmermann. France: Centre Interdisciplinaire d'Études et de Recherche sur l'Allemagne.

Salais, Robert & Robert Villeneuve (eds.). 2004. *Europe and the Politics of Capabilities.* Cambridge: Cambridge University Press.

Sanders, Todd & West, Harry G. 2003. Power Revealed and Concealed in the New World Order. In *Transparency and Conspiracy. Ethnographies of Suspicion in the New World Order*, edited by Todd Sanders & Harry G. West. Durham: Duke University Press.

Schwartzman, Helen B. 1989. *The Meeting. Gatherings in Organizations and Communities.* London: Plenum Press.

Scott, James C. 1998. *Seeing Like a State. How Certain Schemes to Improve the Human Condition Have Failed.* London: Yale University Press.

Serrano Pascual, Amparo (ed.) 2000. *Tackling Youth Unemployment in Europe.* Brussels: ETUI

Shore, Cris. 1993. Inventing the 'People's Europe:' Critical approach to European Community 'Cultural Policy.' *Man*, 28(4):779-800.

___. 1996. Transcending the Nation-State?: The European Commission and the (Re)-Discovery of Europe. *Journal of Historical Sociology*, 9(4):473-496.

___. 2000. *Building Europe. The Cultural Politics of European Integration.* London: Routledge.

Shore, Cris & Susan Wright (eds.). 1997: *The Anthropology of Policy. Critical Perspectives on Governance and Power.* London: Routledge.

Simon, Herbert A. 1961[1957]. *Administrative Behavior. A Study of Decision-Making Processes in Administrative Organization.* New York: The Macmillan Company

Sisson, Keith & Paul Marginson. 2001. *"Soft Regulation" – Travesty of the Real Thing or New Dimension?* ESRC "One Europe or Several?" Programme Working paper 32/01.

Smith, Anthony D. 1979. *Nationalism in the Twentieth Century.* Oxford: Martin Robertson and Co.

Soysal, Yasemin Nuhoglu. 1994. *Limits of Citizenship. Migrants and Postnational Membership in Europe.* London: The University of Chicago.

Spencer, Paul. 1971. Party Politics and the Processes of Local Democracy in an English Town Council. In *Councils in Action,* edited by Audrey Richards and Adam Kuper. Cambridge: Cambridge University Press.

Standish, Paul. 2000. Fetish for Effect. *Journal of Philosophy of Education,* 34(1):151-168.

Starr, Paul. 1987. The Sociology of Official Statistics. In *The Politics of Numbers,* edited by William Alonso & Paul Starr. New York: Russell Sage Foundation.

Stewart, John & Kieron Walsh. 1992. Change in the Management of Public Services'. *Public Administration,* 70(4):499-518.

Stone, Deborah. 1997[1988]. *Policy Paradox. The Art of Political Decision Making.* London: W W Norton & Company.

Strathern, Marilyn (ed.). 2000a. *Audit Culture. Anthropological Studies in Accountability, Ethics and the Academy.* London: Routledge.

Strathern, Marilyn. 2000b. The Tyranny of Transparency. *British Educational Research Journal,* 26(3):309-321.

Stråth, Bo. 1996. *The Organisation of Labour Markets. Modernity, Culture and Governance in Germany, Sweden, Britain and Japan.* London: Routledge.

de Swaan, Abram. 1988. *In Care of the State. Health Care, Education and Welfare in Europe and the USA in the Modern Era.* Cambridge: Polity Press.

Tallberg, Jonas. 2001. *EU:s politiska system.* Lund: Studentlitteratur.

Thedvall, Renita. 1998. *Flexibel arbetskraft som EU fråga - aktörer, arenor och perspektiv.* Report.

___. 2004. 'Do it yourself:' Making Up the Self-Employed Individual in the Swedish Public Employment Service. In *Learning To Be Employable. New Agendas on Work, Responsibility and Learning in a Globalizing World,* edited by

Christina Garsten & Kerstin Jacobsson. Houndsmills, Basingstoke: Palgrave Macmillan.

___. 2005. *The Meeting Format as a Shaper of the Decision-Making Process: The Case of the EU Employment Committee.* Score working paper series 2005:1.

___. 2006. Transparency at Work: The Production of Indicators for EU Employment Policy. In *The Politics of Transparency: Unveiling Organizational Visions for a New Global Order*, edited by Christina Garsten & Monica Lindh de Montoya. London: Edward Elgar Publishing.

Treaty of the European Coal and Steal Community. 1952. http://www.europa.eu.int/abc/treaties/index_en.htm Last visited 2005-12-09. Print-out in author's possession.

Treaty of the European Economic Community. (Treaty of Rome) 1957. http://www.europa.eu.int/abc/treaties/index_en.htm Last visited 2005-12-09. Print-out in author's possession.

Treaty of the European Atomic Energy Community. (Treaty of Rome) 1957. http://www.europa.eu.int/abc/treaties/index_en.htm Last visited 2005-12-09. Print-out in author's possession.

Treaty of the European Union. (Treaty of Maastricht). 1992 http://www.europa.eu.int/abc/treaties/index_en.htm Last visited 2005-12-09. Print-out in author's possession.

Treaty of Amsterdam. 1997. http://www.europa.eu.int/abc/treaties/index_en.htm Last visited 2005-12-09. Print-out in author's possession.

Trubek, Davis M. & Louise G. Trubek. 2005. The Open Method of Co-ordination and the Debate over "Hard" and "Soft" Law. In *The Open Method of Co-ordination in Action. The European Employment and Social Inclusion Strategies*, edited by Jonathan Zeitlin & Philippe Pochet with Lars Magnusson. Brussels: P.I.E. Peter Lang.

Turner, Victor. 1969. *The Ritual Process. Structure and Anti-Structure.* New York: Aldine de Gruyter.

Urla, Jacqueline. 1993. Cultural Politics in an Age of Statistics: Numbers, Nations, and the Making of Basque Identity. *American Ethnologist*, 20(4):818-843.

Vandermeeren, Sonja. 1999. English as a Lingua Franca in Written Corporate Communication: Findings from a European Survey. In *Writing Business. Genres, Media and Discourse*, edited by Francesca Bargiela-Chiappini & Catherine Nickerson. Harlow, Essex: Longman.

Vaughan-Whitehead, Daniel C. 2003. EU *Enlargement versus Social Europe? The Uncertain Future of the European Social Model.* Cheltenham, UK: Edward Elgar.

Vifell, Åsa. 2004. *(Ex)Changing Practices. Swedish Employment Policy and European Guidelines*. Stockholm: Score working paper series 2004:11.

van Vree, Wilbert. 2002. The Development of Meeting Behaviour in Modern Organizations and the Rise of an Upper Class of Professional Chairpersons. In *The Civilized Organization. Norbert Elias and the Future of Organization Studies*, edited by Ad van Iterson, Willem Mastenbroek, Tim Newton & Dennis Smith. Amsterdam: John Benjamins Publishing Company.

Vos, Ellen. 1997. The Rise of Committees. *European Law Journal*, 3(3):210-229.

Wallace, Helen & William Wallace (eds.). 2000. *Policy Making in the European Union. 4th edition*. Oxford: Oxford University Press.

Walters, William & Jens Henrik Haahr. 2005. *Governing Europe. Discourse, Governmentality and European Integration*. London: Routledge.

Weber, Max. 1958 [1946]. *From Max Weber: Essays in Sociology. Translated, Edited, with an Introduction by H.H. Gerth and C. Wright Mills*. New York: Oxford University Press.

Weiss, Gilbert & Ruth Wodak. 2000. Debating Europe: Globalization Rhetoric and European Union Unemployment Policies. In *An Anthropology of the European Union. Building, Imagining and Experiencing the New Europe*, edited by Irène Bellier & Thomas M. Wilson. Oxford: Berg.

Westerlund, Uno. 1995. *Den sociala dimensionen i EU. En analyserande faktabok*. Stockholm: TCO.

Williams, Raymond. 1976. *Keywords*. London: Fontana.

Wilson, Thomas M. & Estellie M. Smith. (eds.). 1993. *Cultural Change in the New Europe. Perspectives on the European Community*. Oxford: Westview Press.

Wood, Dan B. & Richard W. Waterman. 1994. *Bureaucratic Dynamics. The Role of Bureaucracy in a Democracy*. Boulder: Westview Press.

Woolgar, Steve & Geoff Cooper. 1999. Do Artefacts Have Ambivalence? Moses' Bridges, Winner's Bridges and Other Urban Legends in S&ST. *Social Studies of Science*, 29(3):433-449.

Wulff, Helena. 2002. Yo-Yo Fieldwork: Mobility and Time in a Multi-Local Study of Dance in Ireland. *Anthropological Journal on European Cultures, issue on Shifting Grounds: Experiments in Doing Ethnography*, 11:117-136.

Zabusky, Stacia E. 1995. *Launching Europe. An Ethnography of European Cooperation in Space Science*. Princeton: Princeton University Press.

References

Zeitlin, Jonathan & Philippe Pochet (eds.) with Lars Magnusson. 2005. *The Open Method of Co-ordination in Action. The European Employment and Social Inclusion Strategies.* Brussels: P.I.E. Peter Lang.

Zimmermann, Benedict. 1996. *Die Vielfalt der Wirklichkeit und ihre Reduktion in der Statistik. Die Diskussion über die Kategorie ,Arbeitslosigkeit' im Kaiserreich and ihr Nachhall im Rahmen der Europäischen Einigung.* Berlin: WZB Papers, FSII 96-106.

INDEX

Index

Stockholm Studies in Social Anthropology

1. *Caymanian Politics: Structure and Style in a Changing Island Society* by Ulf Hannerz. 1974.

2. *Having Herds: Pastoral Herd Growth and Household Economy* by Gudrun Dahl and Anders Hjort. 1976.

3. *The Patron and the Panca: Village Values and Pancayat Democracy in Nepal* by Bengt-Erik Borgström. 1976.

4. *Ethnicity and Mobilization in Sami Politics* by Tom Svensson. 1976.

5. *Market, Mosque and Mafraj: Social Inequality in a Yemeni Town* by Tomas Gerholm. 1977.

6. *The Community Apart: A Case Study of a Canadian Indian Reserve Community* by Yngve G. Lithman. 1978 (Available from the Univ. of Manitoba).

7. *Savanna Town: Rural Ties and Urban Opportunities in Northern Kenya* by Anders Hjort. 1979.

8. *Suffering Grass: Subsistence and Society of Waso Borana* by Gudrun Dahl. 1979.

9. *North to Another Country: The Formation of a Suryoyo Community in Sweden* by Ulf Björklund. 1981.

10. *Catching the Tourist: Women Handicraft Traders in the Gambia* by Ulla Wagner. 1982.

11. *The Practice of Underdevelopment: Economic Development Projects in A Canadian Indian Reserve Community* by Yngve G. Lithman. 1983.

12. *Evil Eye or Bacteria: Turkish Migrant Women and Swedish Health Care* by Lisbeth Sachs. 1983.

13. *Women of the Barrio: Class and Gender in a Colombian City* by Kristina Bohman. 1984.

14. *Conflict & Compliance: Class Consciousness among Swedish Workers* by Mona Rosendahl. 1985.

15. *Change on the Euphrates: Villagers, Townsmen and Employees in Northeast Syria* by Annika Rabo. 1986.

16. *Morally United and Politically Divided: The Chinese Community of Penang* by Claes Hallgren. 1987.

17. *In the Stockholm Art World* by Deborah Ericson. 1988.

18. *Shepherds, Workers, Intellectuals: Culture and Centre-Periphery Relationships in a Sardinian Village* by Peter Schweizer. 1988.

19. *Women at a Loss: Changes in Maasai Pastoralism and their Effects on Gender Relations* by Aud Talle. 1988.

20. *'First we are People...': The Koris of Kanpur between Caste and Class* by Stefan Molund. 1988.

21. *Twenty Girls: Growing Up, Ethnicity and Excitement in a South London Microculture* by Helena Wulff. 1988.

238

22. *Left Hand Left Behind: The Changing Gender System of a Barrio in Valencia, Spain* by Britt-Marie Thurén. 1988.

23. *Central Planning and Local Reality: The Case of a Producers Cooperative in Ethiopia* by Eva Poluha. 1989.

24. *A Sound Family Makes a Sound State: Ideology and Upbringing in a German Village* by Karin Norman. 1991.

25. *Community, Carnival and Campaign: Expressions of Belonging in a Swedish Region* by Ann-Kristin Ekman. 1991.

26. *Women in a Borderland: Managing Muslim Identity where Morocco meets Spain* by Eva Evers Rosander. 1991.

27. *Responsible Man: the Atmaan Beja of North-Eastern Sudan* by Anders Hjort of Ornäs and Gudrun Dahl. 1991.

28. *Peasant Differentiation and Development: The Case of a Mexican Ejido* by Lasse Krantz. 1991.

29. *Kam-Ap or Take-off: Local Notions of Development.* Edited by Gudrun Dahl and Annika Rabo. 1992.

30. *More Blessed to Give: A Pentecostal Mission to Bolivia in Anthropological Perspective* by Göran Johansson. 1992.

31. *Green Arguments and Local Subsistence.* Gudrun Dahl (ed). 1993.

32. *Veils and Videos: Female Youth Culture on the Kenyan Coast* by Minou Fuglesang. 1994.

33. *Apple World: Core and Periphery in a Transnational Organizational Culture* by Christina Garsten. 1994.

34. *Land is Coming Up: the Burunge of Central Tanzania and their Environments* by Wilhelm Östberg. 1995.

35. *Persistent Peasants: Smallholders, State Agencies and Involuntary Migration in Western Venezuela* by Miguel Montoya Diaz. 1996.

36. *Progress, Hunger and Envy: Commercial Agriculture, Marketing and Social Transformation in the Venezuelan Andes* by Monica Lindh de Montoya. 1996.

37. *Shunters at Work: Creating a World in a Railway Yard* by Birgitta Edelman. 1997.

38. *Among the Interculturalists: An Emergent Profession and its Packaging of Knowledge* by Tommy Dahlén. 1997.

39. *Shamanic Performances on the Urban Scene: Neo-Shamanism in Contemporary Sweden* by Galina Lindquist. 1997.

40. *Cherished Moments: Engaging with the Past in a Swedish Parish* by Bengt-Erik Borgström. 1997.

41. *Forests, Farmers and the State: Environmentalism and Resistance in Northeastern Thailand* by Amare Tegbaru. 1998.

42. *Pacific Passages: World Culture and Local Politics in Guam* by Ronald Stade. 1998.

43. *Under One Roof: On Becoming a Turk in Sweden* by Judith Narrowe. 1998.

44. *Ambiguous Artefacts: Solar Collectors in Swedish Contexts. On Processes of Cultural Modification* by Annette Henning. 2000.

45. *"The Hospital is a Uterus": Western discourses of childbirth in late modernity – a case study from northern Italy* by Tove Holmqvist. 2000.

46. *Tired of Weeping: Child death and mourning among Papel mothers in Guinea-Bissau* by Jónína Einarsdóttir. 2000.

47. *Feminine Matters: Women's Religious Practices in a Portuguese Town* by Lena Gemzöe. 2000.

48. *Lost Visions and New Uncertainties: Sandinista profesionales in northern Nicaragua* by Inger Lundgren. 2000.

49. *Transnational.Dynamics@Development.Net. Internet, Modernization and Globalization* by Paula Uimonen. 2001.

50. *Gold is Illusion. The Garimpeiros of Tapajos Valley in the Brazilian Amazonia* by Enrique Rodriguez Larreta. 2002.

51. *Lucknow Daily. How a Hindi Newspaper Constructs Society* by Per Ståhlberg. 2002.

52. *Only For You! Brazilians and the Telenovela Flow* by Thaïs Machado-Borges. 2003.

53. *"They call for us". Strategies for Securing Autonomy among the Paliyans, Hunter-Gatherers of the Palni Hills, South India* by Christer Norström. 2003.

54. *'Our Fury is Burning': Local Practice and Global Connections in the Dalit Movement* by Eva-Maria Hardtmann. 2003.

55. *Species Aid: Organizational Sensemaking in a Preservation Project in Albania* by Peter Green. 2004.

56. *India Dreams: Cultural Identity among Young Middle Class Men in New Delhi* by Paolo Favero. 2005.

57. *Irish Scene and Sound: Identity, Authenticity and Transnationality among Young Musicians* by Virva Basegmez. 2005.

58. *Eurocrats at Work: Negotiating Transparency in Postnational Employment Policy* by Henita I hedvall. 2006.

Books in this series can be ordered from
Almqvist & Wiksell International
P.O. Box 7634
SE-103 94 STOCKHOLM
SWEDEN
Phone: +46 8 613 61 00
Fax: +46 8 24 25 43
E-mail: order@akademibokhandeln.se